# Don't Let Them Scare You

ELMER DAVIS

# Don't Let Them Scare You

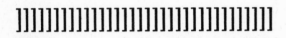

THE LIFE AND TIMES OF
## ELMER DAVIS

By Roger Burlingame

J. B. LIPPINCOTT COMPANY
PHILADELPHIA AND NEW YORK

To
PAUL KIEFFER
Elmer's Friend and Mine

# ACKNOWLEDGMENTS

This book grew out of a conversation with Elmer Davis's oldest and closest friend, Paul Kieffer. When Paul suggested the biography, it seemed to me that he was suddenly meeting my most urgent unexpressed wish; yet I was unsure of my capacity to fulfill so bright a hope. Paul persuaded me that it was worth a try and offered to help me by opening whatever avenues of approach were accessible to him. As he was executor of the Davis estate, these were considerable. Though nothing in the nature of a subsidy was ever considered by either of us, he was able to obtain for me certain exclusive privileges such as that of examining documents in the control of the family and to establish a liaison with Mrs. Davis and her children which was essential to my enterprise. The cooperation that the family has given me so generously and so wholly without commitment has brought me a confidence which, in my early uncertainty, was scarcely anticipated.

The Davis-Kieffer friendship goes back to Elmer's Oxford days. Himself one of the first batch of American Rhodes Scholars in 1902, Paul Kieffer's interest in succeeding groups led him to make the acquaintance of the boy from Indiana in 1913. Later he became as welcome in the Davis home as if he had been a member of the family. The children called him "Peke" and looked forward eagerly to his visits.

My own acquaintance with Elmer Davis was more casual but

it was against a background of admiration as great as any I have ever felt. To me he was not only the only broadcaster who really understood the news but the only one who could make me understand it too. When I missed one of his talks, I felt as hungry and dissatisfied as if I had gone without a necessary meal. It is true, as occasional passages of this book imply, that I sometimes disagreed with him, but always after he had fairly presented me with the grounds for disagreement.

I know from the many people I have talked to and the letters and editorials and citations I have read that thousands or even millions of Americans felt as I did. To count the confused and doubting folk he has taught to think with clarity or the scared men and women to whom he has given courage would be an exercise in arithmetic progression toward infinity. Though he is dead, the progression goes on: the growth from his words will be sturdy in our children's future.

From those who worked or played with Elmer Davis, I have had abundant help. To the family—Fliss, Robert Lloyd and Anne—I owe most for they have made every step easy, extending hospitality to me on my visits to Washington and supplying me with personal details I could not have otherwise found. To my sorrow, Fliss did not live till I had finished the book.

Of his colleagues in radio, Edward R. Murrow gave me most, but I must also thank Eric Severeid and William Paley of CBS. In ABC there were John Daly and Thomas Velotta, with whom Elmer was associated in his postwar work; both made valuable contributions. In my study of his work for the government I was helped by Jonathan Daniels, Arthur Sweetser, Archibald MacLeish, Edward Barrett, Edward Stanley, John Mason Brown, Victor Weybright, Carl Lokke, Joseph Barnes, Samuel Williamson, Katharine Pringle, Harold Guinzburg, Armitage Watkins, Francis Brennan, Robert Hale, and Whitney Shepardson.

At the Library of Congress, my old friend David Mearns, head of the Manuscript Division, put at my disposal the very considerable body of Elmer Davis papers which were given to the

8

Library by the family after his death. In all my work at the Library Mr. Mearns, his extremely knowledgeable assistants, Messrs. Vance and Thompson, and the entire staff of the Division did everything possible to make me feel at home in the Library and to make my way there easy.

On my first visit to the Library of Congress, I had a special stroke of luck. A young employee of the Library, who introduced himself as Jerry Love, told me he had heard I was writing Elmer Davis's biography and that he wanted to offer his help as a citizen of Aurora, Indiana, Elmer's native town. Mr. Love had been a Davis fan since he had heard him talk at the Aurora High School commencement in 1951 and had kept the story about the speech from the local newspaper. He then gave me abundant assistance in the most difficult part of my project—Elmer's boyhood days— by putting me in touch with a number of elder citizens who knew the Davises senior and the Severins.

From these people, I got great assistance. Mr. W. D. Backman, president of Elam Davis's First National Bank of Aurora, told me of the family ancestry. Mrs. Esther W. Roache, secretary-treasurer of Hillcrest Historical Foundation of Aurora, also gave me detailed information about the family and suggested others who could enlighten me about Elmer's high school days.

Fellow students in the Aurora High School were Messrs. Bernard H. Schockel and Frank C. Hopping from whose letters I have quoted at length. President Harold W. Richardson of Franklin College supplied me with a complete record of Elmer's courses and grades there. I had an extremely illuminating letter also from a fraternity brother at Franklin, Mr. Edwin L. Deming.

For information about the Oxford days and about the Rhodes Scholarships in general I am indebted to my friends Paul Kieffer and Whitney Shepardson, to Mr. Courtney Smith, American Secretary of the Rhodes Scholarship Trust, to fellow Scholars Professor William Greene, Messrs. H. Gary Hudson, C. F. Zeek, E. H. Eckel, and Robert Hale.

A detailed account of Elmer's career on the New York *Times* was provided by my lifetime friend Samuel T. Williamson who was a fellow reporter there—excerpts from which I have used in the text. Memories of Elmer's life in New York in *Times* days and later were contributed by Mr. and Mrs. W. W. Rogers, Messrs. Lee Crandall, William Bridges and Robert Keith Leavitt. I owe Mr. Leavitt a special debt of gratitude not only for his delightful and instructive letter about the lighter side of Elmer's life in New York—including much about the celebrated "Baker Street Irregulars"—but also for putting me in touch with other informative persons.

Among those who sent me copies of letters to and from Elmer Davis, I owe most to the late Carolyn Wilson, whom he first met on the Ford Peace Ship and who became a lifelong correspondent and a friend of the family. In the last year of her life, despite severe physical handicaps, Miss Wilson let me visit her in her home on Elmer's old stamping ground, Mason's Island, and told me much about his early journalistic career.

Others who sent correspondence were Messrs. Edward L. Bernays, Peter Viereck, James Thurber, Joseph Barnes and Mrs. Kenneth Littauer. Mr. Thurber put me in touch with Mr. E. B. White who, in turn, steered me toward *The New Yorker*—for many years a treasury of Davisiana—and pointed out to me an editorial in which he proposed Davis as Director of the OWI. Both of these gentlemen suggested that I ask the help of Miss Ebba Jonnsen, *The New Yorker*'s librarian, who gave it generously.

Two revealing views were given me by Elmer's radio agent, Thomas L. Stix, and Dr. Bernard Cohen, his physician. Mr. Stix lent me a record of that celebrated voice which was a catalyst to my work. Dr. Cohen showed an appreciation of his patient's humor which was refreshing in a doctor.

I have made constant use of the New York Public Library and I want to acknowledge the patience, kindness and courtesy of those members of the staff whom I have consulted. Here, Mr.

Robert Hill of the Manuscript Division introduced me to the Library's collection of Davis papers.

In the editorial offices of the New York *Times*, my distinguished fellow writer, Robert L. Duffus, provided me with many back issues of this paper to whose columns—news and editorial—Elmer anonymously contributed and he pointed out their true authorship.

Several of my sources were confidential and I have reluctantly acceded to the requests of some of my most enlightening informants to withhold their names. I thank them just the same.

I have always welcomed reasonable editorial advice and that of George Stevens of Lippincott has been wise and patient. George is a real editor. He refuses to follow the current fashion of running a manuscript through a copy desk on a belt conveyor.

Kenneth Littauer has shared with George the editorial function. My wife, a trained critic, has read every word more than once with her usual stern detachment. For stenography, typing and collaboration on the index my thanks go to Mrs. Russell A. Loring.

Of the many books I have consulted for historical background, I can name only a few. In constant use were Churchill's volumes on the second World War. Eisenhower's *Crusade in Europe* and Robert E. Sherwood's *Roosevelt and Hopkins* were essential. One of the most valuable books I have seen is an English publication entitled *The War* (not to be confused with the recent American volume with the same name), edited by Desmond Flower and James Reeves. It is a collection of eyewitness and first-hand accounts of events, the authors of which range from generals to corporals, from prime ministers to government clerks. I have also used Fleet Admiral William D. Leahy's *I Was There,* the *Memoirs* of Harry S Truman, *Senator Joe McCarthy* by Richard Rovere, *Only Yesterday* and *Since Yesterday* by Frederick Lewis Allen, *Ford: Expansion and Challenge* by Allan Nevins, *The American Republic* by Richard Hofstadter, William Miller and Daniel Aaron, *The Time for Decision* by Sumner Welles, *This is London*

## Acknowledgments

by Edward R. Murrow, *The American Rhodes Scholarships* by Frank Aydelotte, *The World Between the Wars* by Quincy Howe, *The War, First Year* by Edgar McInnis, and Volumes 3, 5 and 6 of *Our Times* by Mark Sullivan. Other books and periodicals from which I have quoted I have credited in the text.

*Danbury, Connecticut, October 1, 1960*

12

# PROLOGUE

## 1

THERE ARE YEARS in our history that, as we look back on them, are scarcely credible. Such are those immediately following the Civil War, when corruption in North and South made this country "the scandal," as Kipling said, "of the elder world." Such, too, are the years of the 1920's, when, parallel with the progress of national prohibition, we embarked on a career of madness that ended with the depression, a calamity second only to civil war in horror and depth. But the most recent lapse came when we had succeeded to leadership of the world, when the war-tired nations looked to us for counsel and strength, yet when, obsessed by fear, we failed not only them but ourselves.

It was precisely in mid-century that the meaningless, groundless wave of panic hysteria swept us. It began with the speech of a psychopathic demagogue on February 9, 1950. There are those who say it was the demonic power of the late Senator Joe McCarthy that created the panic wave out of vacuum. It seems more likely that the stage had been set for the rabble-rousing Senator to rant on.

Since the closing years of the 1930's we had been put through a series of mental gymnastics probably unparalleled in history—at least in that span of time. In the 'thirties, beginning with Roosevelt's recognition of the Soviet Union in 1933, a considerable number of the American intelligentsia had softened toward communism. Several philosophical writers had dallied with its ideology; some, even, had joined the Party. Then with the Stalin-Hitler pact of 1939, these converted adherents fell away in droves. Their bitterness against their former comrades grew with the Russo-Finnish war of 1940, but suddenly, the following year, we must all love the Russia which fought so valiantly against the Nazis! The injured people, stabbed in the back by the unspeakable Führer hypocrite, had at last seen the light; communism—or at least its evil features—was on the wane and Russia and the West might go on together like the lion and the lamb after Armageddon into a millennium of peace.

But when "peace" came (with the echoes from Hiroshima and Nagasaki still jarring the American conscience), with it came the shattering disillusionment from Moscow where, phoenix-like, the Comintern rose from the synthetic ashes, and Stalin repudiated every war-inspired promise. And, in the postwar years, certain Americans wondered if we had been fighting the wrong enemies, and we were asked by our policy-makers to turn forgiving eyes toward Germany and Japan, for they, after all, were the great bulwarks against communism; perhaps, even, they should be rearmed by Nato and Seato, whatever those were besides pronounceable combinations of initials.

Was it surprising, then, that the American people should withdraw into themselves, into something they could understand or thought they could understand and, because fear had become the fashion in the world, should create their own little bogy man, the American Communist? The fact that this bogy had no tangible existence except in negligible quantities and weakened convictions made no difference, he was American and therefore comprehensible (however un-American he might be!) and more immediately frightening.

The American legend, hung over from the invulnerable isolation days, taught us to turn our eyes away from the obscure and essentially evil Europe and Asia to something we could know

14

and touch, that had been purified by wilderness, sanctified by pioneer hardship and become, finally, independent, no longer dependent upon a foreign wellspring. Yet now, in conflict with this ideal, had come the phenomenon of communication: the radio brought a fear which could no longer be allayed by the floating comfort of Ivory Soap or the fast relief of Anacin. This fear, being nameless, might just as well be turned homeward as toward its unclear source and it awaited only its crystallizer, its interpreter who would make it appear concrete. So along, at this moment, came Joe McCarthy, waving in his hand the alleged names of alleged American Communists—alleged to be engaged in subverting the United States government from within.

It is undoubtedly true that the Wisconsin Senator did not at first realize what he was doing. Those who, like Mr. Richard Rovere, have tried to analyze McCarthy's elusive mentality, believe he thought he was merely making campaign speeches in which he had inserted a novel gimmick; that no one was more surprised than he at its effect. But it is plausible to assume that he lit, by those words, a fuse of fear which had been laid into the farthest and darkest corners of confused, bewildered and bedeviled America.

Having lit the fuse, McCarthy, watching with surprise the speed with which it burned, saw that it served his personal ambition and followed it, blowing upon it to enhance the haste of the burning. We know what happened—all but the youngest of us know; in the search for Communists led by McCarthy's wild and obfuscating statements the lives of innocent men and women were ruined, distrust was spread across the land and we became the laughingstock of the world. The rabble-rousing Senator held the Congress in the hollow of his hand, including many of those members who hated him most, intimidated one President and gained the temporary support of such otherwise intelligent statesmen as Robert Taft. That he was able to humiliate the Army, to cause the FBI to circumvent its rules, and to render inoperative portions of the Constitution itself was not because of his personal

15

power, appealing as it was to the vulgar, but because he was the spokesman for an inarticulate fear—a spokesman who seemed, for a moment, to give it meaning and could furnish victims for the panic rage.

Many Americans today are deeply ashamed of their faith in this false god and take comfort only in the truth that so many others were in the same rudderless boat. But now, in this aftermath when all but the far echoes of the tumult and shouting are stilled, it might be well to consider some of those who were not in the boat; who consistently spoke calm and guidance from a firm American shore and brought the unhappy people back to sanity.

There was one in particular. . . .

2

In the most desperate days of the panic, when many dared not move or speak without looking over their shoulder for the fancied specter, a slow, even, Middle-Western voice brought reassurance into millions of American homes. It presented the extreme contrast with the reckless shouts that rose from the Senate floor. It appraised, it reasoned, it recalled to an America unafraid; its tone and cadence were those of an old Yankee—perhaps a puritan—certainty; of the stubborn vision that made the impossible feasible through the tough march that once joined the oceans. And the words were the words of the Founding Fathers, infused with wise biblical advice but couched in the colloquial usage of the rural fireside.

Again and again, in various words but never in any that obscured the basic meaning, the voice said:

The first and great commandment is, Don't let them scare you. For the men who are trying to do that to us are scared themselves. They are afraid that what they think will not stand critical examination; they are afraid that the prin-

16

ciples on which this Republic was founded and has been conducted are wrong. They will tell you that there is a hazard in the freedom of the mind, and of course there is, as in any freedom. In trying to think right you run the risk of thinking wrong. But there is no hazard at all, no uncertainty, in letting somebody else tell you what to think; that is sheer damnation.

Then, in the year before the voice began to fail from a man's overwork in the effort to bring his people back to a rational view of the true American way, these words, paraphrasing Lincoln, spurred the courage that was beginning to return.

This nation was conceived in liberty and dedicated to the principle—among others—that honest men may honestly disagree; that if they all say what they think, a majority of the people will be able to distinguish truth from error; that in the competition in the market place of ideas, the sounder ideas will in the long run win out. For almost four years past we have been engaged in a cold civil war—it is nothing less—testing whether any nation so conceived and so dedicated can long endure.

I believe it will endure, but only if we stand up for it. The frightened men who are trying to frighten us, because they have no faith in their country, are wrong; and even wronger are the smart men who are trying to use the frightened men for their own ends. The United States has worked, the principles of freedom on which it was founded—free thought as well as political liberty—have worked. This is the faith once delivered to the fathers—the faith for which they were willing to fight and, if necessary, die, but for which they fought and won.

Two years after these words were spoken, the voice that spoke them was stilled and the tired man went into the long suffering

**17**

## Prologue

which led to his death, but the cause in which they were said has,
for the time at least, been won. And, as someone has said, words
are seeds, and if the soil has deep feeding, they grow. And it is
not easy to believe, even in this still uncertain age, that the
American ground has turned sterile.

18

# 1 ]]]]]]

## 1

THE DECADE that ended the nineteenth century has been called "the gay nineties"; Thomas Beer wrote of it as *The Mauve Decade,* and other deprecatory terms have been thrown at it from the pinnacle of today's space-conscious superiority. We think of it as leisurely, slow-moving, romantic, complacent and hypocritical.

But this is hindsight. To the men and women who lived in them, the times were stimulating and robust. The American continental frontier had, to be sure, officially closed. Yet a new expansion westward to the Far East began in 1898, as one result of a war of which, today, we are vaguely ashamed, and the expansion has troubled us ever since. But this flight of the eagle across the Pacific was hailed, at the end of the 'nineties, as a final demonstration of Manifest Destiny, and only a few skeptical prophets shook their heads.

To those of us who were boys when the curtain began to fall on the century, there was a sense of sharp change, of new acts and new actors that would crowd the stage when the curtain should rise again. Politics were for our elders. We heard meaningless echoes of the jingle of free silver and the death rattles of Populism, and we had difficulty with the picture of mankind being "crucified upon a cross of gold." But the immediate and tangible war news was thrilling provided one did not have to bother about causes or results, and, for such of us as lived in the urban centers, the new technologies and industrial expansion brought daily excitement.

News of the X-ray came from Europe in '95. The following year, wireless telegraphy was born. Niagara Falls was "harnessed" in mid-decade and the long-distance transmission of electric juice in the late 'nineties brought light into the darkest corners and power into transportation. The telephone was still a marvel and scarce in the back country and Edison's phonograph with its wax cylinders and big brass horn was still a fascinating novelty. To the boys who heard it no news was more urgent than that which came from Kokomo, Indiana, where Elwood Haynes had demonstrated a horseless carriage. For many years thereafter this "toy" was an object of derision to the majority of adults—the same adults who thought experimenters with flight belonged in an asylum—but even the boys scarcely dreamed that this engaging contraption would one day remake the map of the United States.

That map had already been twice drawn. First settlers followed the rivers and established towns on their banks and when the Industrial Revolution came, the factories, needing both water power and transportation, were built in the river towns. But the railroads changed this design. As trains brought coal for the new steam power and carried both raw materials and factory products, cities grew up along the tracks ignoring the waterways. Thus Pittsburgh and Cincinnati, for instance, were river bred—flatboats brought the people and steamboats the industries—but it was locomotives that gave life to Indianapolis. In the state of Indiana, therefore, there was a distinction between rail-built Indianapolis and the towns on the bank of the Ohio, a short distance down river from Cincinnati. In the 1890's this distinction was sharp and there was dispute as to whether the river-town folk or those up north were the real "Hoosiers." Certainly the river towns came first in time while the rest of the state was largely a swamp, malarial and swarming with mosquitoes, and the first Indianans were immigrants who came either down or across the Ohio. All this changed, to be sure, when Elwood Haynes's

Kokomo toy developed into the third map-maker; then all were good Hoosiers together, unified, and some thought too arrogantly proud of their state—"hoosier than thou," Robert Benchley is said to have said.

But in the "mauve decade" the river towns of Indiana were still mainly agricultural, innocent of factory soot and, by ambitious urban Americans called "backward."

## 2

One of the backward towns, less than thirty miles across the state line from Cincinnati, was Aurora, named for the sunrise which it faced. (Another river town a few miles away was named by one less impressed by mythology, simply, Rising Sun.) Aurora is still there, somewhat enlarged, and prouder since one of its sons talked, nightly, to twelve and a half million people.

In the early years of the nineteenth century, the settlers of Aurora came from two directions: from Pennsylvania in flatboats and from Kentucky in enlarged canoes called pirogues. One from each group led in establishing the town: Jesse Lynch Holman and Thomas Gaff. Gaff started a whiskey distillery and Holman wrote a book.

Actually Judge Holman's book was written in Kentucky before he crossed the river, but after it was published, he so regretted it that he burned the edition—or as much of it as he could buy in —in Aurora's public square. The book was a novel called *The Errors of Education*. It seems that Holman, grown older and wiser and perhaps more ethically sensitive since he had moved north, looked on this youthful creation, when he saw it in print, with horror as certain to corrupt the morals of the young. The event was, as a later historian of Aurora wrote, "the first and, so far, the only book-burning in Indiana."

The distillery, on the other hand, was not thought corrupting in that robust age, and survived. The Gaffs were solid citizens,

21

respected by young and old. They made good whiskey—rye and bourbon—and these things were as much part of the pioneer diet as bread and meat. It has been said that liquor helped combat the rigors of climate and gave strength for the chopping of trees; that it began to affect morals only after the physical work was done and men had become otherwise corrupted by warm houses and prepared food.

By 1890, the whiskey distillery in Aurora had been joined by another enterprise—a coffin factory. Aurorans insist there was no connection between these industries; that the products of this new concern were largely exported—perhaps to the malarial midlands of the state. There was also a flour mill and a very respectable First National Bank. Two railroads had come in to supplement the river transportation—the Monon and the B. & O. Aurora had some quite prosperous citizens—and some lowly ones too.

Above the riverbank, the town rises steeply and the streets and their lines of houses are on tiers. From the beginning, these tiers have graded the citizens. On the river level, the people live in shacks, raise a patch of tobacco for their own smoking and chewing and subsist mainly on river fish. On the top tier are the big houses of the rich and great; in between are the homes of the middling gentry, small businessmen, storekeepers, doctors and lawyers. In the spring of every year the river threatens to flood; when it carries out its threat, the lowly folk run for their lives up the hills, invading the barns of the better-off, but they have always come back after the waters have subsided.

In a large house on one of the middle tiers, lived Elam Holmes Davis. He was, in 1890, cashier of the First National Bank of Aurora. He was a respected citizen. He was active in the Baptist church. His wife had been Louise Severin, daughter of a Palatine German who had found his way to Aurora after the German revolution of 1848. She was Elam's second wife. She and her spinster sister, Huldah, both taught in the Aurora High School and Louise Davis eventually became its principal. Louise was as articulate as Elam was laconic. To these people a son was born on January 13, 1890. They named him Elmer—a hick name, he used to say later with a characteristic winking pride in the circumstances of his birth, and appropriate to the "backward" town on the Indiana bank of the Ohio.

## 3

Sixty-one years later, in 1951, Elmer Davis went back to Aurora to give the commencement address to the high school's graduating class. It was an adult speech, for this man, who had read aloud to his own eleven-year-old son from James Jeans's *The Universe Around Us,* never talked down to boys and girls. He told them about the traditions of their river and their town. He told them of the people who had come as immigrants in his grandfather's day.

> They left us [he said] an honorable inheritance, those residents of Aurora who went before us—a way of life that suits us, a freedom that makes that way of life possible; freedom to think, to say what we think, and to act according to our conclusions.

In that same address, he gave an uncommon picture of the town and a brief glimpse of his boyhood against its background.

> What distinguished Aurora from the other towns of its size was the universal interest in music and the almost universal capacity for performing it. I say almost universal, for I was one of the very few people around town who couldn't sing. Even buried in the back row of Charlie Gardiner's male chorus, I did better if they couldn't hear me. And to be unable to sing, in Aurora of those days, was about as much of a deformity as if you'd had both legs cut off by a freight

23

train. Luckily, by playing second fiddle in the high school
orchestra, and later in the old Interurban Orchestra that used
to play up and down the river . . . I just managed to get
under the wire. . . .

It is an unflattering portrait, but Elmer Davis was not given
to talking enthusiastically about himself. He added a recollection
of the attitude of the members of his own graduating class forty-
five years earlier toward the world they were about to enter.

In our day we could believe that progress was ever onward
and upward with no reversals. . . . We never dreamed then
that there could be hard times as bad as those of 1929 and
after ; . . . and we never dreamed that the human race could
ever again slip back into such an abyss of barbarism as
Germany was in the nineteen thirties or Russia is today.

Inability to sing was not the only thing that troubled Elmer's
growing years. His passionate interest in sports had not, in his
boyhood, the cooperation of his body. He had neither the close-
knit build nor the quick physical coordination essential to good
performance on diamond and gridiron. He has been described as
"ungainly," with a head too large for his slender body. A high
school classmate remembers that "there was something droll
about his appearance, a serious drollery." He gave a first impression of great seriousness, yet those who made an effort to
know him discovered, as his boyhood friend Bernard Schockel
tells, "a sort of wiry, dry, explosive, provocative humor, not
respective of the dignity of the victim, although such humor was
impersonal— . . . his remarks were likely to be general, objective, seemingly unaware of the sensitivity of the listener. So that
his classmates treated him with affectionate drollery, as it were,
and with a bit of caution."

But the physical ineptitude which limited his participation in
baseball was transferred to an intellectual pursuit in Elmer's mind

24

—a profound understanding of the beloved game that lasted through life. In school, therefore, he became manager of the team, which involved the financial arrangements and the scheduling of games. He was an infallible keeper of box scores. In such sports, too, as boxing, he learned rules and fine points which enabled him later to become a sports writer of considerable celebrity.

Yet he never got over the itch to take part. "He gave me the impression," writes his classmate Frank Hopping, "that he would gladly exchange his mental acumen and keenness for the ability to excel in athletics." Perhaps, though, even had some magician offered him the exchange he would not, after all, have excelled. He was too dedicated to scholarship to have given adequate time and energy to sport. For him the "A's" were not those of Aurora's teams but of her classrooms. These he won without apparent effort—to the surprise and envy of his schoolmates.

One would suppose that, with all this smartness, as it was called, this boy would have been a teachers' favorite. On the contrary, he was, apparently, a thorn in their flesh, particularly in that of his Aunt Huldah Severin, who taught science and mathematics in the school. We are much aware, today, of the prevalence of conformity supposed by the social scientists to be peculiar, in the free world, to the United States, and we think of earlier eras as being distinguished by rugged individualism. That this was not true in the small Indiana towns at the start of the century is evident from the reminiscences of Aurora people. In such a Baptist stronghold, deviation from the orthodox in thought as well as in behavior was looked upon with horror by the guardians of youthful morality. And from his earliest high school years, Elmer Davis was a rebel. Whether he had been born into that camp or whether hard-shell Baptist Aurora put him there, that is where he remained. When, later, he supported the New Deal, certain citizens of this Republican stronghold eyed him with suspicion and, despite his persistent attacks on communism, labeled him a "fellow traveler."

25

4

At sixteen, in the fall of 1906, he went to Franklin College in Franklin, Indiana, twenty miles south of Indianapolis. The college had been founded in the mosquito days before the railroads. Indiana had always taken education seriously. The pattern of it had been laid out in the great documents which had established the Northwest Territory—the Ordinances of 1785 and 1787—and which were embodied in her constitution when Indiana became a state.

The boy's appearance and manner as he arrived on the campus were not immediately appealing to the worldly wise sophisticates from the north. Those upperclassmen who were gunning among the freshmen for fraternity brothers watched him with negative expressions. There was, in addition to his long, lanky and awkward look, the inimical fact of his coming from southern Indiana. Inter-Hoosier prejudice had lasted until 1906, two years before the Model T was born. So for several months he was left alone to pursue his studies, an exercise which usually consoled him for loneliness.

In a college as small as Franklin, however, it is difficult for any student to remain long by himself. One classmate and then another began to laugh with Elmer's wit rather than at his figure. After a while even the awful barrier between north and south broke down. Franklin and Aurora were, indeed, on the same railroad, and the railroads, Elmer remembered, strung the threads of culture in Indiana. So before the end of freshman year the brothers of Phi Delta Theta changed their expressions and he was pledged.

After that his shyness began to dissolve and he moved into the leadership that later made him, a Phi Delta brother recalls, "the pride of his college and his fraternity." He was an editor and a playwright and at the top in studies. He also found amusement in Indianapolis, rumors of which came to his father's ears. To

26

Elam Davis cards and the theater were works of the devil. In March of Elmer's senior year he wrote, cautioning his son against this waywardness. It was costly, he said, impaired the boy's health and would injure his reputation—especially if, as Elmer then expected, he was to be a teacher. He was disturbed, too, by Elmer's apparent apostasy, his expressed "contempt" for prayer and his willingness to listen to the "idiotic sayings" of agnostic professors.

But a month or so later, Davis, senior, changed his tune. "Order your clothes," he wrote, "and get all you will need, so that you will be prepared for your journey and I will take care of the finances." What journey, he does not say, but not, surely, the short rail trip on the Monon road from Franklin to Aurora. Between Elam Davis's letters, his son must have won the Rhodes Scholarship to Oxford. There must have been other letters—letters of congratulation, and it would have been characteristic of Elmer to throw them away. But this one he kept: perhaps because there was a reference in it to a girl to whom he had become engaged (but never married) or possibly because on the back of the envelope, in pencil, was the box score of a ball game he wanted to remember.

But scholarship or not, there was good reason even for this austere father to be proud of the youth as he emerged from his gangling adolescence, his wisdom already balanced by worldly humor. In his four years at Franklin Elmer had only twice slipped below the grade of A. The slips came in psychology and geology. In Greek, Latin and German; in mathematics, chemistry, history and political economy he had won top marks in every semester. In Greek he had read the *Anabasis,* the New Testament and the *Iliad;* in Latin, Livy and Horace, Plautus and Terence and even *De Rerum Natura* by Lucretius—an uncommon but a wise assignment for the times—and he had studied both European and American history. And, in the end, to his Bachelor of Arts degree was attached the parenthesis of *magna cum laude.* In the face of these triumphs, Elam Davis could scarcely support his allegation

27

of wasted time even if, in winning them, his son had cracked the hard shell of Aurora's orthodoxy.

In the fall of 1909, the boy had felt equal to the stiff "qualifying" examination for the scholarship. The Rhodes trustees laid emphasis on the term. These examinations were not competitive. The best man did not necessarily win. But one who passed the examination was qualified for election. Other criteria were then applied and the candidate who met all the extracurricular requirements was chosen and was notified of his election some time after the first of the year in which he was to enter the Oxford college to which he had been assigned.

In the six years that the Rhodes Scholarships had been given there had been 397 Scholars from all the countries named in the founder's will. Elmer Davis was Number 398.


5


Cecil John Rhodes had lived in the prime years of the British Empire and was, himself, an empire builder. In his youth he was torn between two desires: to be educated and to be rich. In pursuit of this dual avatar, he shuttled between Kimberley in South Africa and Oxford in England. It was not an easy commutation in the 1870's when the voyage took seventy days. At about the time of his first visit to the Cape Colony, the fabulous Kimberley diamond mines were discovered and exploited and Rhodes, a common laborer digging with his pick and shovel, saw his future in the sparkling stones he turned up. Yet the world of books and study never ceased calling to him. It took him eight years to get his Oxford degree and he cherished it as dearly as he did the colossal wealth that gave him the kind of power that has long since disappeared from the Western world. This uncommon dualism of mind has been a happy thing for the beneficiaries of his most celebrated will.

This last of his seven wills, with its codicils testifying to this strange man's restless thinking and his reach toward the perfection of his scheme is one of the signal documents in the history of international scholarship. The scheme covered first the English-speaking countries—the Empire and the United States; then a codicil let in Germans who knew English.

In these days it is hard to recapture the spirit of Cecil Rhodes's dreams. But they were the epitome of British imperial thinking in the nineteenth century. English schoolboys were brought up on the slogan, borrowed from Spain, that the sun never sets on the Empire. In the last decade of the century, Britons swelled with pride at the poem that Kipling in one of his less humble moods composed:

> The poor little street-bred people that
> vapour and fume and brag,
> They are lifting their heads in the stillness
> to yelp at the English Flag!

But there was no vainglory, no flag-waving or lion-roaring in the long dream of Cecil Rhodes. He honestly believed that mankind would be better off if it was wholly dominated by the Anglo-Saxon race. He wanted the entire continent of Africa to be part of the Empire; he wanted men and women to go out from England and settle in the Middle East and in South America until the population in those lands was predominately British, and he spoke for the "recovery of America"—protesting that he had no wish to make of the United States a subject nation, but rather that it should be an integral part of the Empire with the central government alternating between London and Washington. If these things were accomplished, Rhodes believed that there would come to pass an eternal Pax Britannica with no more wars or hates or international disharmony. Whether that grandiose scheme would have produced, in the new century, the beginning of the Scriptural millennium instead of the bloodiest of all times is a question

29

which belongs with the ifs of history—a difficult game to play since all empire except the Soviet has so utterly dissolved.

Rhodes first stated his dream at the age of twenty-two when wealth and power lay far in the future. But it was the inspiration of his impulse toward riches. From this point to the last of his seven wills, there was a progressive moderation of his aims until at last they took tangible form in the educational project of the Scholarships. But meanwhile he had added nearly half a million square miles of South Africa—what has become Rhodesia—to the Empire and he had helped set the stage for the conflict which would add the Transvaal as well. In this land he had become a benevolent despot, a true dictator, yet beloved by the natives and even, for a time, by many of the Dutch as well.

He died in 1902 as the Boer War drew to its close. Immediately the trustees of his huge estate began to work out the complex provisions of his last will. Perhaps most difficult of all were the plans for Rhodes Scholarships in the United States. Basic to the trouble here was the difference between British and American concepts of the higher education.

## 6

In the United States, the extreme ideal of democracy has infused and finally controlled education as it has all other aspects of American life. We suffer today from the compulsion in our schools to consider all students equal and to offer little advantage to the uncommonly gifted. The result is a conformity to a norm set by a low common denominator and boys and girls are kept immature beyond their adolescence. To maintain the pretense of equal opportunity an arithmetical scheme of credits is set up and the pressure of strict supervision demanded by the least adult of the group is applied to all. But this arithmetical scheme further seems to set an equality of values for all subjects so that the student believes himself to be educated as soon as he has gained the correct number of credits. As Frank Aydelotte, a former Rhodes trustee, has written:

> It is so easy for the quantitative method of counting up hours in a registrar's office to get itself translated into a quantitative theory of culture. When . . . the elective system seems to be based on some kind of democracy of courses in which one "hour" is equal to another no matter how many light-years of intellectual distance may separate their origins, it is easy for the student . . . to come to think of education in purely quantitative terms. A man cannot do this in Oxford. The very lack of a system brings him face to face with the reality of education.

This difference tended to frighten Americans away from the qualifying examinations. The requirement of Greek and Latin also excluded many boys, for our schools did not insist on the classics. Thus competition for the Scholarship was reduced. But the trustees had further trouble carrying out the provisions of the Rhodes will. These provided that there should always be two Rhodes Scholars at Oxford from each state or territory. The trustees soon found that, notwithstanding the theory of democratic education, the states were far from equal in levels of learning. So while several boys were eligible from, say, Massachusetts, there were fewer from Mississippi. This varied from year to year but Rhodes's plan of two from every state was a more quantitative scheme than Oxford's traditions warranted.

Today, all of these problems have been met; the United States has been divided into regions of six states each. Returning Rhodes Scholars, full of enthusiasm, have spread the word and the competition is keen. And the Latin and Greek requirements have been abolished. These changes were made possible by those clauses in the Rhodes will which allowed flexibility to the trustees: and told them that the aim was to get the best Scholars rather than

31

to stick to details of method. But in 1910, none of this adjustment had been made.

On the other hand, in 1910, the American committees of selection were determined, whatever the difficulties, to meet the founder's ideals of young manhood. These were carefully specified in the will.

My desire being [it read] that the student who shall be elected to the Scholarships shall not be merely bookworms, I direct that . . . regard shall be had to (1) his literary and scholastic attainments; (2) his fondness for and success in manly outdoor sports . . . (3) his qualities of manhood, truth, devotion to duty, sympathy for and protection of the weak, kindliness, unselfishness and fellowship; and (4) his exhibition during school days of moral force of character and of instincts to lead and take an interest in his schoolmates.

Perhaps there was no one in the state of Indiana in 1910 who could present the requisite B.A. or B.S. degree and, at the same time meet all the other standards. Elmer Davis, however much otherwise he may have qualified, could show little "success" in outdoor sports. "Fondness" he had indeed in theory. But here again the English concept differed from the American. Even in 1910 the American amateur athlete was professional in all but pay. English boys played for the fun of it. "Success" in England was synonymous with "fondness." There was no grueling competition in an English college, no bitterness at failure to "make" a team. You played rugby or soccer because you loved it; the games were incidental to other pursuits.

So Elmer, holding, at twenty, a degree of B.A. *magna cum laude* and already reading the odes of Horace for pleasure, was elected and prepared, as the Franklin year closed, to go out into a larger world than Aurora or Franklin had dreamed of. His fellows looked on him with a mixture of awe and puzzlement. They read the account of his success in the Indianapolis *Times* and asked each

32

other what was Oxford, what was Queen's, what on earth was Litterae Humaniores, the "honor school," Davis had chosen? And why should an Indiana man want to go that far from home with all the opportunity there was here? Some shook their heads and said well, that was the kind of thing that happened to a man once he forsook the good Baptist faith, and they predicted he'd be sorry when he found himself in that godless foreign place. The young men thought and said what all groups of undergraduate Americans think and say when they see one in their midst who knows precisely where he is going and why.

7

In 1910, William Howard Taft was in the second year of his Presidency. In England, Edward VII died and the people shouted Long Live the King to George V. In Germany, the Emperor, William II, said, "Looking on myself as God's instrument, I shall go my way without regard to the ideas and opinions of the time"; the cruiser *Moltke* was launched at Hamburg and a battleship squadron took permanent station at Wilhelmshaven. In the Far East, Korea was annexed to Japan.

In the United States, the Boy Scouts of America, the Rockefeller Foundation and the Carnegie Peace Fund were established. Mark Twain, O. Henry, Winslow Homer, Julia Ward Howe, John La Farge and Mary Baker Eddy died. The Pennsylvania railroad began running trains under the Hudson River to Manhattan. Glenn Curtiss made a new record by flying sixty miles in one hour and eighteen minutes; Barney Oldfield broke the world automobile record at $27\frac{2}{3}$ seconds a mile, and the trotter Uhlan trotted at the rate of 1.58 minutes a mile, thus establishing a new record on the harness track. In Highland Park, Detroit, Henry Ford opened a vast new plant to be devoted to the manufacture by assembly-line techniques of the Model T. The year was remarkable for its abundance of strikes and trust-busting. Philadelphia was victorious in the World Series, winning four games to Chicago's one.

In October, after inventing a highly ingenious way of crossing the ocean without paying his passage, Elmer Davis enrolled at Queen's College, Oxford. In his case the hope of Cecil Rhodes that men might come to England to study "without . . . withdrawing them or their sympathies from the land of their adoption or birth" was abundantly realized. For Elmer remained not only American but indomitably Hoosier as well.

# 2 ]]]]]]

1

THE ENGLISH, in 1910, were just beginning to feel a weakening of their earlier conviction that all Americans were products of the Wild West; if not actual cowboys, at least they were rugged folk accustomed to nightly attacks by grizzly bears and Indians. This had been normal enough, for people always believe what they want to believe about foreigners. Such a romantic view of America was long cherished by Englishmen and their final awakening to the drab truth that we were, indeed, much like themselves was disappointing.

Mr. Hugh Moran, a Rhodes Scholar of 1905, writing more than fifty years later in the *American Oxonian*, recalls his first days at Wadham College. A white-haired Fellow (member of the faculty) dropped in to call. "I say," he asked Moran, "do tell me, did you ever know Billy the Kid?" When Moran said no, the Fellow was sorry. It then appeared that he knew more about Billy the Kid than Moran knew. He had learned of him years before when he had lived briefly on a ranch in the Far West and Billy had become one of his favorite characters. He forgave Moran his ignorance, then, and took him home to tea. His wife, Moran remembered, "bowed formally and motioned me to a seat, looking me up and down as if astonished that I did not wear a sombrero and buckskin shirt. . . ."

By 1910, however, enough Americans had come to Oxford to alter the traditional opinion. Several American Scholars had brilliantly distinguished themselves. They had not only stood well by

35

comparison with colonials—men from Australia, Canada and
Rhodes's own South Africa—but they had competed successfully
with Englishmen in both studies and sports. Whether or not this
was pleasing to the English youths who might have preferred to
look upon their transatlantic cousins as glamorous savages, the
adjustment toward truth was in accord with the shape of things
to come—with a time of necessary partnership in the defense of
Western civilization.

But, as Cecil Rhodes had wished it, the candid young Americans cherished the differences between themselves and their hosts.
If they had tried to ape the English manners and too readily
accept the English views, one of the purposes of the scholarships
would have been defeated. For both Englishmen and Americans
on this high intellectual plane the divergencies were healthy.
Through the years the liberalization of Oxford from the extreme
conservatism of the past has come partly through contagion from
American students and many of our own educational institutions
have been inoculated by returning Rhodes Scholars who have become professors, with resulting changes in the design and practice
of scholarship. All this was, perhaps, inevitable as the world grew
smaller and alliances between peoples became irresistible, but it
was hastened by the far vision of Cecil Rhodes.

But such a future, in 1910, was dim for most of us, and
England, for Americans of small means, was a fortnight away
from New York and farther still from Aurora, Indiana. To the
Hoosier home-town boy, the journey must have seemed like an
adventure; the horizon both alluring and fearsome. What went on
in the private mind of Elmer Davis as he faced the prospect we
are unlikely to discover; we only know that, when he had covered
the first lap, his behavior was both bold and shrewd.

2

To a young man of twenty, thriftily reared, for whom the doors
of opportunity have suddenly opened wide, money is likely to be

a primary consideration. For young Davis, the transatlantic future was bright enough. The enormous sum of three hundred pounds (in 1910, the equivalent of $1,500) awaited him in Oxford but no part of this was available to him in New York on the eve of the adventure. Most certainly he did not want to be beholden to his father for more than the barest of expenses. There was no enmity there, as later events were to show; only an urgent wish for independence. He knew that he was leaving Aurora for good. That narrow circle of experience was behind him. He might have occasional nostalgic dreams about the home town and he would continue to be proud of the state but he wanted no ties with it. His father might pay for his trip to New York but he would invent his way on from that point.

Forty-eight new Rhodes Scholars were on their way to England that fall. Most of them were embarking at New York. Why not persuade them all to go on the same ship? This would give them a chance to get acquainted before "term" at the colleges began. Also, if one passenger could herd all the others on board a certain ship, might not the steamship company to which she belonged look on that passenger with favor?

Davis asked this question in the office of the American Line. An official said the company would not only look with favor, they would give such a passenger his own passage free. It was not a new device even in 1910, nor was it a particularly brilliant one, but it revealed a distaste for debt—even to a father—that amounted in later years to one of the few fears that ever disturbed Elmer Davis and made him, as a friend said, a sort of financial hypochondriac.

The *Haverford* was not a passenger ship but passengers were welcome for their passage money. Her cargo was mainly cattle. She made her way slowly in the early October winds and landed in Liverpool.

As always, men made cautious acquaintance with Davis. Some were scared of his close-packed wit. Even as a boy, he took quick, strong dislikes. His irony withered the fakers, the pretentious. But others who jumped the first hurdles became deeply attached. Those who understood humor got to know him best; but, in any crowd, the percentage of men responsive to wit is never high.

His cabin mate was Whitney Shepardson who, more than forty years later, was to share with him some of the burdens of the second World War. Shepardson was a graduate of Colgate and was headed for Balliol College. Sharing a small cabin for two weeks on a cattle steamer, men either kill each other or become enduring friends. But there was no casualty in the Davis-Shepardson quarters, and if there were occasional word battles, both enjoyed them, for they were both experts in word marksmanship.

It was raining in Liverpool when the *Haverford* docked there. It was still raining in Oxford on the Sunday night that Davis and a fellow Scholar, Charles Zeek, from Louisiana, arrived. The train had been late and when their hansom cab arrived at Queen's College, the gate was closed. For a while they stood in the cold rain, pounding on the gate breaking the deep Sabbath stillness with their noise. Finally a man in a top hat came and opened the gate. His appearance was impressive. Davis held out his hand.

"I'm Elmer Davis, sir," he said, "and I suppose you are the president of the college."

"No, sir," the man replied, "I am the college porter."

"Such," Professor Zeek remembers, "was our introduction to Oxford, where we found the porter and the messenger to be among the most important people in the college quadrangle."

The clothes-conscious Britishers of those days must have been amused by the American sartorial variety. At Oxford anyone who did not wear the gray bags and Norfolk jacket was conspicuous. What they thought of the peg-topped trousers, the padded shoulders, the high-button shoes and the pork-pie hat that were fashionable at the time in Aurora, Indiana, is not recorded but the looks these Oxford lads cast at Elmer Davis are remembered by his fellow Scholars. In clothes, he eventually capitulated with inroads into his 300 pounds, but it is well remembered that he continued to wear with pride the other marks of his Americanism.

The preservation of what has been called, *ad nauseam,* his "twang" amid the deeper and more resonant tones that surrounded him was probably not consciously rebellious. Persons with sensitive ears almost invariably take on something of the accent of the daily speech they hear. The so-called "drawl" of the southern United States, for example, is peculiarly infectious and many a Yankee, however determined to guard his speech, has returned after a long sojourn in the South to amuse his northern friends with the lazy overlay that has softened his normal staccato harshness. Now we know from Davis's own statements that he did not have a sensitive ear. He was never able to acquire anything resembling a proper French accent though his idiom and grammar were correct and though he was married to a woman who was nearly bilingual. So the celebrated "twang" was more likely a result of physical inflexibility than of Hoosier stubbornness. In any case its effect was profound because it was so integral with his other traits.

Two things he could never quite take. One was the climate, which he called "un-Christian." The other was the eight-o'clock roll call, that curious institution which seemed so at odds with Oxford's general freedom from restriction. No count, for instance, was taken of attendance at lectures or other functions. Where a man might eat was his own affair. But, for the first two years residence in the college was required and this was checked by a curfew and a rising hour.

It is told that when Davis's "scout" knocked at his door one morning and announced that it was half past seven, sir, Elmer said yes and turned over. In an hour the man returned: It's half past eight, sir. Through the morning this was repeated every hour. Finally the disheartened man called: It's noon, sir, and I'm going home.

Elmer's rooms were on a stair in the corner of the Back Quad.

**39**

On the wall hung an oar from a shell of 1833 when the Queen's College crew won a victory over a Cambridge crew. The oar must have been a reminder of a sport in which young Davis could never excel. Perhaps more important to him was the occupancy of the rooms many years before by the great Jeremy Bentham.

3

The first few weeks of an American Rhodes Scholar were, in 1910, full of surprises. This is less true today since in our universities there is more awareness of English educational systems and since so many returning Scholars have told their tales.

It was disconcerting, for instance, after graduating, perhaps with honors, from an American college to find oneself again a freshman in a hierarchy in which the upperclassmen looked at one down their noses. It was galling to discover that no recognition whatever was given to the American degree or the American honors. At the same time it seemed curious that the student— "fresher" though he be—was left so utterly to his own devices as far as methods of study, choice of lectures to be attended, hours of work and play; and above all that there were no tests or quizzes, no devices by which he or his teacher could keep a periodic check on his work.

As Frank Aydelotte, former American Secretary to the Rhodes Trustees wrote in his book, *The American Rhodes Scholarships:*

The American student at Oxford misses almost all the academic machinery that he has been used to in his native university. At Oxford there are no "courses" in the American sense of the term. There are no record cards in the registrar's office, no "signing up" for the lectures he expects to attend, no required number of hours per week, no daily assignments, no mid-term tests or hour exams. The Rhodes

40

Scholar is a little puzzled on his first Monday morning, and on a great many mornings thereafter, to know just what he is expected to do at a given hour or moment. Shall he read this volume, or master such and such a table of dates, or attend such and such a lecture, or perchance wander down High Street in search of tobacco, or shall he spend a few hours in the shop of one of the delightful Oxford booksellers . . . ? The whole world of work and play . . . is all before him where to choose. His only hard-and-fast academic engagement is to call on his tutor once a week at a specified hour to read an essay on a specified topic.

In short, the American student discovered that Oxford was more interested in educating than in instructing him. Nothing was thrust upon him. The English college is interested in drawing out rather than putting in. It provides abundant opportunity for the student to show his talent, his aptitude or his interest: perhaps never again will he find such wide-open gates for his effort. But he must make his own way through them; no one will push him or try to "get him by." To the tutor he will express himself and a good tutor will listen as much as he will talk. American educators are coming to see the merit in such a pattern, but few of them did so in 1910.

Scraps of reminiscence by men who were at Queen's with Elmer Davis throw some light on activities there that were signposts pointing toward his mature character and career.

I do not recall [writes H. Garey Hudson of the class behind his] that Elmer engaged in any of the college sports. [Another contemporary remembers that one row on the river in a cold rain was enough.] It seems to me that his usual exercise was an afternoon walk adorned with some of his characteristic brilliant conversation. His keen observations and dry wit were well known.

41

And he was a rebel, as always, against tyranny.

On the occasion of a revolt in the Junior Common Room against a small clique of upperclassmen who, though without talent in anything except political manipulation, had arrogated to themselves the control of college affairs including sports, Elmer was a leader in planning the parliamentary strategy through which the bosses were overthrown.

That these bosses were the sacred "upperclassmen" who, Scholar Hudson recalls, were customarily regarded as demigods by those below made no difference to Scholar Davis. Give me Liberty! he shouted, in effect, and won the battle.

That Elmer Davis was mature enough to fit quickly into this unsystematic system is evident from the rapidity with which he made his way. That he was able, in addition to the rigorous pursuit of *litterae humaniores,* to explore Europe as far as Turkey and thus establish in his early twenties a basis for his later international understanding, is still more significant. But the Oxford educational design helped there, too.

Vacation, at Oxford, takes up half the year. There are six weeks at Christmas, another six weeks at Easter and four months in the summer when the student is free to go his own way. He is under no compulsion whatever. But vacation at Oxford is not the same as vacation in an American college. In a subtle but essential sense, the Oxford vacation is part of the curriculum. In America when final exams for the year are done with, the student does his best to forget his college work. Either he goes in for an orgy of rest and play or he gets a summer job usually remote from his college courses. But at Oxford, when he is released from conferences with his tutor and from lectures, his deeper educational work begins. Now, in leisurely privacy, he can digest all that the term has fed him; he can reflect and he can let himself be led into new paths of understanding. In term, he is guided into learning; in vacation he educates himself. In vacation his hours of reading may be supplemented by play but he is never under the pressure to enjoy himself that departmentalizes American school and college and, indeed, business life.

The scholarship stipend makes travel possible and travel is encouraged in the English university tradition. To the purposeful scholar it is integrated with study. The man whose "honor school" is European history finds on the Continent the artifacts that give tangible substance to his reading. If, like Davis, he is pursuing the classics, these will come into high visibility in Greece and Rome.

## 4

From Aurora, Indiana, to Oxford in England is a long stride. But for the English-speaking youth with Anglo-Saxon blood, England is never quite another world. From Aurora to Paris, however, is a jump out of reality. When he first found Paris, England had not drawn Davis entirely out of Aurora. There were other Americans in Paris, then, escaping its unreality by banding together but watching from their safe refuge the engaging strangeness. One of these, a student like himself and living with a group of students, had gone a little deeper into Paris than most; she had worked at it and could interpret it in more universal terms. She was a Boston girl, younger than Elmer, with more, perhaps, of what the snobs called culture and less of book learning. Telling him about Paris, showing him the theater and the opera, the gardens and the Guignols and amused by his occasional derisive appraisals, Florence MacMillan was presently in love.

Elmer, however, had much to think about and much to see in Europe before he went back to Queen's College. There was no question, then, of marriage: it must stand, if at all, far in the future. Marriage forfeited the Rhodes Scholar his scholarship. But in those days, there was plenty of time for everything. Love could be slow or interrupted, and marriage was a serious thing with economic implications in that far-off time when you had to pay for what you bought, and if a young American had hasty thoughts, Oxford soon dissolved them.

It is possible that, after a Paris vacation, a new color or note was added to the already abundant harmony of *litterae humaniores*. Certainly if there had been danger of Davis's becoming that object of Rhodes's dread, a bookworm, Paris mitigated it.

After "term" had begun a few reminders came in the post from across the Channel. Elmer and Florence had found a first bond—one of those ties so eagerly sought by trysting youth—in the coincidence of their birthdays. Both were born on the thirteenth of January. On this thread were hung many of the shy words that began the long courtship.

But before this romance had begun there were other troubles that threw it out of focus. As early as January, 1911, a letter had caught up with Elmer in Dresden where he had gone on his first holiday. The news it contained must have disturbed his entire Oxford stay. It was from his mother. It told of a financial disaster that had overtaken his father. A local company in which Elam Davis had had faith and had become involved had failed. The loss of his stock which he had borrowed money to buy, and his personal endorsement on some defaulted notes, had put him in debt to the extent of nearly $20,000.

To Elmer this news coming so near the start of his new life must have been a shocking blow. His reply to his mother's letter does not survive. It is possible that he offered to come home at once to help her out, for a month later he got a letter from his father playing down the bad news. It began, "Pleased to know you enjoyed vacation" but cautioned him that it was better to stay at school and give time to his studies than to go on trips of recreation. Then:

As for me and the financial embarrassment that has overtaken me, do not let that worry you . . . while we will be

44

very poor, while the Lord gives us good health, and plenty of work, we feel rich, and will be enabled to get on without trouble . . . we are living comfortably, your mother is greatly enjoying her teaching, and I still have my position in the bank.

It must have been about this time, nevertheless, that the determination came to cut the time of Oxford study from three to two years. However much the people at home discounted the consequence of the disaster, the news posed an uncertainty: how long would it be before young Elmer would have to get out and work to help mend the broken fortunes? And when the hint of love came in Paris, that doubt built higher the barrier to eventual marriage.

Yet none of these troubles could dangerously interrupt this levelheaded youth in the pursuit of his education under the immortal aegis of Cecil Rhodes. On the contrary, they spurred him to harder effort, determined him to capture the full loot while there was yet time. The dominant fact about the life of Elmer Davis was its evasion of waste. He filled every hour with mental activity, but not to overflowing, so that nothing was lost and his memory sealed what his mind had embraced.

In June, 1912, he believed he was ready for what was known in Oxford as "Greats"—the examination for his B.A. degree. He had mastered the Greek language and had read deeply in the literature and history of Greece. These things became part of the very currency of his writing and speaking in later years. There are allusions to ancient history in many of his best essays; his letters and addresses composed in troublous years compared the politics of Hellenic or Roman times with those of the current American scene. The effect of some of this study on his radio talks was noted by Professor William C. Greene:

I used to recommend to my Harvard classes in Greek that they listen to Davis, among other reasons because his Oxford training in Greats had contributed to his masterly use of connectives in his brief broadcasts and to his clarity in indicating thereby his shifts of direction,—emphasis, or qualification, or statement of opposing facts.

In Greats, Davis won a Second. Why he did not get a First was explained in a letter written by his tutor, E. M. Walker of Queen's College:

Mr. Davis came to this college as a Rhodes Scholar in the autumn of 1910 and began his reading for the Schol Litterae Humaniores in January, 1911. His original intention was to take the usual period of reading, two and a half years. Circumstances, however, compelled him to enter for the examination a year earlier in June, 1912; and he thus had a full year less for his course of study than is customary. In spite of this, he all but obtained a First Class. This I regard as one of the most remarkable achievements I have ever known in this Schol.

Still, when the examination was over, he did not go home. By getting his degree in 1912 he could hold himself ready for return at any time. But the letters from home were not insistent.

He spent the summer traveling. In Belgrade, he fell into the hands of an unscrupulous money changer who took his good British money and gave him, in exchange, the worthless currency of a dead regime. "I was a stranger," he quoted, as usual from the Bible, "and he took me in." The detailed knowledge of the Balkans and of the complex relationships of central European peoples to Germany and Russia which appeared in later essays was acquired, in part at least, in these vacation travels.

In October he took up "digs" in Walton Street and did postgraduate work through the winter. Letters from both his father and mother at that time told of his father's illness and the cost of

medical treatment but they still urged him not to come home—
yet.

For her birthday on January 13, 1913, Elmer sent Florence
MacMillan thirteen roses. "How," she wrote him that night, "did
you spend our birthday?" They were engaged, then, but further
hope was long deferred. In June, another coincidence strength-
ened the bond that the coincidence of their birthdays had established. Both Florence and Elmer were recalled to America by the
illness of their fathers. Both arrived too late. William Donald
MacMillan and Elam Holmes Davis died within a week of each
other.

The letter telling him of his father's death by heart failure met
Elmer as he landed in Boston on the White Star Liner *Cymric* out
of Liverpool.

With his arrival the lean years began. They were years of
courage and self-denial. They did not tend to reduce the symptoms of financial hypochondria. But they were full of enterprise
and the development of a diversity of talents.

# 3 ]]]]]

## 1

THE YEAR 1913 was the year before the deluge from which we have never wholly emerged. It was more than the end of an era or a delayed turn of the century; more than an eve of revolution. It was the meeting moment of a past and a future more different from each other than any pasts and futures so suddenly juxtaposed had ever been before. It was a moment of dead center when directional movement seemed to have stopped for the sole apparent purpose of letting us enjoy being alive in the security of the best possible world. Tomorrow we—citizens of the civilized world as we called ourselves—expected to continue in the march of progress into an infinity of green pastures.

The march of civilization [wrote Elmer Davis looking back on 1913 from 1940] had freed man from his traditional worries—food and security. Ruinous wars, destructive social upheavals, were as certainly outgrown as famine, pandemic diseases, religious bigotry. Man was free to think; he could think boldly, for the machinery of society was foolproof. If society still needed improvement, that could be accomplished by the direct primary, or the popular election of senators, or the initiative, referendum, and recall; or by giving the vote to women.

48

Actually the change in velocities, or whatever it was that brought the dead center in 1913, had begun earlier in the Edwardian years. Windows had been opened to air out the stuffiness of late Victorian rooms. A new visibility had penetrated the corners hitherto darkened by artificial convention as surely as the electric light had done away with the shadows of the gaslit streets. The resulting change of manners had brought in a new frankness which eventually became as artificial as the concealment which had preceded it but which, in 1913, was still fresh and refreshing.

Before about 1912 it was generally true that the righteous could be seen in certain places, the wicked in certain others; now the two streams intermingled for the first time. . . . So nice girls went to tango teas at cabarets, and drank cocktails, and smoked cigarettes, and talked sex with boys; and of course there was a tremendous uproar.

If we try now to hear that uproar it will be drowned out by the echoes of the guns and bombs that we have been hearing ever since. But those of us that can remember its sound are sure that it was rather pleasing than otherwise to the young people who had inspired it; it was obbligato to the dance melodies—the counterpoint of the tangos. We were spurred to bigger and bolder things when

Our moral mentors told us that it was an age of unprecedented license and corruption, and that we boys and girls who had just cracked our shells were a brood of vipers from the pit.

There was nothing peculiarly American about all this. The same kind of renaissance (as it then seemed) was sweeping over Europe. Men and women were dancing in Rome and Paris and Berlin; women in those places were lost in even bigger smoke

49

clouds than in America, and in the England that Elmer Davis had just left, the tango tea was especially popular because there was tea in it. The night clubs—always international whether they are in London, Vienna or Cairo—were as crowded with young "vipers" as in New York and the horror of the English clerics reverberated in the Gothic vaults of Anglican cathedrals.

To us of that generation all these things that we did in 1913 were gay because there were no strings to them, they were of the moment, uncomplicated, pure fun. The present was so utterly present, so overwhelming that yesterday was forgotten, tomorrow indefinitely postponed. This has never been the same since, perhaps will never be.

## 2

The fringe of all this must have brushed Elmer Davis even in the cloistered ambiance of Queen's College during his last few months in England. Whether his work, bringing alive the dead languages and exploring ancient Rome, had kept him from the tango teas he has not said; at least we know he was aware of them. He was more aware of them in England and of all the moral revolution than in Cincinnati and Aurora where he went to help his mother out of her personal tragedy and out of the financial doldrums in which Elam Davis's death had left her. It was hardly an atmosphere calculated to emphasize the joy of living. To this young man dynamic with energy and feeling the urgency of a world he must live at the center of, an Indiana river town gave no inspiration. It belonged to a past he wanted to shuffle off like an old skin and he was impatient to get into the central whirlpool currents of America. A look at the high school, maybe the college at Franklin, induced a fading of the never too strong impulse toward a teaching career.

It was quite natural for him to want to write. At Oxford he had done essays and theses that were highly praised. What has been preserved of his writing in those days has not the directness or the thrift of words that later set him apart from his lush contemporaries. But anyone who could see latent talent in a manuscript saw it in his. "He writes excellent English," wrote Tutor Clark of Queen's, "and expresses himself with vigour." And H. Garey Hudson, Queen's '11, notes:

> Elmer belonged to a group including Christopher Morley and John Crowe Ransom which set about writing a novel. Each member of the group in succession was responsible for a chapter, his aim being to leave the plot so tangled as to defy the efforts of the next writer to solve it.

He had come to grips with his mother but he had done that before (along with Aunt Huldah) and won. Louise Davis was a persistent woman; it was said she could talk such a stream that interruption was nearly impossible. She was dead set against the career of a free-lance writer—an idea Elmer had played with at Oxford—and she had written him that he could not possibly support himself so: advice which was, of course, quite sound. But he *must* teach, she said, teaching made money, then if he insisted, he could write "on the side."

Elmer had learned the expediency of silence. It was Elam Davis's way to let Louise talk. Elmer privately approved the technique. He let his mother have her say and did not try to argue. But after she was through he went his own way—which was to New York—and took her with him.

There must have been some money somewhere. (There nearly always is.) It is certain that he could not have supported both his mother and himself on the wages from his first job on *Adventure* magazine—ten dollars a week. But it was equally certain that even in 1913 when ten dollars was ten dollars that, at week's end, there was little left for either saving or dissipation. He lived as far west as you can get on 113th Street in New York. It was there that, in September, a wistful letter reached him after being

51

forwarded from Aurora in which Florence MacMillan, now in Brookline, Massachusetts, said that she was still wearing his pin but would send it back to him whenever he should find someone he liked better.

*Adventure* irked him in the winter and he began casting about for something into which he could more deeply get his teeth. Early in 1914, a letter from Arthur Greaves of the New York *Times* told of a possible job there. "I got it," Elmer scribbled in the margin of Greaves's letter, and the letter with the young man's exuberant annotation is among the handful from those days that have survived.

## 3

It was a broad jump from the quiet of Queen's College to the tempestuous city room of the New York *Times,* even with Aurora and adventureless *Adventure* in between. To the cub reporter who chased fire engines, turned up at the spot of a murder before the body was cold or, at short notice, covered a sports event, the Latin poets were of little immediate use. It is true that the *Times* was more consistently aware of erudition than the other New York papers, but on a more leisurely floor than that on which Davis worked, and its scholarly sallies usually waited till Sunday to emerge. Also, the *Times* screened the news so that only that which was "fit to print" appeared—on its front pages at least. And the editors, too, followed a code of rhetoric and a prescribed vocabulary which pleased young men who had taken on the English language as their mistress.

When this young man of twenty-four began his job on the *Times,* there was plenty of news. We are surprised, looking back over the yellowed or microfilmed papers, that there were so few portents even in the foreign dispatches. The cloud no bigger than a man's hand that hung so pregnant over Europe was scarcely visible. There had been war, there was unrest in the Balkans, but there was always unrest in the Balkans and the Balkans were too far away to be worried about by New Yorkers—or, for that matter, Londoners or Parisians. But New Yorkers took the domestic news seriously.

Woodrow Wilson had been in the White House long enough to arouse the ire of the conservatives who regarded any interruption of the *status quo* as a threat to the life of the Republic. Wilson was critical of business and industry. The tariff, he said, "makes the government a facile instrument in the hands of facile interests." He appeared to favor what was not yet called a welfare state. He planned a reform of banking and currency. He considered private monopolies "indefensible and intolerable."

In the year before, the state of Wyoming had ratified the income tax amendment; now it was a reality and to cap the horror, taxes were publishable and therefore incomes could be fairly accurately guessed at by the public. Businessmen, accustomed to almost countless years of cut-throat competition and a *caveat emptor* policy, were uneasy before the newly created, powerful Federal Trade Commission. Was it really true that business was now going to be regulated from Washington? Was the sacred *laissez-faire* which had brought the nation to industrial leadership of the world about to be abandoned?

In Panama, the canal was opened to traffic from ocean to ocean. In Colorado, one of the bloodiest battles in the history of American labor, between striking coal miners and gunmen whom the operators hastily pushed into the militia, resulted in the death of twenty-five persons, including eleven women and two children. The violence ended only when President Wilson sent Federal troops to Ludlow, Colorado.

It was in the spring of 1914 that President Wilson ended the tradition whereby, in the event of national insults from abroad, honor could only be satisfied by humble apology or war. Indeed, for a few feverish weeks, there was a true war scare in such inflammable centers as New York. It had nothing to do with Europe where the fuse would soon start burning. The controversy

53

was between us and Mexico. Victoriano Huerta, who had become Mexico's President by the expedient not unprecedented in Latin America of murdering his predecessor, had ordered the arrest of some United States Marines in Tampico. Huerta apologized but the pacifist Secretary of State, William Jennings Bryan, also demanded that he salute the American flag. This he refused to do. While the American warmongers were screaming for blood, President Wilson quietly adopted a policy he called "watchful waiting." He did seize the custom house at Vera Cruz to prevent the landing there of a shipment of arms. But later he accepted mediation from the "ABC" powers of South America. There was no salute to the flag but it was a Pyrrhic victory for Huerta: a new revolution forced him out in July. This patient act for which Wilson was bitterly criticized marked the beginning of a new era of international relations.

In New York, Charles Becker lost his appeal from conviction for instigating the murder of Herman Rosenthal—a 1912 crime so sensational that other news had been pushed off the front pages of every paper except the *Times*. But even the *Times* ran stories of the retrial which centered round such legendary characters as Gyp the Blood, Dago Frank, Lefty Louie and Whitey Lewis. In otherwise dull New York, Theodore Roosevelt arrived after travels in the wilder parts of South America where he claimed to have discovered a hitherto unknown river. Skeptics greeted this news with the suggestion that the "River of Doubt" was well named and one, checking Roosevelt's location of it on the map, said it must run uphill. But the Colonel was ill, had lost thirty-five pounds, and the *Times* extended its sympathy in an editorial headed "The Returning Conqueror." The first widely publicized demonstration of radiotelephone (which would one day become the means of broadcasting) was a half-hour conversation between the Wanamaker stores of New York and Philadelphia. And, at the end of May, New Yorkers to whom the memory of the *Titanic* disaster was still vivid, were shaken by the news that the steamship *Empress of Ireland* had sunk in the St. Lawrence with a loss of 954 lives.

These things happened against a background of serenity in the United States. The news from abroad was no more disturbing. The most violent news in Britain was of the behavior of militant woman suffragists who slashed a Velasquez painting in the National Gallery, attempted to force an entrance to Buckingham Palace and tried to blow up a viaduct of Glasgow's water supply. In Germany a new record for balloon flight was established and the editor of a newspaper was imprisoned for laughing, editorially, at the Crown Prince. There was a secret convention with France concerning Northern Anatolia and Syria. In France, an airplane pilot flew over Mont Blanc and there was a general election in which eleven political parties figured. There was also a four-party election in Austria-Hungary and laws were passed there for the compulsory education of children over six. And then, at the end of June a shot was fired. After it nothing in the world was ever quite the same.

4

It took not only the newspapers but even the experts in international politics quite a while to clarify the connection between the assassination of Austria's Archduke with the battles of Vimy and the Marne. To New Yorkers, the sparks along the fuse from Sarajevo were quite incomprehensible. A few were so horrified by the jumping of the fire from Serbia through France, Belgium and across to England that they began to wonder if, eventually, it might also leap the Atlantic.

Elmer Davis, reading the flash news in August and September, must have felt acutely the plight of his English friends. Already England had mobilized and young men were streaming across the Channel. Many of them, he knew, were trying to carry the happy mood of the year past into the unknown trenches. Later he read

**55**

of the young officers who leapt on the parapets and, with their swagger sticks, waved their troops into the attack until the impersonal traverses of the German machine guns convinced them that they were no longer on the playing fields of Eton and Rugby.

In London, when all the English orchestras went into the minor, the dancing still went on but now there was an urgency that came among the boys and the girls so that the whole of sex had to be crammed into the minutes before the train or the boat left. The inconsequential mood was there no longer. If there had been love in 1913, it was, as Elmer remembered it, "a delicately flavored blend of reality and illusion, of candor and mystery." In 1914, it was, perhaps, even more unreal, yet it had a momentary starkness; its candor was a necessity, not an adventure, and its only mystery lay in the question whether or not death would end the story.

Sex, of course, has always played a supporting role in war and so it did in 1914, though less elegantly and less chastely than in the Age of Chivalry. But overnight, the relatively slow, shy sex of the English tango tea had altered. Now everything had a string attached. Even the dancing and the cabarets, even the cocktails and the cigarettes, suddenly had a purpose. The curious thing was that the beetle-browed moral critics found that the activities against which they had railed a year before were now noble, as if all sin might be forgiven and even glorified once a patriot's grave appeared this side of the horizon.

From then on through the years of war and peace and war, the human mind has been trying to catch up with the facts. Probably, if he were alive today, Elmer Davis would doubt that it ever could.

5

The first vivid eyewitness story to come to America—a story which has become a classic in the history of American war correspondence—was printed, not in the New York *Times* but in its rival morning paper, the *Tribune*. To New Yorkers it brought a sense of the war's immensity and of the ruthlessness which would distinguish it from all other modern wars—a sense which, in the years to come, would grow to fever height. Without today's syndicate pattern, however, in which such a story would be repeated in a hundred provincial newspapers through the country, this remarkable piece of reporting had little effect on the inland population, much of which was still angrily pro-German.

The story was written in the city of Brussels while the veteran American correspondent, Richard Harding Davis, watched the invasion, there, of the destroying enemy.

The entrance of the German army into Brussels has lost the human quality. It was lost as soon as the three soldiers who led the army bicycled into the Boulevard du Régent, and asked the way to the Gare du Nord. When they passed the human note passed with them.

What came after them, and twenty-four hours later is still coming, is not men marching, but a force of nature like a tidal wave, an avalanche or a river flooding its banks. . . .

At the sight of the first few regiments of the enemy we were thrilled. After, for three hours, they had passed in one unbroken steel-gray column, we were bored. But when hour after hour passed, and there was no halt, no breathing time, no open spaces in the ranks, the thing became uncanny. . . . You returned to watch it, fascinated. It held the mystery and menace of fog rolling toward you across the sea.

To the shocked Americans who read this account and the same correspondent's story of the burning of Louvain, it was evident that whatever glory had, in the past, attached to war, had now departed. From these inhuman forces, no gallantry could be expected. Even in our Civil War there had been gentlemanly intervals under flags of truce, prisoners were exchanged, and something of a distinction had been maintained between soldiers and civilians. The image of Appomattox with its honorable generals acknowledging mutual respect at the very moment of surrender when Lee became immortal, would fade in this new mechanical carnage. Yet even these shocked Americans clung to a belief in the enduring validity of the "rules of war," so recently agreed to at The Hague.

The battle of the Marne was normal war (except for the taxicabs that carried poilus and their arms out of Paris) and the victory, turning back so immense a force with apparent piecemeal strategy, was glorious in the strategic legend. But when, in May, 1915, a passenger ship was torpedoed and the passengers denied ordinary civilized succor, this was barbarity. To those who knew little or nothing of Genghis Khan, it was unprecedented. That the *Lusitania* was loaded to the gunwales with ammunition to be used by the Allies against Germany was, at the time, inadmissible evidence. Even if it had been admitted it would have been far outweighed by the fact that Americans, traveling under the umbrella of neutrality, had perished side by side with belligerent Britons. This infiltrated across the Hudson into the Middle West as no other "atrocity" could have done and, even in Milwaukee, there were red faces.

From this point on, the pro-Germans, the isolationists, and both the professional and the conscientious pacifists fought a losing battle. Many a sincere peace advocate, not troubling to weigh moral causes, pronounced "a plague o' both your houses," setting up the abstraction "war" as the monstrous villain; if some high-minded St. George would come forth and kill *that* dragon, it would not be necessary to take sides, for both sides would then admit their error.

That this St. George turned up in Detroit shows how far the dark European cloud had moved westward. He was already believed to be a saint by all those who were not convinced that he was the devil incarnate. He had already demonstrated his saintliness and his sin by establishing a minimum wage of $5 per day in an automotive factory which, by 1915, had the first moving assembly line in the history of quantity production.

Once the germ of ideological pacifism had bitten Henry Ford, he worked fast. He was richer, apparently, than any other American citizen and therefore his power was virtually unlimited. So confident was he in this power that he believed he could stop the war, now in its second year, with the aid of other idealists. It was, perhaps, the most grandiose combination of the sublime and the ridiculous that has ever been created even in these incredible United States; yet it possessed a quality that, in its naïveté, was almost mystic—the sort of thing that has more than once scared Europeans. For reporters, editorial writers, wags and paragraphers it set a field day of almost unprecedented dimensions. Like a ribald dance in a graveyard the comedy was shocking against the tragic background; yet the comedy was all that was necessary for the journalists, and there was plenty of that. It was only over the years that the event produced long afterthoughts.

# 4 ]]]]]]

## 1

IN THE DAYS of preparation for the voyage of Ford's Peace Ship, whose "delegate" passengers were committed to the job of "getting the boys out of the trenches by Christmas," the *Times* editors scanned their reportorial staff looking for someone sardonic enough to do justice to the project. The man they picked was only twenty-five; he had been with the paper little more than a year; but his stories had had precisely the dead-pan quality that was needed for the objective reporting of a crazy episode. A better choice than Elmer Davis could scarcely have been made.

Having set, late in November, 1915, the goal of Christmas, Ford had to organize the preliminaries with the racing speed that he understood so well in another context. He had some dynamic assistants, notably the writer Louis Lochner, the Hungarian pacifist firebrand, Rosika Schwimmer, the clergymen Jenkin Lloyd Jones, Dean Marquis and Charles Aked; Judge Ben Lindsey, the publisher S. S. McClure, and the Ford manager employee, Gaston Plantiff, who had not the faintest idea what the expedition was about but was an efficient executive. Yet, as the weeks moved on, there was nightmare confusion in the Biltmore suite where the arrangements were being made. The ship had been chartered—the *Oscar II* of the Scandinavian-American Line—and telegraphic invitations had been sent out over a field that stretched from William J. Bryan to Thomas A. Edison, from Jane Addams to John

60

Wanamaker. As the replies came in, it was obvious that most of those on the upper echelons of importance were availing themselves "with regret" of the excuse that the time was too short for busy people to commit themselves to such a voyage, however worthy the destination. Yet there were many acceptances from men and women whose imagination had been fired by the bold gesture, and a considerable group who elected to go "for the ride." And, naturally, there was a large crowd of uninvited persons who flooded the headquarters with telegrams trying to persuade this obvious "sucker," Mr. Ford, to extend them his hospitality.

Because of the supposed educational value of the pilgrimage, a group of students was invited. But what proved to be the deepest thorn in the flesh of the idealists was the press delegation. Reporters, in Ford's view, were supremely necessary because news of the expedition must be sent to the corners of the earth, but the cruel lampoons in their messages—in some cases demanded by the editors—were not anticipated. In addition to the representatives of such important papers as the New York *Times* and the Chicago *Tribune,* there were a ragtag and bobtail from obscure provincial papers which the regular press people regarded with contempt.

Whether the sailing on December fourth was as broad a comic opera as the papers made out is a question that only an eye-witness with an enduring and photographic memory can settle today. In the long retrospect the whole drama must be seen in a much-mellowed light. Certainly there were many sincere and prayerful folk among the 3,000 who saw the *Oscar II* leave her Hoboken pier; perhaps, too, there were fewer jokesters than the derisive papers said. But the front-page story in the New York *Times* was orderly and restrained, and only the arrangement and emphasis of the incidents suggested the sly winks of the reporter and city editor. Even then, in the exuberant gaiety of his youth, Elmer Davis was devoted to the truth, but, if the truth was sometimes funny, it would hardly be honest to omit it for that reason.

61

However, the behavior of young Davis aboard the ship was anything but respectful.

At the sailing, there were some irresistible scenes. The "Great Commoner," Bryan, waving his big hat in farewell and pronouncing the Peace Ship a second Noah's Ark, yet refusing the almost physical pressure of Henry Ford to go along, was a piece of tragicomic drama that for a reporter was pure honey. And the famous pacifist inventor, Thomas Edison, there he was, too, sure enough, but on the pier, not on the deck, as the Ark moved into the Hudson. There was the caged squirrel anonymously presented to the delegation with the message that it would be happy in the presence of so many "nuts." Finally, there was the co-author of the classic pacifist song, "I Didn't Raise My Boy to Be a Soldier"— in a rage because, somehow, he hadn't got booked.

The Marconi wireless which Ford called the longest-range gun in the world was incessantly busy from New York to Oslo (Christiania, as it was then called). Entire sermons by the clergy members were transmitted at a cost of $1,000 apiece which Ford paid out of his own pocket. (He had, in that capacious pocket, $10,000 in currency, put there in case anyone tried to curb his extravagance.) But press dispatches also were filed in quantity and it was these that troubled such sensitive idealists as Louis Lochner, secretary of whatever organization there was, and the Reverend Jenkin Lloyd Jones more than they did Ford himself. Indeed, when the ship's captain, after a talk with the wireless officer, brought a handful of what he thought were outrageous messages, Ford (perhaps remembering the success of the deprecatory Model T jokes) said to let them go, there would be no censorship on board.

Some of the news stories were pure fabrications invented by reporters who were bored by the lack of news. At the instigation of Davis, they had formed their own press club at whose meetings much liquor circulated unbeknownst to the teetotaling Ford. This impromptu organization amused the less solemn passengers. The press club, wrote Florence L. Lattimore in a letter to the

*Survey,* "provided practically all the laughs on the ship, their mock trials and initiations into the 'Vacillating Order of St. Vitus' on a windy night being the only relief from peace mission talk on the whole trip over." No one more than Elmer Davis enjoyed this sort of fun. But if he endorsed any of the fantastic news items emanating from those meetings, it is certain that none appeared in the *Times.*

Nevertheless, he was immune to the effect that Ford's personality had on some of the newsmen. Miss Lattimore recorded their confessions to her:

"My chief told me to do satirical stuff . . ." said one. "I'm not going to do it. I can't after seeing Henry Ford's face." "I came to make fun of the whole thing," said another, "but my editor is going to have the surprise of his life. I tell you I believe in Henry Ford and I'm going to say so even if I lose my job for it."

Privately Davis disapproved of the whole affair. Yet his contempt for it did not appear in the anonymous stories the wireless carried for him to the *Times.* He was a reporter of the old school in the days when by-lines were exceedingly rare. Perhaps if there had been broadcasting in those days and his voice had come over the air there would have been, in it, that inflection which editorialized some of his news talks. Nevertheless he was called, by one of the zealots—an unlikely legend says it was Henry himself —a "snake in the garden of Eden," a title which so delighted him that he promptly created a "Snakes in the Garden of Eden Club" into which he initiated his sympathetic friends.

It was on the fifth day out that an irresistible story broke, and if the bored reporters were revived by the prospect of the headline WAR ON PEACE SHIP, they can scarcely be blamed. The bomb that started it was President Wilson's preparedness speech wirelessed to the ship and read to the company. Now of all the words that truly incensed Henry Ford, "preparedness" was the most inflammatory. Back in August in an interview published in the Detroit *Free Press,* he had angrily attacked the concept and stated repeatedly that preparedness was a cause of war. With this belief he had indoctrinated his disciples on the Peace Ship, and a committee proposed a resolution condemning the President's speech. It was then that, according to the delighted reporters, all hell broke loose.

One of them reported "mutiny"; the message was intercepted by a nearby ship whose captain asked if he should come to their assistance. As is often the case, the ministers of the Gospel were the most violent—the Reverend Mr. Jones reportedly shaking his fist at McClure and shouting, "Go to bed, sir"; the reason for this particular command not having been clear. But it came into the *Times* story without slant or comment. Perhaps that was why, when it was proposed by the angriest of the "delegates" to expel the correspondents from the expedition, Snake Davis did not escape censure.

> The leaders of the party [read the *Times* story on December 20] refused to define or name the individuals but the *Times* correspondent is believed to be included.

2

When the *Oscar II* landed in Oslo, the dissension was still so rife that one of the Norwegian reporters said, in the presence of the Reverend Mr. Jones, that the spirit of the devil seemed to be abroad in the ship. The cries of "Shame! Shame!" with which the minister replied were reported in the press of the world, but after that, the stories dwindled away and were submerged in the news of a more important war.

Meanwhile the poor host whose generosity had made possible the enjoyment of so many cynical passengers had disappeared. It was reported that when a wave had washed over him while he walked the deck in a storm he had contracted a severe cold and was in bed in his cabin. Some of the reporters suspected that he had died and, imagining that the greatest story of all was in the offing, broke into his room where, sure enough, he was in bed but still much alive. But it was in the privacy of this cabin that the man who had been called Christlike became disillusioned. Rumors had reached him of the behavior of the unredeemed passengers which had made a farce of his idealism. His spiritual adviser, Dean Marquis of St. Paul's Cathedral in Detroit—who had been opposed to the enterprise from its start—had sat long hours by Ford's bedside persuading him for the sake of his health, his wife and his business to leave the party and go home. On the record, Ford was never again called "Christlike"; after this one completely selfless act of his life, something in his soul hardened and he became the ruthless tycoon of history.

Meanwhile, however, the ruck of the passengers, including much of the press, not caring in the least what had happened to their host, had a field day in the Norwegian city and later in Stockholm, buying in the best shops everything from evening dresses and dinner jackets to sets of china, and charging them all to Henry. Having been legitimately booked at certain hotels, they moved to others where the accommodations were more luxurious, and ordered extravagant meals. It was estimated by Mr. Plantiff, who wrote the checks, that half a million dollars had been spent in European cities by the passengers of the *Oscar II* and that in every community they visited, the exchange rate had risen.

One of the jokes perpetuated by these juvenile adventurers was to forge the name of the Reverend Jenkin Jones on restaurant checks for champagne. Dozens of bottles were therefore credited to this militant teetotaler. These stories were not told until years later; in the meantime, the whole incident faded in the garish light of the war, then, in the early months of 1916, in its most terrible phase.

Elmer Davis and Carolyn Wilson of the Chicago *Tribune*, who afterward became a lifelong friend of the Davis family, stayed

65

over after the *Oscar II* had returned with the other passengers. They visited The Hague, supposed to be the pacifist center of the world and, because they could read Dutch, absorbed the scathing comments on the Ford effort in the Netherlands press. Davis came home, in February, on the *Adriatic* and went back to the city room of the *Times*.

Over the many years which have seen so much madness, the episode of the Ford Peace Ship has drawn back into a gentling perspective. Admitting that it was ill-conceived, ill-managed and lacking in realistic understanding, many who watched to laugh now see a demonstration of faith in an idea that seems, today, to be archaic. On the twenty-fifth anniversary of the December sailing, the Detroit *Free Press* said, editorially, that

> we do not laugh any more, nor joke, when that unique argosy is mentioned. We mourn rather the disappearance of times when men could still believe in progress in human enlightenment, and thought that even those in the throes of blood lust might be led to reason. . . .

And Elmer Davis himself, in the best of all his essays, "On Not Being Dead, as Reported," wrote, in 1939, of the crusaders:

> They were not my enemies really—only a group of high-minded people who held with great fervor ideals on whose practicability I had been compelled to throw some doubt, in print; they were in fact the leaders and delegates of the Ford Peace Party, and they looked on me as one unsaved, who had not seen the light. Very likely there was more in that view than I would admit at the time. I still think the Ford Peace Party was a crazy enterprise; but an endeavor, however visionary and inadequate, to stop a war that was wrecking Europe, appears in retrospect a little less crazy than most of the other purposes that were prevalent in Europe in 1916.

66

3

The salary of a newspaper reporter in the teens of the twentieth century—even when that reporter covered such spectacular episodes as the Ford peace crusade—was scarcely enough to keep body and soul in juxtaposition in increasingly expensive New York. Samuel T. Williamson, a *Times* colleague in those years, gives an idea of the kind of pay he was getting for important reporting.

In the summer of 1916, Elmer covered the Billy Sunday meetings in a big wooden tabernacle up on Washington Heights. Reporting the antics of the acrobatic revivalist for what was then the staid New York *Times* was quite an experience for both the *Times* and the Hoosier recent Rhodes Scholar—for the *Times* because influential personages and models of propriety had financed Billy's invasion of sin-ridden Manhattan, so the newspaper gave him front-page, respectful treatment; and for Elmer because Sunday's one-way conversations with the Almighty lacked the formality of the ritualistic Oxford college chapels, also, because of the *Times* policy of playing up Sunday, Elmer did very well for a *Times* reporter. For in those days seasoned reporters were paid not salaries but according to space. . . . The space system was a complicated one. Basic rate was $8 a column, $10 for an exclusive story. When a reporter was assigned to a story like Billy Sunday, or an important convention . . . which produced columns of speeches and the like, the reporter temporarily struck gold.

Williamson tells of the copy-reader's custom of cutting reporters' stories, but Davis's "facility with the English language made it possible for him to write a long story so phrased that a copy-reader couldn't cut it much."

Fortunately the energy of this wiry young man—not depleted by competitive athletics—could carry him into extracurricular work. Besides the articles and stories he sold to a variety of magazines, Elmer Davis had written, and one of the best publishers of the day had published in 1915, a full-length novel.

*The Princess Cecilia* was light reading in the romantic tradition. Considering that it was in competition with books by Ernest Poole, Theodore Dreiser, Booth Tarkington, Willa Cather, Edna Ferber and Fannie Hurst, it did as well as D. Appleton and Company could expect a first novel to do. The story is set in an imaginary Far-Eastern country; the inhabitants are Malays and Arabs. After four years at Harvard, the sultan of this nation, "Ambok," brings home with him an American classmate whom he names poet laureate although the young man has never written a line of verse. As Ambok's constitution provides that the poet laureate shall rank below the royal barber in the hierarchy, the young American is ostracized by the large American community in the capital, but his love affair with a Malay princess brings a happy ending.

The book has the tricks of its genre: the impossible literary dialogue and the long, detailed descriptions of scenery and costume down to the last sarong. Yet the author's private laughter at his own story sets it apart from the ruck of the vogue: the sapient reader soon becomes aware of the satire and is more amused than thrilled. *The Princess Cecilia* was the first of a line of such novels, but Elmer's wit had not yet been honed to the razor sharpness of later days. In 1915, before he had any by-line in the paper, it was probably useful in bringing his name out of the dark anonymity of the close-packed news columns of the *Times*. And it laid a foundation for free-lance writing.

But Davis's serious, critical attention to the great crisis of these years had already begun. It is a prop to the morale of those writers who must simultaneously write and live, to see the realistic separation in this young writer's mind of potboilers from reflective, topical essays. He could hardly have been lavishly re-

68

munerated for "Concerning Fatherlands" published in the *Forum* two months before the German torpedoes sank the *Lusitania* with its two precious cargoes of people and bullets. What, he asks, is the true fatherland of the Germans who had come to Cincinnati —from one of whom he was descended—to Milwaukee or Chicago in mid-century? Was it the Germany that forced them into exile, or the land of exile itself with its wilderness freedom and its ultimate reward of prosperity for honest labor? In the answer to these questions, Davis resolves the conflict of loyalties that, for a time after the outbreak of war, had puzzled him.

It was true, he wrote in the *Forum* essay, that the sons of the Germans who had come to America were, at this moment, "headlong in their allegiance to the Germany of William the Second." But that was because

> they have so idealized the Germany builded by the men who drove them out that they think it is the same sort of Germany that their defeated and exiled fathers would have built had their dreams reached fruition.
>
> The typical South German of those days was Victor Scheffel—the melancholy yet genial singer of Heidelberg. . . . A still better type, perhaps, is that character of Scheffel's whom Scheffel loved—Hiddigeigei, the chivalrous, humorous, sentimental and philosophical tomcat. . . .
>
> There you have the tolerant South German with his zeal for personal liberty—the man who in America furnishes the solid backbone of the resistance to militant censors of the people's habits, and who in Germany has hardly been reconciled by a long course of Prussianization to the mystic phrase, *"Polizeilich verboten."* Liberty and comfort, peace and quiet—freedom to manage their own affairs, and a little music and a glass of beer when the day's work was over—it was not much that the ancestors of the German-Americans asked. But they had to come to the Ohio Valley to get it. The Germany they were trying to create was mortally wounded

in 1848, and died when Bismarck became the helmsman of Prussia.

Davis's own grandfather Severin was, to be sure, a Prussian "whose brother had fallen by his side on the Berlin barricades" —one of the relatively few who had lost faith in Prussia and were too embittered ever to return from the Ohio Valley. Perhaps that was one reason why his grandson had jumped back, in his thinking, over the heads of the Midwestern pro-Germans of March, 1915, and a reason, too, for Elmer's certainty that

> should the day come when the Germans in America must decide between their old and their new home, they would to a man be loyal to the country in which they now live.

The essay is peculiarly worth reading today. It recalls a situation unique at the time, but inevitably American. For however happy the exile and whatever of newness the American land may have given to compensate for the oldness that had been lost, the nostalgia remains. The essay points the experience of all the generations of immigrants, of voluntary and of forced exiles from Ireland and Russia and the south of Europe who have built the New World—much of it out of their own sorrow. Yet their grief was a sublimated grief and, for their children, only an abstract grief. In the German case, it was an abstraction from something that was dead, something to which, concretely, they could never return.

> For the Fatherland for which the German-American hurrahs and argues and spends his money and his prayers is a No-Man's Land, a Utopia, existent only in his own fantastic dreams.

In conclusion, Davis wrote with the scorching irony that came to flavor so much of his later speaking, of the world we should face if Germany won. Americans who saw this clearly were relatively few in that first spring of the war, and these words whose truth we all recognize today must have brought conviction to thoughtful minds in that confused time. And perhaps for Henry Mencken this piece, if he ever read it, may have forecast the afterthoughts of later years.

Perhaps [wrote Elmer Davis at the end of "Concerning Fatherlands"] Mr. Mencken and his followers are right. If the Germans win this war we shall see a new Heaven and a new earth—a new earth wherein Germany shall be the keystone of the structure; a new Heaven, for it will behoove all of us to get rid of our beaten gods and turn to those whose aid is of avail. For some time past England and France and Belgium have given their adherence to the red-capped goddess of Liberty. True, they have given her but lip service much of the time, with no little falling away after strange gods; but nominally she has headed the Pantheon whose other members are Virtues of the Christian type. A German victory means the triumph of the new Walhall wherein the seat of honor is held by Germania, clad in shining armor—Germania, whose mystical worship is abroad from the Niemen to the Meuse and has suddenly startled a world which knew it not. Her high priest is none other than William himself; and in her train is the God with whom William converses, a deity half Lutheran, half Old Testament Hebrew, as well as the reborn Aesir of the ancient Teutons—Wotan and Donar the warriors, and the diplomat Loge. It is a formidable array; and should its devotees prevail, it will be for us who formerly worshipped the red-capped goddess to overthrow her images, and, following the eminently sensible example set by the races conquered by the Saracens, to go over bodily to a god who can protect his people.

In that day German-Americans may worship the Fatherland with seeing eyes; but it will not be such a Fatherland

**71**

as is now enshrined in their hearts. "Whom ye ignorantly worship him declare I unto you." That Fatherland is and will be, in the Platonic phrase, a model in the skies.

This, then, in another mood was the romantic novelist, the irreverent burlesquer on the *Oscar II,* the newspaper reporter with a nose for news and an eye for fun. But it is the Elmer Davis we have come to know, the American who stood in a dark hour and remembered that we were born free, who saw on the clock-face of his mind that it was only two minutes till midnight.

# 5 ]]]]]]

## 1

PERHAPS because he was a member of its staff, the New York *Times* of February 6, 1917, gave a couple of inches to the wedding, on the day before, of Elmer Davis and Florence MacMillan. The quiet ceremony in the rectory of the Prospect Park Baptist Church in Brooklyn was attended only by the families and close friends of the principals and by the best man, Edward Klauber, destined to play a significant part in the groom's later career. So ended the four years of engagement, punctuated only by rare occasions of meeting and by the annual thirteen roses that marked the common birthday.

Two months and one day later, the New York *Times* printed President Wilson's proclamation, following a resolution by Congress, that a state of war existed between the United States and the German Empire.

Day by day through February and March, the fever of the American people had risen. In the wave of feeling that followed the German policy of unrestricted submarine warfare and its rapid implementation in the sinking of ship after ship of American ownership and registry, pacifist and pro-German protest had been drowned out. Before March was done the prospect of war had become a certainty. Thus, the vote in Congress and the President's solemn words brought a sense of relief. The tension broke; to many, American honor had at last been saved and what lay ahead was all action. As the gay posters told us, we must put our

73

shoulders to the wheel for Uncle Sam and all would be well. And we "won't," George M. Cohan told us as the bands beat out his tune, "come back till it's over over there."

Looking at this whole scene today, from the point of maturity to which experience has brought us, our behavior, as a people, in 1917, seems almost unbelievably callow. From the extreme of angrily determined neutrality and isolation, the national pendulum swung overnight, as it were, to a jingoistic opposite. Men and women who had hailed Wilson's apparent pacifism of a year before and applauded his "too proud to fight" speech, rushed into exhibitionist patriotism. With apparent blood thirst they shouted "Hang the Kaiser" and told one another in all seriousness that "the only good German is a dead German." Hysteria brought abuse to everyone remotely suspected of pro-German sentiment. The most innocent American who happened to have a German-sounding name—whether of Alsatian, Swiss, Belgian or even Scandinavian origin—was persecuted by panic hounding. A German-American socialist was lynched by a mob in Illinois. There was a general boycott of German music and German singers were heckled.

But these things were not confined to the mobs. With the Espionage Act, the Trading-with-the-Enemy Act and the Sedition Act (echoes of which have occasionally plagued us ever since), government made the reign of terror official. The barring of certain newspapers and pamphlets from the mails curtailed freedom of the press, and the arrests by the Department of Justice for so-called "disloyal utterances" brought freedom of speech to an end. Some of this, to be sure, must always be expected in wartime, but the unjust and often ludicrous extremes of 1917 and 1918 have not, in American history, been surpassed.

There was a sharp distinction in the public mind between the military and civilian fronts. Work on farm or in factory or office, however essential to the war effort, was considered soft, "cushy" or cowardly. Any healthy young man not in uniform was likely to have a white feather waved in his face by a female firebrand.

74

Thousands of men, therefore, evaded stern responsibilities to escape the stigma; often enough, the army job turned out to be the soft, safe one while the family of the uniformed "patriot" suffered. Glory attached to the soldier and many a romantic girl cheered her man proudly away to war with the sentiment characteristic of the Age of Chivalry that he must come back with his shield, or on it.

All this has long been archaic. Since war became a business rather than an adventure, the flags and the bands have faded out; concentration is on efficiency. Whatever mistakes may still be caused by the huge problems of conscription, there is no moral pressure on a man to shoulder a rifle when he is better equipped to do something else. The great wartime bureaus in government make new manpower demands: a man or woman with linguistic or geographical or economic knowledge is needed in a hundred office spots; new techniques of psychological warfare, intelligence, communication and news need experts who would be wasted in combat. Also, bombers and missiles have merged the fronts so that home is often the most perilous place to be.

But in 1917, it took courage to be realistic. To know that a good journalist is a better war asset than a bad shot in an infantry outfit or that even a good family provider is a greater stimulus to home front morale (which is, after all, what keeps the army in the field) than an inefficient soldier to a combat unit—and to act upon that knowledge—required guts in the days of the first World War.

2

In April, 1917, Elmer Davis was supporting not only his new wife but his mother and contributing to the support of a half brother as well. This he could not have done on a soldier's pay. He could, to be sure, go overseas, if he was paid on a civilian basis, and this he hoped to do, for the *Times* had promised him a correspondent's job. Yet, through the spring, he was repeatedly passed over: the jobs he knew he was best fitted to do were given to others.

As spring grew into summer, the elephantine processes of government moved to create an army from the materials of raw men and imitation rifles and arms and ammunition out of factories geared to the making of bedsprings and women's compacts. At the same time, new officers with creased olive-drab serge blouses and shiny insignia poured out of the officers' training camps. War was in the air and the question What are you doing? was on everyone's lips. Posters depicting Uncle Sam with his accusing finger pointing at YOU were on every street corner.

Davis's unease in this time was hardly concealed by the cloak of humor he threw over the revelations in his letter to Carolyn Wilson in September, 1917:

Aside from motives of patriotism, sensitiveness, and reactions of conscience which could probably be explained away, my pride is affronted at the idea that they can maintain the war without any cooperation from me. To stay in the same old job while everybody else is in it makes one feel like a eunuch amid the Follies chorus.

By year's end, however, he was making little effort to hide his impatience.

After waiting around for some months [he wrote in December] expecting to be sent as a war correspondent . . . I was grabbed by the draft in August, eventually exempted by the district board, [on grounds of family responsibilities] which does not relieve the disturbance of the soul. . . . I feel like a piece of cheese out of it, but don't see how I can get in it at present without working undue damage. . . .

It is possible to extract a minute quantity of satisfaction

from the thought that even the present job gives an opportunity to be of some use now and then. . . .

His criticism of other men—two in particular—who were sent to Europe while he was passed over probably understated his true appraisal.

Eye-witnesses allege that both of these were formerly newspapermen, but there is little evidence of it in their stories. [One] appears to regard the war as a convenient excuse for dining with ministers, and news as whatever is small talk at the ministerial table. [The other], whose work was not devoid of excellence early in the war, has apparently let it go to his head; and divides his stories between rhetorical blurbs in which he disdainfully mentions the alleged matter of news briefly in the third paragraph and then drops it out forever, and disquisitions on how the war would have been won a year ago if they had only done what he told them to. No doubt neither of these worthies is judged fairly by those of us who want their jobs, but it is painful to see stuff that the most amateurish night city editor would stick on the spike and raise hell with a reporter for writing printed under an A head, having been ennobled by the fact that it carries ten cents a word cable charges.

Miss Wilson's reply to this letter, written from Europe where she had been a correspondent since 1916, suggested several possibilities of jobs which he might fill nearer the front than New York.

As for me, friend Carolyn [he answered in January, 1918], you are right; I ought to be over there. But the draft regulations preclude my attendance on the war in any of the amiable and harmless occupations you suggest. Not having foreseen the Times' unwillingness to recognize merit, I am left in a position—Class III of the registered manhood of the

77

nation—where it is impossible for me to go in any of the graceful demi-military occupations. . . . I can enlist in aviation, I can be drafted as a buck private. These are the only possibilities. I do not aspire to the first; finances precludes the second. . . . Strange and unconvincing as it may seem . . . I'd really like to get a shot at the Boche.

In June, although he never let any humorous aspect escape his reflection, there were overtones of sadness in his description of wartime New York.

These correspondences . . . can hardly overlook the momentous changes coming over the surface of things among us. Greenwich Village, for instance, has lost much of its reputation for daring. . . . Marriage, for example, used to be in supreme contempt among villagers. There were many who were married but few who had the nerve to brave public opinion by admitting it. Now comes the draft and the male halves of these alleged free unions are coming forward and claiming deferred classification in 4A on the ground of dependent wife. The draft board has been giving serious consideration to the question of when is a marriage not a marriage, and in general has decided that those who feared to confess their shame before their free-thinking comrades, but now profess matrimony in order to escape carrying a gun, must run along to [training camp]. . . .

These are hard days . . . but the populace of the United States seems to be settling down to it pretty well. People are beginning to realize that the war requires not only worthy emotions but hard thinking, and a larger proportion seem to be trying to think than one could have thought possible a year ago. Not least in Washington. To those who have not been in Paris or London, New York seems to have got itself creditably on a war basis, though doubtless we have a long way to go even yet.

3

In comparing the American newspapers of 1918 with the picture of the first World War that historians have since given us, we find glaring discrepancies. There were few correspondents up front with the combat troops and those who were there had difficulty in getting their stories to their papers in time for them to be news. Meanwhile those reporters who were at the communication centers made broad guesses. By the time the guesses got into the papers they had usually become slanted in the direction of optimism. The impossibility of taking photographs at the front and the absence of techniques for the quick transfer of such pictures had they been taken, made it necessary for home publishers to hire artists to make the guesses graphic. These imaginative persons depicted scenes not unlike those of the Civil War showing victorious American soldiers running across no man's land and attacking German trenches with bayonets while all about lay dead or dying enemy men and horses.

It is true that the *Times* did not do quite this sort of sensation-mongering; it did, however, print items about the lack of food in Germany and the consequent decay of German morale. This caused Davis to remark that "if they fight like this when starving God help us if they ever get anything to eat."

To the trained journalist with a mind that intuitively threshed the wheat out of the chaff this was irritating. Davis not only detected impossibilities in the news items; he was also aware that editorials were sometimes based on incredible cables. He managed to bring this to the attention of the brass in the editorial offices and got a reputation for having a nose for the truth. He was rewarded by being assigned, in September, to censorship of the editorial page.

The censorship rules were evidently strict though Davis characteristically exaggerated when he wrote a colleague that he was expected

to go over the proof and throw out (a) anything I don't like;
(b) anything I think the owner wouldn't like; (c) anything
I suspect any one of our 400,000 readers might not like.

Finally, on November 8, 1918, he told Miss Wilson of the false
armistice report and its effect in New York.

The news motivated our city to an expression of feeling which
I will not attempt to describe, having tried it in three columns
of the New York Times and failed, though apparently with
a lesser degree of unsuccess than any of my colleagues. Nobody but Walt Whitman could have conveyed even a faint
impression of what it was like. . . . At this writing peace
may be three hours away or three months. . . . Whenever it
comes, however, it will be an awful strain on a lot of us for
we shall having nothing left to think or talk about; nor, as it
seems now, any moral incentive at all comparable with the
one that has kept us all going for some time past.

The *Times* then wanted to send him to Berlin; he would refuse:
". . . imagine having to fraternize with Hun households before
the blood was dry on the family bayonet." But he had hopes

of being shipped in the next year or two on a grand tour of
the lately oppressed but newly liberated nationalities of
eastern Europe, if they can be restrained from fighting among
themselves to make travel profitable; I ought to have a good
many friends in Prague, Warsaw and Belgrade, having propa-
ganded heavily for those oppressed races; though my observation has been that a friend in need is forgotten with great
rapidity when the need has passed.

There is no comment in these letters on the peace settlement
that followed the Armistice: it was characteristic of Davis to
reserve judgment on this and like him not to express exuberance

over the "war to end war" or voice his assurance that the world had become "safe for democracy." That he was not moved by the mystic idealism of Wilson which brought women to their knees in the streets of Paris was in tune with his characteristic realism.

In that interval between Armistice and Peace, men were able at last to turn to homely things. The most intimate thing in Davis's life was the birth in May of a seven-pound boy, his and Florence's first-born. Immediately afterward, with the weariness common to floor-pacing husbands, he wrote "everybody doing well, thanks, though I think this method of perpetuating the race has damn few merits about it."

4

Actually, in the war years, Davis had made himself more useful to the *Times* than he knew. His exploratory travel during the Oxford vacations had engraved the map of Europe upon his brain. He had learned much of the ways of the various peoples that had become belligerent. He could, then, supply the men who had to edit or rewrite the cabled dispatches from the war zone with background for the stories. He could also weigh and judge the emphasis the news should assume.

That he had made a penetrating study of the war in its military, economic and social aspects is evident from the by-line articles which, late in 1917 and in the following spring, appeared as Sunday features. The first of these came in November soon after Wilson's controversial statement about peace without victory. It is on the whole unexciting and, but for occasional flashes, lacking in the animation that spiced most of his essays. It is labored in spots and the historical parallels are farfetched. Yet, reading it today after the long sequence of compromise, appeasement and new conflict there is a quality of prophecy about it that is arresting.

The main parallel is with the Peloponnesian war which was

suspended by the uneasy Peace of Nikias. In the years of exhausting war, punctuated by no important military decisions,

> Nobody's objects had been attained; everybody was wearied of the war and appalled by the prospect that it might drag on for years longer with no conclusive result.

The peace was, in short, a peace without victory: the kind, in Davis's view, that Wilson appeared to advocate.

> So [he went on] the actual specific grievances which led up to the war were ignored; it was like a peace which should leave the Germans in possession of Alsace-Lorraine, Posen, Bohemia, Croatia, Transylvania, and should give France and Belgium only the option to start again under the German shadow.

This was, of course, an extreme conclusion from the parallel, but it was a warning.

> The parallel could be continued, between our own immediate future and the later years of the Pelopponesian war. . . . It is not conjecture to point out that the formula of peace without annexations and indemnities failed to settle the Peloponnesian war and failed to erect any solid structure for the world to live in after the balance of power had proved inadequate.

Yet it had not been a causeless conflict any more than the present fight with Germany had been without reason.

> The war was about something, the Greeks had gone to war to settle certain things, and they would not be at peace until these things were settled one way or another. The sorry success of the peace patched up by Nikias and his lukewarm counterparts in Sparta ought to remind the student of ancient

and modern history of the comment made by James J. Hill in September, 1914: "This war will end when somebody is licked; and until somebody is licked it will not end."

Four months after this article appeared it looked very much as if the Allies were the ones destined for the licking. The drive of the German armies in March, 1918, before which British units melted away and which was stopped at the very gates of Paris in the last days of the spring brought such despair in England that American units arriving there in May were greeted by the question, "Why did you come? The war is over." Morale returned in the summer with the successful battles at Château-Thierry and in the Argonne; yet historians later pointed out that when the Armistice came in November, the Germans were by no means licked—at least, not in 1945 terms.

As Davis watched the Versailles meeting in June, 1919, convened to confirm the November armistice, and to revamp the European balance of power, he must have been reminded again of the peace of Nikias. There were sharp differences, to be sure: the Versailles reparations, as John Maynard Keynes later argued, were impossible of fulfillment; some of the remaking of Europe's map—such as the creation of the Danzig corridor—was wholly impracticable, the terms of German disarmament were easy to evade, as Hitler showed, and Wilson's Fourteen Points, ideal for the world he visualized, dominated by the League of Nations, proved tenuous indeed when that instrument failed to gain the support its creator had foreseen.

So, despite the breakdown in spots of the parallel—and historians say that parallels are never quite valid—it is clear that Davis's view even in this early time was far more realistic than most of the emotionally or sentimentally colored views in America at the end of her first year of war. Then, in the years between 1919 and 1940, it became evident to others than Charles de Gaulle that France's victory in the first war had not only exhausted her for the second but had produced a defensive rather than an aggressive concept in her military staff at the very time when technology was favoring offensive strategy. In 1940, then, it appeared that the wrong nation had been "licked" in 1919 and that the first World War had, in fact, defeated France rather than Germany.

All this, of course, was long before the revolutionary change in the aspect of war ushered in by the atomic bomb. Yet even then the need had come not only for altered strategic concepts but for the addition of new factors. The airplane had brought the home front into the zone of hostilities. The course of war was becoming altered by political considerations. As Elmer Davis was to learn during the most strenuous activity of his life, between '42 and '45, psychological and communication additions had affected both strategy and tactics. But when the A and H bombs came, the argument that someone had to be licked was no longer valid for, as no one saw earlier or more clearly than he, nuclear war would lick all participants and the human race into the bargain.

5

To return, however, to the last year of the first World War, we find that Davis, in May, 1918, when the mammoth German drive of March had been stopped, did another war piece for the Sunday *Times* which again won him a by-line. Its truth, when it appeared, was less obvious than hindsight has made it. The headlines were:

AUSTRIA'S FATE HANGS<br>ON WEST FRONT BATTLE

Oppressed Nationalities of Hapsburg Empire<br>Will Doubtless Rise if Germans Are Checked<br>by Allies in France

Publication by the *Times* of this article suggests that many Americans still needed clarification of the Balkan complex and

84

were not yet fully aware of the restlessness of the Slavic peoples under Austrian domination. But for Davis, all these nations had been an old stamping ground. His classmates at Oxford had been amused by the stories of his lighter adventures during the vacations, some of which ended with jokes on himself as if he had been an Innocent Abroad. He had made friends in Prague and in Belgrade; these included the great Masaryk and the lesser Beneš and, in the land along the Adriatic, he had learned, before the fact, of the insurgency behind the shot that lit all the fuses in 1914. Now he saw clearly that the tottering Hapsburg regime would fall when Germany fell and with an even louder crash, for when the showy Dual Empire went, its pieces would fly off in all directions to independence. Davis's admiration for these oppressed peoples was one of the dominant influences upon his international thinking.

In the postwar years in New York, Davis settled, like most of us, into the happier ways of peace. His production grew more and more abundant. In these variegated years it never struck him as singular that he could read himself to sleep with the odes of Horace in the original and, in the morning, go out to report on the condition of boxers preparing for the evening's prize fight.

# 6 ]]]]]]

## 1

MARK SULLIVAN saw the American mood of 1920 as one of nostalgia.

That homesickness [he wrote in the first chapter of his book *The Twenties*] was responsible for many of the votes that Warren G. Harding got when he ran for President of the United States in 1920; of all the speeches he made in his campaign, the three words that most appealed to the mood of the country, the one phrase for which he was most applauded, was "back to normalcy."

The nostalgia was, like that German dream of the forever dead Germany of Heine, for a past that for some five or six years had been in its grave. Later historians have seen the nostalgia of 1920 as the springboard for a decade of retrogression; some have thought that the mood produced an effort to recapture the spirit of frontier days. Actually, much of that spirit was, indeed, recaptured by Henry Ford's Model T car which led to a whole new set of frontiers in the ghost-lands left by the railroads. But there was, too, a return of the lawlessness that had characterized the earlier frontier era and of the corruption in high places that had gone along with the continental conquest. This was abetted by national prohibition, in itself a frontier product, and by the financial boom that ended in disaster at the decade's close.

Wilson's exhausting campaign for the League of Nations which ended in the breakdown from which he never recovered; the rejection by the United States of the League—which proved to be the kiss of death for that experiment; the nomination for the presidency of an obscure Ohio newspaper editor for the specific reason that he *was* obscure; his election by an electorate that made no effort to penetrate the obscurity, and the new President-elect's abandonment of power to a group of rascals that came to be known as the Ohio gang: these were the events of the second postwar year in America.

The follies of the 'twenties were not, however, confined to the United States. Some, to be sure, spread from these shores and took grimmer shape overseas. Others had their root in the war's devastation, most of which America had escaped. For one thing a curious romanticism affected certain political leaders in a traditionally cynical Europe and led to such anomalies as the Locarno Pact and other hollow agreements to "outlaw" war. But the most disastrous folly of all was Italian fascism, which emerged from a synthetic revolution designed and carried out by the followers of the ex-socialist Benito Mussolini. Its ultimate consequences in 1922, when the "march on Rome" seemed to answer Italian demands for extravaganza, were incalculable.

2

In the summer of 1920, however, before the portents of disaster were visible in the apparently cloudless sky, our nation was still basking in the sunlight of Millennium after Armageddon. Even national prohibition was regarded with complacency, the cellars being still stocked, and drinking not yet a patriotic duty. Workers were said to be arriving at their factories sober, on Monday mornings, and the industrialists were happy about this, being secure in the possession of amply filled country-club lockers. It is true that the millennial atmosphere had not persuaded political lions and lambs to lie comfortably together, and there was still a kind of war between Democrats and Republicans in this election year. It did not amount to much because the Republicans were the nostalgic party and any one who waved the banner of homesickness for the *status quo ante* was fairly sure of being elected. The Democrats, however, were looking at the future; they regarded that future with less serenity than their opponents; they went so far as to implement the dictum of the "War to End War" with a League of Nations and uttered echoes of the voice of Wilson crying in the wilderness. This irritated the nostalgists because it implied European contacts, and their hope of an eternal Pax Americana lay in total isolation from the Machiavellian princes.

At the same time, League or no League, millennium or no millennium, a considerable part of the American people had not yet lost its sense of humor. That was why it was possible for even the solemn *Times* to print, in addition to the detailed coverage of political conventions and campaign battles, a column of the most engaging spoofing that had been created since the immortal dialogs of Mr. Dooley and Mr. Hennessy.

From the town of Amity, Indiana, there emerged, late in June, 1920, the "oldest living conventioneer," Godfrey G. Gloom. Mr. Gloom had been a Democrat since Civil War days, and in the years between he had learned a great deal about the ups and downs (especially the downs) of the Democratic party. He carried a gold-headed ebony cane on which in his despondent moods he leaned heavily; though he was capable of considerable excitement with the proper stimulus. His English was not always that of the *Times* nor did he maintain those standards of accuracy that were traditional in its columns. But the *Times* washed its hands of him; he was an independent observer who happened to be one of the many knowledgeable observers whom the *Times* correspondent interviewed.

88

Literal-minded readers searched in vain for Amity on Indiana maps, nor could they find any trace of Amity's newspaper, *The Grapevine Telegraph*. Civil War lists revealed no Godfrey Gloom and no Indiana citizen would admit that Gloom was a Hoosier name. The column about him and his views, however, grew in popularity through the hot days of oratory and balloting and many turned to it first before plunging into the sea of detail that spread itself over page after page of convention news.

Mr. Gloom made his first appearance at the Democratic national convention in San Francisco. A *Times* correspondent would meet him in the auditorium or in the street outside or in the lobby of a hotel and ask questions which Gloom was never reluctant to answer. His comments suggested that he was less impressed by the eloquence of the convention speakers or the dignity of the occasion than the delegates might have wished.

Godfrey G. Gloom [ran the column for July 3], the old-fashioned Jeffersonian Democrat from Amity, Ind., was found this afternoon by a TIMES correspondent in front of the Exposition Auditorium, pensively picking his teeth.

"I suppose you have come from that great hall yonder where the fate of a nation is being decided," he remarked. "As for me, I came away some time ago, and I don't figure to go back today. I was moved to tears by Mr. Bryan's oratory and had to get off here by myself where none could see me weep."

"What particular passage moved you to tears?" the correspondent asked.

"There were several," said Mr. Gloom. "For example, when Mr. Bryan said that the Democratic Party was expected to think. Them words stirred a number of painful memories in me. I looked back over the course of American history, and I found it simply studded with occasions when the Democratic Party was expected to think and disappointed all expectations. I surmised that nobody expects it to think except Mr. Bryan, and he expects it to think of him.

But what most affected Mr. Gloom was a reference that called forth a bitter reflection on prohibition, then just beginning.

"My heartstrings was stirred principally by Mr. Bryan's remarks about the sanctity of the home, and how we must preserve it against them as would violate it. It called back an episode that occurred in my home town of Amity this spring. I had opposed Baz Overturf when he ran for Town Marshal, and since I opposed him of course he was elected. Well, Baz was always a vindictive person, one to cherish bad blood. My wife always puts up some raspberry cordial, and one day not long after he took office he came stalking around to the kitchen door.

"You can infer the rest. That cordial was meant to be non-intoxicating, but having been left around the house quite a while, nature had took its course. Baz Overturf took it all away, and if he poured it down a drain nobody seen him do it. My wife's gray hairs, four grandchildren and two great-grandchildren saved her from arrest. But Mr. Bryan's reference to the enemies of the home brought the whole scene back to me with vivid poignancy."

This gentle dig at the arch-prohibitionist William Jennings Bryan was characteristic of Godfrey Gloom. On July 4 he became disgusted with the whole affair and the headlines on his column read:

GODFREY G. GLOOM
QUITS CONVENTION

With a Parting Shot at Those
Who Criticize His Loyalty to
Jackson

90

INDIFFERENT TO OUTCOME

After Watching a Number of
Ballots He Decides He Doesn't
Care Who Gets the Nomination

A friend, however, induced him to see the day out.

"Yes," he observed to a TIMES correspondent, "I am here by courtesy of my friend Walter J. Woof, Washington correspondent of the Amity [Ind.] *Grapevine Telegraph.*

"Seems he had two seats, one of which had been occupied all through the week by a flashin' brunette from out Pacific Avenue. Today her husband come back, so I get to set down and rest my weary bones. . . .

"The South is not so solid this year as it might be; in fact a good deal of it is highly gaseous.

"It's all the fault of this false notion of fair play. The Republicans went and picked out a man that nobody wanted and few had ever heard of, and some here seem to feel that it would be unsportsmanlike to take advantage of them. The campaign, according to these views, should be a generous rivalry in attempted suicide."

The following day:

MR. GLOOM UNABLE
TO QUIT THE SCENE

Veteran Democrat Becomes
Fascinated With the Study of
Political Animosities

and, of course, he remained until the bitter end.

91

"I don't care [he concluded] who's nominated, nor do I think the party will care much. When these delegates go back home the boys are not goin' to ask 'em, 'Who did you nominate?' They'll ask 'em, 'Who did you beat?' "

Through the summer and fall up to November, Godfrey Gloom had special articles, illustrated by John Held, Jr., in the Sunday Magazine section. These included "Money Has No Terrors for Mr. Gloom"—about campaign funds, "Mr. Gloom's School of Politics," "Mr. Gloom on Princes and Potentates" and "The Morals of Mr. Gloom."

But on July 12, a telegram was addressed to Elmer Davis from his boss, Carr Van Anda of the *Times,* which read:

I would like to say that your account of the session that nominated Cox was one of the finest pieces of convention reporting I have ever seen

and from Elmer's colleagues, the *Times* correspondents who had been obliged to cover the San Francisco convention with true *Times* solemnity, there was a letter in verse which read:

> Dear Mr. Godfrey Gloom of Amity,
> It would have been a real calamity
> Had you not come to town to cheer us up;
> Despite your gloomy pseudonymity
> You've won the journalistic primity;—
> There ought to be another Davis Cup.
> Yours, with unanimity . . .

Gloom reappeared in 1924, 1932 and 1936—though Davis was not, in those years a regular *Times* employee—and breathed his last at the close of the 1936 Democratic convention. There was, then, an obituary and an article on his career.

92

3

Some three years later and two years after President Harding took office, the symptoms of madness and badness later said to mark the decade of the 'twenties began to reveal themselves. Already in the spring of 1923, the failure of national prohibition was evident to everyone whose eyes were not sealed by bribes from the illicit liquor dispensers. Each drinker had his favorite speakeasy: these in New York expanded into night clubs with orchestras and floor shows under the expensive protection of the police. In Washington—though still behind the scenes—what proved to be the hottest scandal of recent American history was beginning to boil over a slow fire fed largely by the "Ohio gang." That this was known only to a few was due, perhaps, to the diversions furnished by the other madnesses: the Coué craze based on a practice of self-hypnosis supposed to engender peace of mind; the marathon dance in which men and women collapsed and sometimes died after days of continuous dancing; the behavior of the young folk with their hip flasks, rolled stockings and automotive sexual experiment, and the controversy over Nicola Sacco and Bartolomeo Vanzetti, victims of the red-baiting hysteria which had caught so few reds but so many innocent citizens. But in the spring of 1923, the doings of the Ohio gang and its disciples were becoming known to the President of the United States and would soon, after his tragic death in August, engross the attention of most of the American people.

As spring moved into summer, however, in that tragic year, 1923, public attention was further diverted by a flurry of excitement in the state of Montana. Writers who reflect on the phases of American history have since seen that episode as peculiarly symptomatic of the age—of all our frontier ages, indeed, when a last-minute miracle saved the lucky adolescent nation from disaster.

93

The thing has happened often in this country [wrote Elmer Davis more than fifteen years later] on a larger scale. The European crop failure that got us out of the slump of the Seventies, the Klondike gold that helped cure the hard times of the Nineties, were as unpredictable as the discovery of oil in Montana, and such things created the state of mind of the Twenties, in which everything was possible.

The oil seemed to the people of that northwestern state the direct expression of the Almighty's gratitude for good works. For Montana's powers-that-be had gone far out on a limb to save the newly poor of that land.

All the dry-farming areas were going broke in the early Twenties and families were moving away by the thousand. The leading men of Toole County, Mont., decided to stop that drift; they set all the destitute dry-landers to work building country roads, and paid them off with county warrants. The roads led to nowhere in particular, the warrants were a local currency of dubious and diminishing value outside the county, but when at last the shortage of foreign exchange was about to wreck the experiment, somebody struck oil. Then the roads were needed to get to the oil fields and the warrants were easily paid off with taxes on the oil companies.

But like many a community in the high, wide and handsome days of the expanding frontier, Toole County was not content to relax and enjoy the return of prosperity. No, they must assist Divine Providence in leading them on to a bigger and better place in the sun.

No wonder that men who had had such a signal proof that Destiny was on their side overreached themselves by offering a second challenge to probability.

94

The particular challenge had a comic look to more adult and realistic outsiders, though its consequences were serious enough to its promoters. The challenge was a prize fight. If Champion Jack Dempsey and Challenger Tommy Gibbons could be induced to stage a bout in the town of Shelby, county seat of Toole County, the community would become the Mecca of fight fans from coast to coast, from Canada to the Gulf. Shelby (population 2,000) would become a thriving and splendid city and the future of the county if not of the entire state would be assured.

The reason Elmer Davis so long remembered this ephemeral episode was that he was objectively involved. As they had foreseen the sardonic overtones of the Ford peace crusade eight years earlier, the editors of the *Times* were quick to perceive the Shelby possibilities and sent a reporter to cover the fight whose wit, they knew, would be equal to it.

The fight was scheduled for Independence Day. When Davis arrived, the week before, it was raining in Shelby. Perhaps it was the weather—the deep mud through which he had to wade and the leaden look from the skies with which Destiny was regarding the whole of Toole County—that made his preliminary by-line columns so pessimistic. It was not, certainly, any shadow of foreboding among the people. The Fate that had disclosed the gusher at the precise brink of bankruptcy could not let them down. That by June 30 they were already $100,000 short on the money they had promised the Dempsey management led the reporters who had forgathered to wire their papers that the fight would be postponed if not canceled. But none of them understood the true gambling spirit of Shelby, once it was sure that the Almighty had loaded the dice.

Meanwhile, Davis took the pulse of the people. He pointed to the fact that the wife and kiddies of Tommy Gibbons were already at Shelby.

Domesticity [he wrote] is one reason why the populace of the Northwest is mostly pulling for Gibbons. A family man

**95**

who wants to have his family near his work, a breadwinner who shows the public the family that is supported by his efforts . . . naturally appeals to the moral, home-liking element in the community.

It seems to be Dempsey's luck, good or bad, that those who challenge him always become symbolic figures. Gibbons stands for the domestic virtues, Carpentier represented embattled and heroic France, the mother of arts and culture. Embattled and heroic France lasted a little over three rounds against Dempsey. If the domestic virtues manage to stick four or five rounds, it will be a triumph for American ideals of the Sanctity of the home.

Davis then made his own estimate of the boxers after visiting their camps.

Gibbons, handsome, good natured, easy going, letting his sparring partners off easily, contrasts sadly with Dempsey, whose ferocious ring face is one of his principal assets. Outside the ring Dempsey is anything but ferocious, but this afternoon, with nothing in front of him but a punching bag, he wore a black unshaven scowl that had something of the grim grotesqueness of an Assyrian king setting out to do something mean to his neighbors.

Returning from his visits, Davis discovered that twenty of Shelby's businessmen "have, since yesterday come across with $5,000 each to pay Dempsey." Davis was still skeptical and predicted postponement, but he was wrong. The brave people of Shelby, by their heroic behavior, brought the fight to pass on July 4 as scheduled and remained broke forever afterward. Their only reward was to see Tommy Gibbons, champion of domesticity if not of heavyweights, last fifteen rounds against his fierce opponent, after which the referee gave Dempsey the decision. The box-office receipts came nowhere near paying the costs—an event for

96

which a skeptical press was only partly responsible. In 1939, when Davis recalled the occasion, the population of Shelby, Montana, was still approximately 2,000.

In its small way the Shelby collapse was a forerunner of the national catastrophe that was to come at the end of the decade. There was the same epidemic of blind overoptimism that had afflicted one state in 1923, multiplied, of course, by forty-eight. That the consequences of the national calamity were long-lasting is evident from Davis's note as late as 1939 when he wrote for "Topics of the Times":

> Once more the time has come when we could use one of those interpositions of providence; but the eventual collapse of Shelby is a reminder that we cannot depend on Fate to deal us an ace off the bottom of the deck every time we need a happy ending.

## 4

In 1924, Godfrey Gloom again came out of Amity's seclusion and this time reported both political conventions in his homely way. But in another medium, Elmer Davis wrote more seriously (though no less ironically) of the philosophy behind American party politics as revealed in the odd method of selecting presidential candidates. In the first place, he said, there are seldom any issues at stake—at least by convention time. The only occasion for issues is when a third party arises—as one did in 1924—and usually the issues kill the party.

> Third parties [Davis wrote in "Politics—a Two-Handed Game," published in *Harper's Magazine* for October, 1924] are born of an issue and fed on discontent. Commonly, they die when hard times are over and discontent disappears. The issue goes on and is fought out, but not on partisan lines. For the object of a party is not the triumph of an issue but

97

the acquisition and retention of jobs, honors, and emoluments by the people who run the party. A party based on an issue is ruined whether it wins or loses. If its issue is rejected, the men whose political fortunes are tied up with that issue are finally rejected too. If its issue triumphs, there is no further reason for the party.

The third party in 1924, Senator La Follette's Progressives, in its platform evolved through the convention, "has done its best to avoid controversial questions and to prove that it is just like any other party." Controversy on principles must be avoided at any cost; differences between the parties, if they involve principles, must not be exploited. Actually, according to Davis, there was, in 1924, no difference in principle between the two major parties.

> The only visible difference of any sort is that the Republican party seems to contain a slightly higher percentage of crooks, and the Democratic party of fools.

In great historical elections, he believed, the issues were based on immediate, practical or personal considerations rather than on basic principles.

> Andrew Jackson showed a sure perception of the practical realities of democratic government when he went to the White House on the slogan of "Turn the rascals out." Democracy, inefficient enough under any system, is least inefficient when it operates through two indistinguishable and arbitrary divisions of the politically interested citizen body. One set of rascals, becoming insufferable, can be turned out and replaced by the other set of rascals whose own self-interest will keep them for some years from being quite as bad as their predecessors. When they forget and in their turn become insufferable, they can be replaced by the first set of rascals, now chastened

98

by enforced retirement and willing to behave with reasonable virtue for a term or two.

As usual, Davis dipped into ancient history for an analogy. Between the two parties of the Roman Republic, there was a fundamental difference of opinion. This resulted in such violence that the side that got the upper hand "killed off all the leaders of the other side within reach." After a century of this few political leaders were left. Augustus then assembled those that remained into a "conservative-radical coalition whose sole issue was the preservation of peace and prosperity, and this was the only party of the Roman Empire." Davis does not say directly that this was why Rome fell but he does say that the Byzantine Empire which centered around Constantinople "stood for a thousand years after Rome had been retired to the guide books."

That stability [he adds] was due largely to the fact that political life in Constantinople was organized on the basis of two parties no more different than Democrats and Republicans. . . .

Davis made his second point in a sequel to this article in "The Presidents We Deserve" in *Harper's* for November. Here is an echo of the reflections of Godfrey Gloom in 1920. The ideal candidate as picked in a convention is not a man whose qualities are praiseworthy but a man no one has anything against. The Republicans chose Harding because no one had ever heard of him and could therefore feel no antagonism toward him. The Democrats, however, made their greatest mistake in nominating Cox who had the issue of the League of Nations tied, as it were, to his tail.

5

For Elmer Davis's personal career, 1924 was a key year. On New Year's Eve, 1923, his job as an employed and salaried journalist had come to an end. In the *Times* he had made uncommon progress through the ten years since he had signed on as a cub reporter. He had covered important events in the fields of war, politics and sports. He had written feature articles some of which would stand the test of time. He had created a journalistic character almost as popular as Peter Dunne's Mr. Dooley. He had written—more as a chore, to be sure, than out of exuberance—the official *History of The New York Times* from 1851 to 1921. And he had graduated from the city room to the editorial floor and ended as an editorial writer.

But the *Times* could not confine either his ambition or his talents. He had gone out to the magazines with both fiction and essays. Two of his novels, *The Princess Cecilia* and *Times Have Changed,* had been published and had won fair success. He had just finished a third, *I'll Show You the Town*. More and more, these outside literary activities had cut into his sleep and his home life. Now, like many a young journalist before him, he itched to get away from office hours to devote his full time to writing—to be a free lance!

It was—it always is—a step in the dark. He had his mother and his wife and child to support. He, Fliss and Robin were living in a house not yet paid for. He was, or thought he was, deep in debt. But he felt the thrill of the gambler and, come what might, a great release.

> But can you conceive the relief [he wrote to Carolyn Wilson on New Year's Eve, 1923], after ten years of writing for to-morrow's paper, of cutting loose for once and trying to see if you can do something good? . . . With the awful peril of the abyss, of course, in case you find that even with everything perfect you can't do anything more than hack work.

Truly, it was a night to celebrate!

100

# 7 ))))))

## 1

I N THE LAST HALF of the 'twenties, many, perhaps most, Americans were comfortably sure that they were living in the best possible world. For business, finance, industry and the successful pursuit of happiness our quick and convenient vernacular supplied the phrase "up and up." Coolidge had spread a sort of synthetic balm of Gilead over a nation momentarily worried by the Harding scandals and it was obvious to Republicans that this strong silent man had a good business head. Perhaps, indeed, he had an even better head than they thought when he decided, before the primaries came, that he did not "choose to run" for reelection in 1928. Had he seen the rocks ahead and had this persuaded him to let his successor pilot the ship of state through the perilous waters? To give this lucky Yankee whose laconic ways were thought a symptom of wisdom the credit for such foresight may be too generous, yet it is a Yankee trait to "let well enough alone." To get out while things were on the up and up and let someone else watch them reach the top does not necessarily, for a Vermonter, require advice from a crystal ball.

It was in these years that what we call "mass" activity came into its own in the United States. There were sudden fads or crazes which seemed to draw the entire population to their lodestones at once; such was the Florida boom when prosperous orange groves were bulldozed out of existence to make room for quickselling "home" sites; such was the lure of the rising stock market for which there seemed to be no ceiling. But the enduring thing was radio: for that there was truly no ceiling except the Heaviside layer which bounced the beams into far places.

In 1920, radiotelephony was only a ham's dream. Yet it moved rapidly into a vast commercial enterprise. The results of the Harding election in November were broadcast but few were the possessors of anything other than amateur sets. The press, however, reporting the broadcast, stimulated radio sales and Westinghouse, which first manufactured commercial sets, was also first with a broadcasting station. At this point it was necessary for a genius to arrive and suggest that money could be made by airborne advertising. He appeared in the person of Harry P. Davis, Westinghouse's vice president. By 1923, a million and a half sets were in use; in 1927, there were six and a half million, or one set for every twenty Americans.

To what extent this new medium of mass communication impressed, in those days, the man whose greatest celebrity would one day depend upon it, we do not know. A guess would be that it moved him little. In a short piece published in "The Lion's Mouth" department of *Harper's Magazine* in September, 1924, Elmer Davis observed that "golf, the automobile and the radio are the three common denominators of our age." It is true that the programs of 1924 were not greatly stimulating, though in the years following, there was, with the Locarno Pact, the Hall-Mills case, Daddy and Peaches Browning and the Lindbergh flight, plenty of news to be carried on the air waves.

But Elmer Davis had other interests. As we have seen, he had left the *Times* on the eve of 1924. He had immediately embarked on the career of free lance. Popular belief to the contrary, this career—unless one has other means of support—leaves no time for anything but free-lance writing. It was as a free lance that he wrote, for a month or so in the summer of 1924, under the name— no longer a disguise—of Godfrey Gloom, but the *Times* paid him as an outsider. Then, when the quadrennial political spasm was over, he turned his attention to profitable authorship.

102

The novel *Times Have Changed* was sold to the movies for a comforting sum. In 1924 *I'll Show You the Town* was published. These were admitted potboilers, light, gay and ephemeral, and not taken seriously by author or readers. And there were short stories and an article in *Collier's*. At the end of August, the novel *Friends of Mr. Sweeney* began as a serial, also in *Collier's*. This story, when, the following year, it was published in book form, was met by the reviewers with accolades. "A rattling good up-to-the-minute story of New York," said the *Outlook*'s critic and the reviewer for the *Saturday Review of Literature* wrote that Davis's "style is like a fresh, stiff breeze; and his narrative races." In the *Literary Digest* it was thought "screamingly funny" and an "uproarious satire." We who go back to it in the 1960's find it dated and are able, for the most part, to restrain our mirth, but in 1924, after all, Davis was making a topical approach to quick success and was succeeding.

Sixteen years later, in a Bowker Memorial Lecture delivered at the New York Public Library, he told how a free lance gets his start. That this draws on autobiography in no way diminishes its nearly universal application.

His first novel is likely to be something that he had heavily on his mind, and if he has any stuff it may be pretty good. . . . The reviews will be good and the author . . . will be convinced that a bright future is opening before him. Now probably that first book will not have much of a sale; if it doesn't the author is lucky, for the hour of decision is thus postponed. But he writes another novel—like his first one, in his spare time, at night after his work at the office is over, buoyed up by youth and confidence; and if that one too gets good reviews, if it sells a little better, then the virus of an incurable disease has laid hold on him. He is an author; and it begins to appear an unendurable indignity that a writer of his rare quality has to appear at a desk at nine o'clock every morning and take orders from somebody else

**103**

till five in the afternoon. So he quits his job, and begins to make his living as an author.

Now the chances are that for the first year or two, or three, he does pretty well. His books have created something of a stir . . . and the reputation they have earned for him has brought magazine editors around to see him, asking for short stories or, still more enticing, suggesting that his next novel would probably make a good serial.

A better exposition of the free lance's sequence of thought at the brink of his precarious undertaking could scarcely be made— at least if his aim is profitable fiction. The point that though the money comes from magazines, the prestige which introduces the author to the magazines comes from the books—rarely, in themselves, money-makers—is the important one. But it was in this lecture's very sort of exposition or analysis rather than in fiction itself that Elmer Davis would eventually excel.

## 2

Even then, as he was riding high on the wave of success and making money, if not hand over fist, at least abundantly enough to pay his bills, he could not defy the occasional impulse toward reflective writing. Fiction—or at least the kind he wrote—was no outlet for the thoughts and ideas bred of his studious inquiries into the international scene or his unrestrained reaches into every sort of book.

In midsummer, 1924, there appeared in the *Annals* of the American Academy of Political and Social Science a realistic piece on "The Character of American Influence on Eastern Europe." In it Davis pricked the bubble that had been so big and iridescent immediately after the Armistice of 1918—the bubble of America's mystic sway over the arrangements of a peaceful world. The illusion in those days when many of Wilson's Fourteen Points such as that dealing with the self-determination of peoples were thought to be of divine inspiration, was hard, even six years later, to dissolve. But Davis saw through this to the changed facts. No one remembered better than he the moving ceremonies at Pittsburgh when, with American assistance, the new state of Czechoslovakia was created and placed in the hands of his friend Thomas Masaryk. Nor could he forget the great American donations toward the rebuilding of the bombed Rheims cathedral. But floods of water had gone over the dam since then, unnoticed apparently, by the idealists.

> There is, perhaps inevitably, a pre-millennial tone about most contemporary writings on the immediate future of Europe; all the misfortunes of the age are to be ended by the second coming of America. It is not my business to compete in prophetic prediction with veteran soothsayers, but . . . I see no reason to anticipate any such active collaboration of America in Europe as was expected early in 1919, and seems still to be expected by some persons on both sides of the Atlantic. . . . Even if America should come back into Europe, should enter the League, America will not be "in" Europe as she was in the few months immediately after the Armistice.

In another interval between his own bursts of fiction, Davis turned his attention to the fiction of others. His essay on this, published in the *Saturday Review of Literature,* in October, 1925, was entitled "Tohu and Bohu"—the Hebrew words which, in the first chapter of Genesis, the King James version translates as "without form and void." The burden of the piece (and today's abstract painters may find the argument debatable) was that, however chaotic life may be, art must have order and pattern. Davis's contention was that even when a writer can see no coherent arrangement in the universe about him or in the social setting of which he is a part, he must invent such an arrangement

105

when he sits down to write a novel. A mere reflection of emptiness, Davis argues, is not art.

After this piece was published, he evidently thought about it for a couple of years for, in 1927, a revised version was incorporated in his volume of essays, *Show Window,* under the title of "The Age of Impotence." The revision in no way softened the irony—on the contrary it hardened it—but it included some reading the writer had done in the years between, and there was an evident if not wholly successful effort to tighten the essay and intensify its impact. Although some pretty cogent stuff was excised in the revision, it seems fairer to the author to quote from the later version.

For the writers of the literature of Impotence, he devises the term "Futilitarians."

If you believe [he says] the textbook on geology prescribed for the schools of Tennessee, the earth, prior to nine o'clock in the morning of September 21, 4004 B.C. was tohu and bohu, without form and void. If you believe T. S. Eliot, William Gerhardi, Rose Macaulay, Aldous Huxley, John Dos Passos, Ernest Hemingway, John Gunther and the rest of their school, it is that even now. Life is meaningless, effort is futile, the perceptible phenomena of existence have no interrelation.

I am far from denying it. I do not pretend to discern any unifying or arranging principle in the data of human affairs. . . . But even if life is without form and void, it does not follow that novels dealing with life must also be without form and void. Suppose life is chaos—full of sound and fury, as Miss Macaulay assures us, signifying nothing. Whatever life may be, two dollars is two dollars; and two dollars will buy a current novel or a quart of kitchen stove gin. . . .

The manufacturing novelist goes into competition with one great advantage over the bootlegger; he knows, as a rule, the charms of the rival attraction; the novelist usually drinks gin, whereas the bootlegger rarely reads novels. The novelist

knows exactly what gin gives the consumer; how then, is he
to persuade him to buy a novel instead? Obviously by meeting the needs of the trade; and by failing to do this, novelists
of the Chaotic, Invertebrate, or Futilitarian school have
worked considerable harm to the interest of the industry at
large. . . .

For if the customers on whom novelists depend for their
bread and butter find in fiction only the futility and chaos
they have already found, and are likely to keep on finding, in
life, they will go to gin, quite sensibly, for the illusion that art
ought to furnish.

The diatribe, spiced with sarcasm and occasionally over-
seasoned with indignation, goes on for long—too long, no doubt.
Moreover it lacks the clarity which usually marks Davis's essays.
Possibly this is because he was not entirely sure of his ground. If
the writers he attacks were truly "futilitarian" and all of the
reading public bought gin in place of their novels, it would be
futile to attack them. But the fact was that several of the Futilitarians were achieving a considerable success by answering a
precise public demand. Part of the demand came from the rebels
against the upsurging financial boom and Coolidge complacency.
Such rebels were comforted by the thought that nothing mattered
and that the earth and their existence upon it were accidents. The
other part came from the post war disillusioned who wanted to
have it proved to them that all their effort had been in vain. For
these folk gin was not enough: their ecstasy of despair needed the
support of art, or what they thought was art, and, indeed, much
of it was. That Hemingway and Dos Passos and Huxley and
O'Neill were in phase with the prevailing literary mood did not
diminish their talent, as their later products proved.

Yet the essay is a demonstration of a fighting mood not wholly
uninspired by Davis's own struggle. Here was this young man,
suddenly a professional writer: was this the sort of thing he must
write to appease the critics? Potboilers such as *Times Have*

*Changed* were not, of course, in competition with any work of art but, like all starting writers, Davis had secret frustrated aspirations.

> But oh for that great novel [he wrote to Carolyn Wilson in December, 1924], that was to lift me up into the range of those who might be considered for the Pulitzer, if not the Nobel prize; harrow and alas for the distinguished work of incisive realism. Where is it? Where the woodbine twineth.

Meanwhile, in his search for an ideal of realism, he drew his angry line between sheep and goats. It may seem to us that he picked dubious examples. In some cases hindsight leads to that judgment, but surely some of those he disparaged stood high in contemporary literary appraisal.

## 3

With the successes of 1924, considerable for a starting free lance, Elmer Davis at last admitted that things were looking up. It had been a hard pull; the weaning away from the *Times* had not been easy and the final plunge had been induced by an almost unbearable schizophrenic harassment. Even now there was not a complete separation, but now he could go to the *Times,* always sure of a welcome, offer his special services and more or less write his own ticket. But there were no regular hours in an office, no boss to say Yea or Nay, no anonymous writing.

The house in Kew Gardens had been sold; the Davises had moved into an apartment on Morningside Drive whose proximity to the Cathedral of St. John the Divine would presently prove a sardonic stimulus; "the Robin," as they called their son, was big enough to go to school; and for the hot months a kind friend lent them a country house.

Perhaps because the Robin was coming into his most inquiring age, Davis found it convenient to hire a room in the old Brevoort on Eighth Street and Fifth Avenue for his more intense concentration. Here he distracted the other guests by the "mitrailleuse rattle of the Underwood," yet this was better than letting himself be distracted by events at home. But he went home whenever an interval permitted, to be asked by Robin if he had finished his book. (Because when you do you can stay home and play with me.) Meanwhile one of his letters told that

We have regained our freedom of movement, spiritual as well as physical. It was a hard job climbing out of that long lane with no turning that lies between the Times editorial page and a commuting suburb on Long Island, but I think we're out at last. All three of us. To begin again to live dangerously, even in a mild way . . . is quite a bit, after some years of the prudent life conditioned principally by many mortgages. . . .

I don't know whether all this is of any interest to anyone but me, but I am highly excited by the fact that after a lifetime of playing it safe I've at last climbed out of the shell. May I stay climbed. The thing had been bitten into me ever since I first learned in college that I'd have mother to look after; it became the dominant obsession, and of course the editorial page and commuting and mortgages only made it worse. . . .

Of course all this rests on some fundamental presuppositions, one of which is now present for the first time. Meaning, of course, the red gold. I haven't reached the Big Money yet but it looks as if it is right around the corner and in the meantime we are pretty well off for us.

He was to learn, however, that the fortunes of a free lance have ups and downs, and in the downs his "financial hypochondria" would come back. One of the downs arrived when a story had led him away from the strait and narrow path of formulated magazine

109

fiction into thoughtful writing. It "started out to be only a rough-neck football thriller but it filled up, as I went along, with excerpts from the more sightly portions of my philosophy and personality; became, indeed, an amused and tolerant picture of things as I see them . . . and alas . . . there is grave doubt of its sale." *Collier's* said no serial; it was too long for *Liberty*. "Poverty" may drive him to do some quick fiction for the pulps. "This literature business is amusingly insecure. I have been within arm's length of about twenty-five thousand for months, but whenever I reach out for it it recedes like the grapes of Tantalus." Shall he start looking again for an editorial job? The conflict was beginning that would one day take him away from fiction forever.

There were in this free-lance time, periods of depression which only the family saw. His look of taking everything in his stride, his easy going manner, the gaiety his friends knew, would drop away from him when he came home. To his wife and children he conveyed a sense of failure; of frustration in the attainment of a constantly receding goal.

This susceptibility to changes of mood is not, of course, uncommon among creative writers. What was striking in Davis's case was that it was not visible away from home. At the evening meetings of "The Baker Street Irregulars"—a society that was not wholly dedicated to the study of Conan Doyle—and other more exclusive gatherings, Davis gave the impression of having no cares. And the many pieces he wrote for *The New Yorker* in the 1920's are not only immensely funny but full of fun; reflecting, one would suppose, a happy outlook on the life about him.

There were a few blows that were a real cause for melancholy. His son remembers his winning a prize novel contest and then losing it again because he was at a ball game when the news came.

> They kept calling mother every half hour or so [Robert Davis recalls], until finally they decided their publicity gimmick had to be saved at all costs, so they gave the prize

**110**

to . . . a lady writer. The "gimmick" in question was a radio show scheduled for five o'clock on which the winning author must speak.

Again, once when he had spent all summer on a serial with constant encouragement from the magazine he thought was going to use it, he met refusal when it was done; the editors explained they had merely given him a "green light"—a phrase used by certain periodicals to stimulate without commitment. But these things happen to the most successful authors; it is simply an insight into Elmer Davis's inner self to learn how much they disturbed him and how little he showed it.

Through the summer of 1925, Fliss was looking forward to the birth of her second child. The baby came on the second of September—a daughter—and they named her Carolyn Anne for their friend and Davis's newspaper colleague, Carolyn Wilson.

## 4

In 1925, the growing Cathedral of St. John the Divine cast its shadow over his consciousness and his conscience. Suddenly he had "a recurring attack of moral earnestness, which I thought I had got over with." It is, he thinks, "like malaria, an infection caught in childhood that never gets out of the system." The cause here was a drive to raise money to complete the cathedral as a "spiritual home of all the people" when God and Elmer knew that it would belong lock, stock and barrel to the rigid and exclusive Episcopalians, who would continue to operate it no matter how big it got. Whether it was pure righteous indignation or the old hard-shell Baptist reasserting itself after all these years, Davis leapt to his typewriter and wrote "Dr. Manning's Pious Anachronism," which only *The New Republic* would print. Having once laid hold of this clergyman, however, he would not let him go and a year later refined his rage into "Portrait of a

**111**

Cleric," which *Harper's* could not resist and which readers generally concede is the most thoroughly Davis piece of all his articles.

In it, he tells of the rise of William Thomas Manning to the bishopric of New York, of the controversies over his Anglican birth and his Anglo-Catholic penchant, of his conflicts with other clergymen about their heretical views of the Virgin Birth, of the angry battle with Hearst which brought his enemies to his support and finally, as bishop, of his drive for money to complete the cathedral. The irony throughout the muted diatribe is masterly, stretching but never breaking restraint, and it is only at the end that he mobilizes all his artillery in a diapason of sound.

By a clever pretense, according to Davis, largely formulated by lawyers, people of all faiths including the Jewish were induced to contribute to the building fund under the impression that it was to be a "house of prayer for all people." Once the money was in, however, it turned out that the cathedral was to be owned and operated by only "one per cent of the people" of New York; a sop was thrown to the other sects in the forms of three interdenominational services in which non-Episcopal ministers were allowed to preach from the pulpit though "their unordained feet did not tread the holy ground of the sanctuary," and the humble suggestion by John D. Rockefeller, Jr., a Baptist, who gave half a million dollars, that the "large outside friendly interest should be represented by a small number of laymen of sister churches to the Board of Trustees," was summarily turned down.

The cathedral was, Davis concedes, "a beautiful building if you like Gothic architecture; an impressive building, if you do not require architecture that expresses something of the life around it." And then the final paragraph:

> In the fulness of time our Bishop (he may be an Archbishop by then) will be gathered to his reward; but the cathedral will remain. Perhaps his monument may be more enduring than his brass.

Some time later, praise came from within the church itself.

> Like great numbers of liberals in the Episcopal Church [read
> a letter to Davis from an extremely prominent churchman]
> I got a primitive thrill from your "Portrait of a Cleric." . . .
> It was a magnificent piece of work.

It is in this essay, limited in its subject matter and in its subject, appealing to a small circle of readers, that we may see the Elmer Davis that became celebrated getting into his stride. It is, coming after the "breezy" fiction phase, a very pointed landmark.

## 5

In the almost total unawareness of its people, America moved in the decade's last years toward the nation's greatest catastrophe since the Civil War. Least aware of all, apparently, were the "hard-headed" businessmen. Whether, as some have said, these persons are truly the most incorrigible romanticists of all, it is certain that on the day of judgment in 1929, they were the most bewildered. To those, on the other hand, who professed to no understanding of finance, the bust seemed no stranger than the boom. Unhappily some of these ignorant citizens, persuaded by the alleged knowledgeable or, perhaps, carried away by the boom hysteria, had speculated and lost.

But in 1929, we were still well above the bottom and the slight reprise in 1930 induced a good many badly frightened Americans to welcome the wishful thinking of their President, Herbert Hoover, himself a businessman and hard-headed. It was the President's romantic spasm and not any positive or negative act that made him the eventual scapegoat for the entire depression and swung the electorate away from him in 1932. For nothing is so disheartening as the unfulfilled optimistic promise: the words about recovery being round the corner and "a chicken in every pot" echoed back from the nadir with such volume that some even predicted bloody revolution.

All through the early years of the new decade what Franklin Roosevelt was to call "fear itself" swept across the land. The suffering and disillusion were far greater than those caused by the war or by its immediate aftermath. And it was the generation that grew up in these years rather than the one the war caught that was the truly lost generation.

Perhaps of all those hit by the catastrophe, the writers suffered least. The writer's normal impulse is either to spend the money he earns or to put it in a sock. He is wary of the so-called securities. The whole realm of the money market is under suspicion and the free lance does not enter it except under uncommon pressure. It is his strong subconscious conviction that all financiers are crooks; they deal with a substance the writer welcomes but never quite believes in, and if one is lucky enough to acquire some of that strange commodity it is wise to keep it out of the financier's hands.

The free lance's earning power was not greatly curtailed. Few of the magazines, even in the darkest times, closed shop. They lost advertising and they paid their contributors less. The Hollywood extravagance was reduced. But those industries which produced entertainment suffered less than those which manufactured motor cars or fur coats. Such entertainment as that furnished by the "slick" magazines provided escape and any cheap means of escape from the pervasive ambiance of horror became greatly in demand.

Straight through the depressed years, Elmer Davis was able to sell his fiction. But his real growth in this period shows in the sequence of his essays—some dealing with the here-and-now events, others reaching out into philosophy and religion.

His predictions as late as 1931 seemed to favor recovery during the next, election, year, although he was cautious about express-

114

ing opinions on politics. In the July *Harper's,* in an article entitled "Repressible Issues," he wrote:

> Bread and business not only should be, but certainly will be, the dominant issue next year—if bread is still scarce and business still slack. In that case it will not matter what issues are written into the platform; almost anybody can beat Hoover. But if business is definitely on the upgrade—which seems more likely than not, after eighteen months—nobody can beat him, unless some other issue replaces bread and business not only in the platforms but in popular interest.

He saw the President's position—as he saw many things, in terms of his favorite card game. (It was said that Davis was not a top player of contract, as he was no player at all of baseball, yet he was expert in the theory of both.)

> Mr. Hoover is like a bridge player with no biddable suit but several high cards. He can say nothing and let his opponents bid against each other, higher and higher in the confidence that he can double and set them no matter what their final contract may be. His calculations may be wrong; some of his aces may be ruffed; nobody can tell what will happen till the dummy is laid down, and we see how the Democratic declarer plays his hand. But it seems to me a pretty good bet that Mr. Hoover will continue to inhabit the White House till March 4, 1937.

By October, he was taking a sardonic view of business cycles. He looked back at some of the panics and booms of the past and then into his crystal ball. There he saw another boom and in his most ironic vein, he wrote a piece, again for *Harper's,* called "Happy Days Will Come Again," counseling his readers to

> plunge headfirst into it [the boom] when it comes; for it's

115

going to be a good one and it may be the last. . . . If you really want the pearl necklace or the round-the-world cruise you decided not to buy in 1928, don't let the next chance go by.

Parallel with these articles, however, he published some gayer and more diverse ones—less preoccupied with politics and economics. "The Cause and Cure of God" he wrote for the *Saturday Review of Literature,* and "God Without Religion" and "Miniature Golf to the Rescue" for *Harper's* in 1930; "Good Old 1913" for the *Forum* and "On Lying Fallow" for *Harper's* in 1931, and "Purest of Pleasures," about contract bridge, and "Notes for a New Bible" for *Harper's* in 1932. In those same three years, he published more than fifteen short stories and two novels.

As the critical election of 1932 approached Davis's disgust with the national administrations of the 'twenties grew apace. This had been cumulative since Godfrey Gloom's appraisal of Harding before the first postwar election. But now that the figure of Franklin Roosevelt began to loom on the horizon he was inclined to pronounce "a plague o' both your houses." What he did, at last, at the polls in this presidential year was what many another bewildered American did. It showed a political state of mind that was still far from crystallized.

At home, Davis watched the growth of his son with alternate surprise and detachment. The boy, Robert Lloyd—"The Robin" —was developing an intellectual interest which his father could not always follow. In the evenings Davis would sometimes read aloud from James Jeans's *The Universe Around Us* and the boy of eleven or twelve understood it fully. Indeed, he was able to explain the parts that his father found obscure, and it was these explanations that made the reading enjoyable to Davis. At the same time, it was troubling him to realize that scientific study had so largely been left out of his formal education.

Often, in the evenings, Davis's friend, Dr. Edwin Hubble, the celebrated astronomer, would drop in and he and the boy would talk until Davis was far over his depth. It was in these times that Davis looked on his son with detachment—as if the boy had been an adult stranger.

Carolyn Anne was easier; she was six years younger and convinced that her father was God—a faith that must have given him a lift in uneasy moments.

# 8 ]]]]]]

## 1

THE AMERICAN MIND, if by then there still was such a thing, was truly in a tailspin as the election year arrived. Never in the nation's history had there been such a collapse of confidence. "Confidence in Whom?" asked Elmer Davis as he reviewed the collapse in an article of that title in the *Forum* for January, 1933. He disposed of the possibilities, one by one, and came to the conclusion that Confidence itself, the very abstraction, had vanished. And a good thing it was, he said: Americans had had too blind a faith in too many false gods for too long. Now we must forget the old conviction that

> because we are Americans we shall get more than we deserve. Just at present "Oh yeah?" "Is that so?" and "Says you!" are safer mottoes for this country than "In God We Trust."

It was a time for skepticism. It was a time for the rearrangement of values. It was a time to look with doubt on the promises of recovery especially when they were expressed in such material terms as Mr. Hoover had used. And if and when it begins to appear that these promises will be fulfilled, then we must be most skeptical of all. For

> the test will come when business recovers . . . and it is once again possible to get rich on the stock market. If we forget

our lesson then . . . why, then I would sell my share of the
United States short for anything I could get, and would try
to escape to a desert island before the purchaser came gunning for me.

The fact that Franklin Roosevelt had already been elected
when this article appeared had done nothing to strengthen
Davis's own confidence in the future. He had not, indeed, voted
for Roosevelt. He had cast a protest ballot for Norman Thomas.
That, nevertheless, he was opposed to socialism is revealed in a
letter he wrote Miss Wilson in the summer of 1932. His guess,
he said, was that

> four years more of Hoover would at last make the class
> struggle a reality in this country. If Roosevelt does what he
> promises it may be enough to drain off the pus; but I doubt
> if he can, or will. Anyway, I'm working for the Socialists this
> year, hoping to God we won't have to come to that but very
> much afraid we may in a few years more.

But however he may have felt about socialism, he left no doubt
of his attitude toward business. To prove his point about the
maladjustment of business to individual and social requirements
he quoted from an advertisement he had seen—evidently one of
the "institutional" advertising efforts of the time intended to
stimulate acceptance of the current American industrial economy.

> "Low-priced commodities," quoted Davis, "merely mean that
> everybody can have them. But automatic line production
> means that everybody must have them. . . . Economic
> America has no other problem than that of getting enough of
> its commodities into the hands of the masses of wage-earning
> America in order to keep the wheels of its mass-production
> turning at the other end."

119

Davis inserted this statement of the reverse of the democratic process in an article in *Harper's* in March, 1931, entitled "Can Business Manage Itself?"—a question the article answers in the negative.

> There you are [he wrote]. Individual initiative is a privilege not permitted to the consumer. He *must* take the goods, not because he wants them but because somebody has to sell them—somebody who has not brains enough to make a living by any other method than continual overproduction of goods which the consumer is asked to buy to help out the manufacturer.

That Davis overstated his case in attributing a lack of brains to the "somebody" who overproduced via the production-line technique does not detract from the importance of his comment. In the thirty years since this piece was published we have learned that the maladjustment he saw had a larger frame of reference than he gave it. The problem, in spite of the application of considerable brains, is still with us. The service he did in 1931 was to call attention to the apparent pride with which the industrialist advertised the system's failure and, indeed, to point out the growing gap between industrial production and a society which tried to observe democratic practice. And this defeat of individual initiative in the 1920's was the beginning of the group dominance and the obsession of organization that we have heard so much about in later years.

In the same article he aligned himself with the most advanced (then thought radical) opinions of the time. He advocated unemployment insurance—although

> the average emotional business man roars at the idea. . . . The dole! Well, it is not the dole . . . the dole is something

120

we are paying now in bread lines and soup kitchens. This is not unemployment insurance; it is unemployment damages, of a most uneconomic and immoral sort.

This and other reforms were later put into practice in the Roosevelt administrations and with Roosevelt's support, but Davis remained dubious about the President-elect up to the moment of inauguration. His article, "If Roosevelt Fails," appeared in *Harper's* for March, 1933, and was probably read by many people after the celebrated inaugural speech of March 4. In it he tells of the doubts that obstructed his own vote and explains again that a vote for Thomas did not necessarily mark the voter as a Socialist or a proletarian.

Those of us who supported the Socialist program in 1932 because we thought it less unsatisfactory than any other can make no reply, on the record, to the gentlemen who assure us that Socialism is only a fad of middle-class mugwumps; for all the evidence indicates that Mr. Thomas got a very much higher percentage of the middle-class vote last November than of the working-class vote.

Davis then gave his conditional answer to the question in his title:

If Mr. Roosevelt lives up to the creed he set forth at the Commonwealth Club [in San Francisco], if he steadfastly preaches this new faith to the nation, he gives us something on which we not only can stand but may go forward. If not, you and I may pay for his mistakes at an even higher price than we have paid for the mistakes of Coolidge and Hoover.

Like many Americans, Elmer Davis lost his doubt in later years.

121

2

On the fourth of March, the mood of the country suddenly and sensationally changed. It would, perhaps, have undergone some sort of change no matter what successor to Hoover had delivered, on that day, his inaugural address. Most of the people, in that drowning time, looked hopefully at any straw that might float toward them. But when this crippled man rose above his weakness to speak, the men and women listening in every dark corner of the nation were able, for the moment, to rise above their despair.

> The money changers [he said] have fled from their high seats in the temple of our civilization. We may now restore this temple to the ancient truths. The measure of that restoration lies in the extent to which we apply social values more noble than mere monetary profit. . . .
> This nation asks for action, and action now!

He would recommend "the measures that a stricken nation in the midst of a stricken world may require" and if these recommendations were not followed, he would not

> evade the clear course of duty that will then confront me. I shall ask the Congress for the one remaining instrument to meet the crisis—broad executive power to wage a war against the emergency as great as the power that would be given me if we were in fact invaded by a foreign foe. The people of the United States have asked for discipline and direction under leadership. They have made me the present instrument of their wishes.

These were not words of optimism. They were not an invocation to trust in the Lord. They made no promise except the

122

promise of action. They offered no opportunity except the opportunity to fight. They admitted that our backs were to the wall. Hope was not "around the corner" but on a remote hilltop, the road to which would be hard and up-grade all the way.

For the action, those who had been heartened by the address did not have to wait long. March 4 was a Saturday. In the next day, Sunday, Roosevelt called a special session of Congress for the following Thursday. On Monday, the sixth, he prohibited the export of gold and stopped dealings in foreign exchange. He then declared a "bank holiday." There would be an investigation of individual banks and only those found to be sound would be permitted to reopen.

This closing of the banks followed a sequence of state "holidays" proclaimed by many governors. The New York banks had been shut by order of Governor Lehman on the very morning of the day the President spoke. All this was consequent upon two years of progressive disaster. The money changers had, indeed, fled from the temple and banking institutions all over the country had suffered from their flight. From 1930 on, nearly 800 national banks had failed and there were failures in more than 3,600 state banks. The deposits involved came to more than two and a half billion dollars.

Whatever loss of memory of that time hatred may later have brought, it is historical fact that the people, in the first months of his administration were, almost to a man, behind the President.

The whole country is with him [wrote Will Rogers, the cowboy philosopher]. Even if what he does is wrong they are with him. Just so he does something. If he burned down the Capitol, we would cheer and say, "Well, we at least got a fire started anyhow."

The people of America were, in this spring of 1933, far too preoccupied with the prodigious task of pulling themselves out of the depths to be much concerned over what was happening in the

123

rest of the world. It was long after that we remembered how the rise of Hitler to supreme power in Germany had been almost exactly coincident with Roosevelt's assumption of a very different sort of leadership. It was only when the consequences of these two events came face to face in the crisis at the start of the next decade that those sensitive to the dramatic connected the two beginnings.

It was on the fifth of March while Roosevelt was issuing his call to Congress that the elections in the Reichstag gave the Nazis and their Nationalist allies 52 per cent of the vote. A week later while, under the terror in Germany, thousands were arrested or went into hiding, Roosevelt, in his first "fireside chat" said to the people over the radio, "Let us unite in banishing fear." In the coincidence were portents both for Franklin Roosevelt and for Elmer Davis: nine years later they would be working together against the power that Germany had become.

It did not take long for the doubting Davis to swing over to the President's support; a mood in which he continued through Roosevelt's life, though there may have been times when it was not as easy as in the spring and summer of 1933. But then, as the stimuli succeeded each other, week by week—the banking reform measures, the abandonment of the gold standard, the legislation for banking reform and the NRA, the Securities Act and the later Securities Exchange Act—he knew that here was a leadership in which a confidence that was no longer "blind" could be placed.

It may seem trivial, today, to recall that one of the effective shots-in-the-arm of that spring was the President's recommendation to the Congress that it modify the Volstead statute to permit 3.2 per cent beer. But it was not trivial in March, 1933. In the years before the election, the National Economic League had put prohibition ahead, even, of unemployment as a "paramount problem" of the nation. Before the inauguration, the "lame-duck" Congress, suddenly aware of the nationwide change of feeling

124

toward what Hoover had called "a great social and economic experiment, noble in motive and far-reaching in purpose," proposed the repeal of the Eighteenth Amendment, and by April the states were already voting on ratification.

Roosevelt had been aware of the national temper for a long time. While Hoover and the Congress were still supposing that the majority sentiment was dry, Roosevelt knew it had become overwhelmingly wet. Although, as Elmer Davis noted in his article "How the Wets Won" in *Current History* for December, 1933, the President said very little on the subject, what he did say was timed with the astuteness of an expert politician. His recommendation about beer (which was almost immediately adopted and the innocent beer put on sale) was not a mere stimulus to recovery; it was a human gesture, a sign that other problems than that of depression were being taken care of. It brought celebration everywhere with something tangible to celebrate with, and whether or not the people drank to the New Deal, the toast was in their hearts.

The speed of ratification that came through the summer as state after state expressed an overpowering sentiment for repeal was a proof of popular conviction that had left the people's representatives far behind. It was, as Davis observed, one of the greatest triumphs of democracy in American history. For the people had spoken loud enough for the driest and deafest member of Congress to hear and those who up to the very last minute had voted for prohibition ran like scared rabbits to the other side.

Again, as ratification progressed, the President added a perfectly timed spur. He connected the two problems most grievously confronting the nation. If liquor were taken out of the hands of the bootlegger and made a legitimate commodity, he said in effect, think of the revenue that would come from its sale! And what, my friends, would this do to the tax burden now so heavy on the people whom the depression had rendered unable to pay!

Davis remarked on these breaches in the President's skillful silence on the wet-dry issue. Roosevelt knew well enough what the outcome would be. It only needed a word or two at psychological moments. As traditionally dry Indiana and Alabama voted wet, the prohibitionists conceded defeat. In December, Utah joined the procession and on the fifth, the Eighteenth Amendment passed into history.

Davis's piece on "How the Wets Won" makes dull enough reading in 1961, after our effort of more than a quarter century to forget that national prohibition ever existed. But it is historically valuable. It traces step by step and state by state, the progress of the Twenty-first Amendment. It gives quotations from the speeches of both sides and tells a striking story of the last stand of the drys. But its main importance is in its picture of the ideal democratic process.

In May, 1934, Davis came out in full support of the President in a *Harper's* article, "A Blow at the Foundations." In his last campaign speech, Hoover had said,

> Our opponents . . . are proposing changes and so-called new deals which would destroy the very foundations of our American system. . . .

Roosevelt, Davis said, was destroying those foundations. He gave as an example of this the cancellation of the air mail contracts which, in the Hoover administration, had resulted in graft, special privilege, the end of competitive bidding and the enrichment of unscrupulous individuals. If this sort of thing constituted the foundations of the American system—as Davis insisted they had come to do—then the system ought to be destroyed, root and branch, and Roosevelt should be applauded for doing it. As it turned out, the contracts had to be restored when the Army to which Roosevelt delegated the carrying of the mails failed in its function, but they were restored on a far sounder basis. In any case, this article is a sort of landmark for it indicated the position

126

that, after much thought, Davis had finally taken and would continue to hold.

Through these years that sometimes seem to mark the low point of the nation's history, the Davises did better than most American families. "The Robin," fourteen in 1933, was in Culver Military Academy, and was continuing his interest in science and mathematics. Carolyn Anne was a charming child and developing into a strong swimmer. At eight, she could swim across the bay at Mystic, Connecticut—a good half mile. That the family could spend their summers in a rented cottage and the children go to private schools in the winter—all this in the dark times of the early 'thirties—was evidence that no hungry wolf was growling at the door.

## 3

In most of the first half of the decade of the 'thirties, the bulk of Elmer Davis's work was fiction. His reservoir of ideas for short stories seemed inexhaustible. *Collier's* printed most of them. They were gay and ephemeral. Few of them are remembered today. His novel *White Pants Willie* came out in 1932; *Love Among the Ruins* in 1935 was his last book of fiction.

As he looked back, in 1934, on his career as a novelist, it seemed to him that *Giant Killer*, published in 1928, was his best. But even that, he reflected, though it was "the one idea I ever had out of which something really good might have been written," had not quite come off.

I ought [he wrote to Miss Wilson in March, 1934] to have laid it aside for a year, then worked it over. . . . It's a much better book than the majority of the critics would admit; they said it was too long and too dull, and five years had to pass before the case of *Anthony Adverse* proved that the only reason it failed to be saluted as great was that it was not long enough or dull enough. Still I did a bad technical job, and am accordingly more grateful to the people who recognize its merits in spite of its faults—a very curious company including Cabell, William Allen White, one or two rock-ribbed Republican manufacturers and quite a number of theologians.

The reason, of course, that the theologians had seen good in it was that it was based on the biblical account of the slaying of Goliath.

But by 1934, Davis's ambitions for a "great" novel were fading. He had come to realize that when he set his sights too high, he missed: "It was aiming," he said, "at effects . . . that only music can achieve." To him then, as it had always been, music was the highest of the arts.

In the summer of 1932, Godfrey Gloom had covered both conventions and his interviews balanced the solemnity of the rest of the *Times*. But in 1936, he met his end. He had just covered the closing session of the Democratic convention which had carried Roosevelt to renomination on a wave of enthusiasm.

A headline of the twenty-eighth of June read:

LAST JEFFERSONIAN EXPIRES WITH CONVENTIONS
Godfrey Gloom a Victim of Modern Devices

BY ELMER DAVIS
Special to The New York Times.

Philadelphia, June 27.—Godfrey G. Gloom, the aged Jeffersonian from Amity, Ind., died this evening as a result of injuries sustained when he was crossing a street in West Philadelphia on his way to Franklin Field.

Mr. Gloom had leaped, with an agility hardly to be expected in one of his years, out of the way of a car carrying a radio commentator, only to be knocked headlong by a motorcycle bearing the plates of a newspaper photographer.

128

The story continues about Gloom's being carried to the sidewalk and being supported there by a crowd of well-wishers while he gave his final comment on politics to a reporter. Conventions, he said, are all decided before they begin.

"And where is the excitement in a story when you know before you start to read it how it comes out? No, sir, the convention system and I have both outlived our time, and I know it even if the national committees don't. . . .

"And in any case," said the old-timer, his voice growing stronger now, "there seems no more place in American politics for a genuine old-fashioned Jeffersonian. Jefferson has now been endorsed by both parties, and there seems as little prospect that the endorsement will ever be repudiated as that either party will ever put Jeffersonian policies into practice.

"And maybe," added Mr. Gloom to the astonishment of his hearers, "that is just as well. For the principles of Thomas Jefferson, I have unshaken respect; but when he translated those principles into concrete policies, he did so according to the peculiar conditions of his time, as any man of sense would have done.

"And surely it is not inexact to characterize his time as the horse-and-buggy days; to return to it, and to return to the possibility of literal application of Mr. Jefferson's theories we should have to cut the power lines, tear up the railroad tracks and in general return to the economy of 1800—

"But most of the people in this country, especially those who are the loudest advertisers of their simon-pure Americanism, have adopted the alien and Marxian habit of thinking what the prophet said a hundred years ago with relation to the conditions of his day was divinely inspired and applies to the conditions of any day. So long as people insist on that in the year 1936 the best place for a genuine Jeffersonian is in the tomb."

129

At this point, says the news report, a motorcycle came up to the group and handed a telegram to Mr. Gloom. In a weakened voice he read it aloud.

"Last-Ditch Jeffersonians hearing radio bulletin of your accident urge you to concentrate every effort on speedy recovery so that you may work with us for Landon and Knox. . . ."

At this point Mr. Gloom emitted a loud groan and expired.

Accompanying the news story was a formal obituary, giving Gloom's ancestry ("his grandfather was the late Charles Carrol of Carrolton Gloom"), his birth in Maryland and his unexplained migration to Indiana and his claim "to have held Jefferson's horse at the first inauguration of the founder of the Democratic party."

After the landslide in November in which only two states cast their vote for Landon, Davis wrote for the *New Republic* one of the wittiest articles of his literary career. It is entitled "Let My People Go"; the title refers to the appeal of God's Chosen People to a Pharaoh. The Pharaoh refused but "the refusal brought so much trouble down on him that eventually he had to pay them a bonus to get out of the country." Davis compares the members of the Union League and Bankers' clubs with the migrating Jews of Scripture and the comparison must have been, in some cases, galling to say the least although it may be doubted if these members would ever be caught reading this "radical" publication.

Quite a number of my acquaintances [the article explains] have told me since the election, that there is nothing left but to move to Canada. My acquaintance is not extraordinarily large; and provided that it is a scientific sampling . . . what I have heard must indicate that about five million people are going to move to Canada as soon as they can collect outstanding bills and get rid of their leases.

130

Citing historical precedents for such mass migrations, Davis recalls the Huguenots forced out of France, the Tories who left home after the American Revolution, the White Russians who fled their sovietized land and the Jews who were now leaving Germany.

But the citizens who now threaten to shake the dust of this debased republic from their feet and move across the northern frontier are on a somewhat different footing. Nobody is running them out; they are not threatened with the loss of life, liberty, or the right to pursue happiness—unless they can't be happy except when they are promoting utility holding companies. They will go, if they go, for one of two reasons—either because they believed all the campaign arguments of Republican orators, or because they refuse to play unless their side can always win. Either way we could get along without them.

But the doctrine of the good neighbor requires that we should pause and consider what this will mean to Canada. . . .

How long will it be before they start blaming the Canadian government "for everything that goes wrong"? After all,

they are in the habit of blaming the government . . . and it will be strange if they can break that habit in a new country. So you can hardly expect the Canadians to contemplate this prospective wave of immigration with unmixed delight . . . and it takes no great imagination to see Canadian political speakers, about 1948, telling the discontented that if they don't like it here they had better go back to Wall Street where they came from.

It was pieces like this that caused the Roosevelt-haters to include Elmer Davis in their catalog of villains, and, at last, when he was in government employ, to call him a Communist.

**131**

As usual the events of the election year of 1936 kept the attention of most Americans at home. There was a minority, however, that, in spite of the sensational political landslide and the repeal of prohibition, kept watching Europe and becoming alarmed over the growing power of Germany's National Socialist party. As we look back on it today, Hitler's unopposed invasion of the Rhineland in May, 1936, was the first war cloud. But few could know, then, that the march to Munich had begun; that a little more than two years later, the point of no return would have been passed.

Even Elmer Davis with Europe always in the edge of his vision could scarcely imagine that from here on his life and thought must become progressively involved with events overseas and that in his analysis of those events, he would employ a medium of communication that was, in 1936, wholly unfamiliar to him.

# 9 ]]]]]]

## 1

AS THE DECADE of the 1930's drew past its mid-point, the shadow of Europe began to darken America. From then on, no matter how fearfully the people retreated from its advance, it caught them at last. And they did retreat—most of them at first—in the old nostalgic hope that the long-blessed American people could evade the evil from overseas. They had had their own troubles, the disaster of the depression—from which no real recovery had yet arrived—but that was domestic; it could be taken care of at home. Indeed the administration had grappled with it bravely, some thought, and even if the problem was still too big for any administration, at least it was an American problem outside the reach of the Machiavellian European political manipulation that threatened the peace of the world.

The sense of this creeping shadow came, as none had ever come before, into the homes of the people. It came daily and nightly, inescapably, following us from room to room, driving with us in our cars. It came on long waves and on short waves and, although electronic scanning could not yet bring us the picture of that little man with the clipped moustache and the lock of hair across his forehead, the incessant voices brought his presence, immediate, among us. And to confirm the words—their horror always eased a little by the romantic commercials suggesting that there was nothing milk of magnesia could not cure—there was the growing stream of refugees; of men and women made penniless and hounded out of their homeland telling us, face to face, that it was all true. This confirmation, to be sure, did not spread far into the interior. Most of the Midwestern cities had no large population of Jews to receive the stricken refugees whereas there was, in some places, a very considerable number of Germans whose first impulse was favorable to the aggrandizement of Germany and its climb back to the level of the great powers no matter under what aegis.

At the same time there were, everywhere, prescient Americans who, listening to remote signals on their radios, reflected on the shrinkage of the world and knew that their continent, protected over the years by oceans and vast spaces, was no longer invulnerable. But perhaps the most immediate fear was that of infection from the fascist philosophy. The most potent factor of this alarm was Sinclair Lewis's novel, *It Can't Happen Here,* published in 1935. This released the minds of many of its readers from the parochial notion that fascism was exclusively a European phenomenon but concerned all society and all mankind.

It was, then, about 1935 that the American people went into that phase of schizophrenia which lasted in greater or less degree right up to the Pearl Harbor attack at the end of 1941. The isolationists, eventually led by an organization appropriately named "America First," included the pro-Germans, the pacifists, the anti-British, those who thought the threat implied in *It Can't Happen Here* a unique American problem and many sincere people who still believed that we could and therefore should go it alone on a path separate from the rest of the world.

This split into two moods had had, by 1936, when Hitler began his drive toward European conquest by invading the Rhineland, abundant preparation. Disillusionment with the last war had infected large areas of the Allied world. Sources of this infection were, among others, the Congressional investigations into the part played by munitions-makers in stimulating the conflict; Walter Millis's book, *Road to War,* "exposing" America's seduction to

134

pull British chestnuts out of the fire; and the resolution of Oxford students not to support their government in another war. There was also the sympathy which had grown among some of the intellectuals with communism under the delusion that hatred of war was a Communist tenet. Odd bedfellows of these in the isolationist camp were the wealthy folk—especially obstructionist in England—who were reluctant to offend Hitler because Germany presented the strongest bulwark against Bolshevism!

Frederick Lewis Allen in his popular review of the 1930's, *Since Yesterday,* reported:

As late as April, 1937, a Gallup poll on the question "Do you think it was a mistake for the United States to enter the World War?" drew a yes from 71 per cent of those polled.

Once bitten, twice shy was the saying that passed back and forth among the peace-at-almost-any-price proponents. To those who pointed with horror to such fascist-imperialist events as the Italian conquest of Ethiopia or the Japanese occupation of Manchuria they answered that these were matters with which the United States had no concern. Why enlarge the area of bloodshed? Wasn't there enough for us to do at home in this time of convalescence from the wasting disease of the depression without interfering in the devious and cynical manipulations of European tyrants?

There were, however, thoughtful Americans—as there were thinking Englishmen, Frenchmen and, indeed, Germans—who saw these things as all of a piece in a world grown small and crowded where the forces were no longer separate. Many of these people could see, again and again, as those fateful years passed, lost moments of decision when a word would have stopped the march toward holocaust. Where was England's "balance of power" that had for so long maintained the Pax Britannica? Where was the French valiant courage when, with backs to the wall they had said "They shall not pass" and held the insistent boche at Verdun? Yet they had done nothing to stop Hitler in the Rhineland at a moment when the Führer was frightened of what he had started, because a single French division could have sent him home.

And, as events accelerated their speed along the road to Munich, the ministers of Britain and France listened with complacency to Hitler's reiterated promise to unite all Germans wherever they might live, watched with complacency his ruthless persecutions of "non-Aryans," were a little bewildered by his *Anschluss* in Austria but would be content as long as the *Drang Nach Osten* remained in the East, and saw reasonableness in his aim to attach the Sudeten country because of its large percentage of alleged German inhabitants.

This sequence of steps toward subjugation by Germany of the continent of Europe—each accompanied by its sop of appeasement from France and England—was deeply disturbing to those who had read, digested and believed a book written some dozen years before whose sale meanwhile had gone above four million. It was a book by an obscure German of Austrian origin, a former corporal in the army that lost the first World War for the Germans. In it a preview of the events now taking place and the philosophy behind them was given with great exactitude. The author, Adolf Hitler, was in jail when he wrote *Mein Kampf* in 1924. In 1936, 1937 and 1938, he was in jail no longer.

The men who were disturbed in the early summer of 1938 included Harold Nicolson, Winston Churchill and Duff Cooper in England; the German exiles Thomas Mann and Albert Einstein; and the Americans Franklin Roosevelt and Elmer Davis.

2

Elmer Davis was in his well-loved Prague when Hitler made his "crazy" assault upon the Rhineland in 1936. Eduard Beneš who had succeeded Thomas Masaryk as President of Czechoslovakia was, like his predecessor, Elmer's friend. The rumble of Hitler's propaganda about the Sudeten Germans was already loud at the gates of the republic. Davis and Beneš talked together about Hitler. At that time, Davis later wrote,

> there were men in the British Foreign Office who took him seriously only because they thought he was crazy and hence incalculable. I mentioned this to President Beneš, who rejected it with vigor. Hitler, he said, was anything but crazy; he was a gambler, but every gamble was based on a cool and accurate calculation of realities. Evidently Beneš knew Hitler better than the British did; also Hitler knew the British better than Beneš did.

That European sojourn in 1936 turned Davis's attention and reflection toward Europe so seriously that his story-writing declined. In the following year, after the election and its immediate aftermath were over, the articles that took the place of fiction focused on Europe. In *Harper's* for 1937, there were pieces on various phases or aspects of the European scene. In March, there was "England's Weak Spot"—London—about which he later had much to say; in April, "England Turns a Corner" shows that he still has faith in the English people, however their government may "muddle through"; in May, "Belgium and Holland, Isolated?" explains these nations' dependence on the great powers; in June, "Czechoslovakia, Bridge or Barricade" is a penetrating analysis of the Sudeten problem. It was, of course, impossible to see the tragedy ahead for that betrayed nation but such a betrayal was beyond belief by any one in 1937 and, as events proved, Davis was a little too optimistic about England—at least about her immediate future.

But no one can read these studies—even today—without realizing his awareness of the forces then in motion or the seriousness of his research into the areas of strength and weakness in the vast potential battleground. This was not journalistic research. It was not digging for facts. Nor was it an alignment of arguments to buttress a thesis. It included an exploration that went deep into backgrounds, into history and folklore and cultural streams; the kind of research that is impossible without a thorough grasp of the heritages and social evolutions of each scene.

There is nothing superficial or reportorial, for example, about his apologia for the Sudeten Germans.

There have been Germans in Bohemia [he wrote in *Harper's* for June 1937] for at least a thousand years; Czech kings in the early Middle Ages deliberately imported a good many to help build up the country, and others drifted in as immigrants coming to a frontier where a better living might be made. Medieval Bohemia was a kingdom of two races; but it was overthrown by the Hapsburg armies in 1620, and for three hundred years thereafter whoever wanted to get ahead had to be politically Austrian and culturally German. A good many Czechs turned German in those days, and still more in the centralizing campaign of Joseph II in the eighteenth century. "A race," says Henlein (of course with particular reference to the German race), "is something made by God"; but nothing is clearer than that a considerable percentage of the German "race" in Bohemia was made by political and economic pressure.

Looking at England he sees not only the government of Chamberlain but those of Disraeli, Palmerston, Gladstone, even Grenville and North.

English governments [he wrote in the April, 1937, *Harper's*] muddle their way through practically any crisis by the same technic. First it is insisted that nothing is wrong; then that even if anything were wrong nothing could be done about it; then, that the government is doing everything possible, and to

138

answer questions about just what is being done would serve no useful purpose; and at last, when the crisis has somehow evaporated, to make it plain that the government foresaw everything long before it happened, and was always on hand with the proper measures at the right time.

No one can quite understand the success of Elmer Davis's later war broadcasts without reading these articles.

## 3

The horrifying events of which the news came from overseas in 1938 did not preoccupy Davis to the exclusion of gentler contemplation. In the most fateful month of the decade—September, 1938—there appeared in *Harper's* what was perhaps the most celebrated of his essays, "On Being Kept by a Cat." Perhaps the feline character has been as well analyzed elsewhere but such an analysis would be hard to find. The piece is personal history, not fiction, but as a penetrating study it is on the level of Kipling's "The Cat Who Walked by Himself"—walking "by his wild lone in the Wet Wild Woods." Friends of the Davis family usually found one of the Persian persuasion ruling the household, moving with the Davises where they went—to Connecticut or Morningside Drive or, later, to Crescent Place in Washington.

To "keep" or to "have" a cat was, to Elmer, a mere *façon de parler*, remote from the truth. In support of this thesis, he cites the story told by "the learned Van Vechten whose *Tiger in the House* is practically the *Golden Bough* of cat lore."

Madame Michelet . . . once computed that she had owned a hundred cats. "Say rather," her husband corrected, "that a hundred cats have owned you." Possibly he was jealous of the creatures who had usurped his rightful place as the domestic pet, but anybody with much feline experience knows he was

139

right—especially people who do not keep servants, and must refuse invitations for week-ends because somebody has to stay at home to take care of the member of the family who cannot open ice-box doors. To the question often asked by the inexpert, "Do you keep a cat?" the proper answer is "No, a cat keeps me."

This "most dignified and independent of living creatures" is self-sufficient if left to himself. Thus the capitalist cat and the alley cat are sisters under the skin; "any cat is a potential alley cat." The most pampered pet could "get along on his own if he had to."

My cat (the possessive is used . . . purely for indentification) is a silver Persian, who in his urban apartment leads a placid and sedentary life for nine months of the year. But when he goes to the country in June he is perfectly at home in woods and fields and fights everything in sight. The cat's high sense of enlightened self-interest leads him to live on his income if he can—but because it is pleasanter, not because he must. The tendency is not unknown among human beings.

Between the alley cat and the feline economic royalist there is another category; the salaried cat. In public or private employ, they resist invasions of mice and rats. Amos was a salaried cat. His so-called owner, a widow, was forced to give him up when she went, after her husband's death, to live with her children, so she took him to the Bide-a-Wee home.

It happened that about that time a certain club discovered to its horror that there were rats in the basement and the Board of Governors empowered the manager to add a cat to the pay-roll. He went to the Bide-a-Wee home, saw Amos and admired him (as who would not?) and employed him—after an exchange of references; for the lady who had been associated with Amos wanted to be sure he joined the right club. Amos came, looked around, and evidently decided that this was not the club for him. The next day he vanished; but six weeks later he reappeared, looking somewhat bedraggled, and has been there ever since.

Meanwhile, he had tried to go home, found that his home had ceased to exist, tried free-lancing for a time "but like many a human being in the same situation, he finally concluded that it was too much of a strain and he had better go back to a salaried job."

The older members of this club which, indeed, was Davis's own, well remember Amos, who eventually died with, so to speak, his boots on. For a moment there was a movement to have him buried in the back yard with a sculptured headstone but the governors stepped on this undignified impulse. In the years that he was there, however, the members were never quite sure whether Amos was an employee or a member, as he used the club's facilities with indifferent abandon. Many a member, for instance, found Amos occupying his favorite chair—a liberty which, in New York clubs, the members themselves do not take, respecting one another's choice of resting places. So, indeed, this club in time no longer owned Amos; rather, Amos owned the club.

4

In the last week of September, the American radio news service was put to its greatest test to date. The communications from Europe were incessant and growing constantly more bewildering. At the same time in the coastal area lying to the northeast of New York the worst storm in the weather annals of that region struck with sudden force, flooding towns, uprooting trees, cutting power lines and drowning people. This area was rendered largely deaf to the words on which the fate of the world hung, by the power

141

failure; yet the transmission must continue telling those who could listen of the two events: Munich and the hurricane. The mind of Elmer Davis was involved with both.

The dominant voice over the radio was that of H. V. Kaltenborn, veteran news commentator for the Columbia Broadcasting System. Since the twelfth of the month he had hardly left the studio at all. He even slept there on an army cot. As bulletins were put before him, he would cut into gayer programs, speaking with his clear, precise, elegant diction as he read the strange news. Then he would bring in European stations: "We take you to London, Prague, Berlin." The older radio listeners still felt a thrill as these once-remote places were brought into the living room. But to minds not trained in the grim European realities, the picture remained unclear.

It is so clear today that a child can understand the whole of it. In one of the best passages of all his writing, the September story is told by Winston Churchill in *The Gathering Storm*, published in 1948—supported then by documents captured in the war. There is so little mystery in the story that it seems incredible that anyone could have been blinded by the events as they transpired through the simple communiqués. But this is hindsight and is forgetful of the fact that *Mein Kampf* had, outside of Germany, so few readers and fewer who took it seriously until Hitler's program showed that he had meant what he wrote.

In the summer, the members of the British cabinet had listened sympathetically to Hitler's demands that Czechoslovakia cede to Germany that Bohemian territory which he said was largely inhabited by Germans. The British government had sent the Runciman mission to Prague to persuade the Czechs that this was simply a question of the sort of self-determination of peoples that Woodrow Wilson had insisted upon. The mission was not successful. Early in September, Hitler's demands were shriller. On the twelfth, in a speech at Nuremberg, he attacked the Czechs so violently that martial law was declared in parts of Czechoslovakia and the pro-German Sudeten Konrad Henlein was expelled from the country. On the fourteenth, the British Prime Minister, Neville Chamberlain, asked Hitler if he might come to visit him and he responded to Hitler's warm invitation by flying to Munich the next day.

> The moment [writes Churchill] was not in all respects well chosen. When the news reached Prague, the Czech leaders could not believe it was true. They were astonished that at the very moment when for the first time they had the internal situation in the Sudeten areas in hand, the British Prime Minister should pay a direct visit to Hitler. This they felt would weaken their position with Germany.

It was, of course, the first step in the progressive weakening carried on by Chamberlain with Daladier clinging to his coat-tails.

Few Englishmen and fewer Americans realized the great potential strength of the Czechoslovak republic. It had a well-trained army. The terrain presented a veritable fortress against land troops. With the support of Britain and of France and Russia (with all of whom it had mutual-assistance pacts) it could resist any invasion. Hitler's generals knew this and, according to Churchill, even plotted to arrest Hitler before he should attack.

But Hitler, the master poker player, kept shouting his demands, at the same time making the most solemn promises to the British and the French that once the Sudetenland was ceded he would never again make a territorial claim in Europe. So, said Chamberlain to his cabinet and to Parliament, were we to court war just to save this unreasonable little nation from a perfectly reasonable partition? And those Englishmen who thought the Czechs were outlandish obstructionists anyway; who could have little respect for a country whose name was not even pronounced the way it was spelled; and who had never even bothered to look at a map of Europe—agreed and gave the premier their support.

Chamberlain went twice again to talk to Hitler and in the

**143**

final meeting it was agreed that neither France nor Britain would support the Czechs against a German seizure of their territory. The Prime Minister then flew back to London and, to a crowd of cheering cockneys who knew even less, if possible, than their M.P.'s, said:

This is the second time there has come back from Germany to Downing Street peace with honour. I believe it is peace in our time.

It was the outcome of these negotiations that finally convinced the generals of the German army that Hitler was so shot, as we say, with luck that he could do no wrong.

## 5

Elmer Davis was, of course, one of the most avid listeners to the careful reporting and comment which came over the air in the staccato speech of Mr. Kaltenborn. While it is true that he did not, in his later career, pattern his own free-wheeling commentary on this model—Kaltenborn could never have pronounced "premier" "premeer"—it is certain that in this critical time he rarely missed a broadcast of this or any other newscaster within reach. It must, then, have been disturbing, to say the least, to be cut off, on the twenty-first—from all contact with the outside world.

As Frederick Lewis Allen reminds us, the New York weather prediction that morning had been "Rain and cool today. Tomorrow cloudy, probably rain, little change in temperature." Before noon the storm struck and by evening there was hardly in the whole of coastal New England enough power to maintain a single radio set. Only those who had cars with sets in the dashboard (and whose cars were not under water) could hear Kaltenborn or anyone else.

One of Davis's favorite summer resorts was a little private island joined by a causeway to Mystic, Connecticut. This was one of the hardest-hit spots. Neighbors on Mason's Island have hinted that the story sometimes told of the Davis family (and cat) half crawling, half swimming in the dark to the mainland is somewhat fanciful. He was reported missing, however, on the front page of the *Times* with the definite implication that he was dead. This produced an essay—at once the most hilarious and the most profound of his career—entitled "On Not Being Dead as Reported."

According to his account in this piece, a radio station, he was told, "went to the length of reporting that my corpse had been seen floating out to sea."

Between the hurricane and Hitler, the papers and the broadcasting stations were overloaded that week; there was little time or space for the correction of misapprehensions. News is the unusual, the not-to-be-expected; so I suppose I have no right to complain if it was news that Davis was dead, but not news, not worth putting in the papers, that Davis was not dead after all.

When he returned to New York and met some of his old friends on the street, he thought they gave him

a look of startled surprise, not altogether unmixed with resentment; for they had done their grieving for Davis, and it could not but be regarded as an imposition when they discovered that it was all a mistake, and that some day they would have it to do over again.

From this point he went on into a philosophic and psychological discussion of time which reached depths Davis had never before touched.

145

> For if I remember correctly [he wrote] the science I once
> studied . . . from the biologist's point of view we start dying
> the moment we are born—which is only another way of say-
> ing that every organism exists in time as well as in space,
> that it is not quite the same at any moment as it was the
> moment before.

It did not take long, however, for his mind to get back,
seriously, to the disastrous happenings in Europe and, when the
end came on the thirtieth, he was again close in touch. He then
wrote, for *Harper's,* an appraisal of what had occurred plus an
accurate prediction of what, as a result of the colossal Munich
blunder, was going to happen.

Two articles were published together in the December, 1938,
issue. One was "The Road to Munich" by Willson Woodside; the
other "The Road from Munich" by Elmer Davis. It is doubtful if,
in the long career of this grand old monthly, there were ever, in
the same number, two more cogent articles based on current news.

Davis led his piece with a translated excerpt from *Mein
Kampf.*

> "A shrewd victor [Hitler had written] will, if possible, keep
> imposing his demands on the conquered by degrees. He can
> then, in dealing with a nation that has lost its character—
> and this means every one that submits voluntarily—count
> on its never finding in any particular act of oppression a
> sufficient excuse for taking up arms once more. On the con-
> trary; the more the exactions that have been willingly en-
> dured, the less justifiable does it seem to resist at last on
> account of a new and apparently isolated (though to be sure
> constantly recurring) imposition."

And Davis commented, thinking, perhaps, at once of the different calamities that had hit two of his best-loved nations:

**146**

There, set down twelve years ago, is a preview of the history of Europe after Munich—a Europe which, at the end of 1938 stands about where it stood at the end of 1811, with this difference: In 1811 England was not only the implacable but the impregnable enemy of the man who dominated the Continent. The England of 1938 is something else, strategically and morally.

He doubts, later in the article, if Chamberlain had ever read *Mein Kampf*. Perhaps, in spite of regulations, neither had the members of the German general staff. What, after all, they thought in their arrogance, could a corporal know about war?

# 10 ]]]]]]

1

IT SEEMS, looking back at that last uneasy year of peace, as if the sequence of events was uninterrupted—as if each crisis led, immediately, to the next. But this was not the sense of the time. Always there seemed to be hope; hope that the German monster would be appeased by the concessions that were made to him; hope that each broken promise would be the last. Today, after years of cold war when broken promises in certain quarters have become routine, we wonder that, in 1938, we could have been so naïve.

Less than six months after the meeting at which Adolf Hitler pledged his solemn word to Neville Chamberlain that he had no further territorial ambitions in Europe, he entered Prague at the head of his army and then, secure in his possession of Czecho-slovakia, laid his plans for the conquest of all Europe. A first step, obviously, was Poland but, to the hopeful, it seemed unlikely that even Hitler would defy the British and French guarantee and risk world war by taking it. Thus, in the Western world, business as usual became the rule and, in the United States, business seemed to have awakened from the long sleep of the depression.

In the summer of 1939, two symbols of the hope appeared in two simultaneous world's fairs in New York and San Francisco. Most of the visiting nations—conspicuously missing was Nazi Germany—staged large, expensive and sometimes beautiful exhibits. The glamorous architecture and movement of New York's

148

"world of tomorrow" and the lovely lighting of Golden Gate's island dispelled foreboding. The irony of New York's project was not yet visible as the crowds gazed into tomorrow's prospect and, in both fairs, the triumphs of gadgetry promoted the sense of security.

And how, it was asked, if there was international tension, could the King and Queen of England cross the Atlantic in the summer of 1939, to visit Canada and the United States? Would they not, above others, be aware of a near brink of disaster? Yet, the skeptical insisted, they must share with their Prime Minister, that veil of ignorance whose fabric was faith in the integrity of a head of state. The frettings and fumings of a Churchill, the warnings of the chronic gloom-caster Nicolson, the dark doubts of Duff Cooper could not fluster the serenity with which royalty moved under the shelter of the Chamberlain umbrella.

As always, however, there were reasons for the royal visit resolved in the midnight sessions of the men who believed their fingers to be on the pulse of international sentiment. Three years before, King George's predecessor had abdicated his throne in order to marry the woman he loved who, accidentally, was an American divorcée. Had this, wondered these wise men, posed a rift in Anglo-American relations? Was not "David" popular in New York; "Wally" in Baltimore? Was this an appropriate time for a rift between traditional allies—no matter how trivial the cause? Already it was conceded in realistic circles that a colossal blunder had estranged the valuable (if unpopular) potential ally, Russia. Yet once the Americans had seen David's nobler brother in the regal panoply they secretly loved, all would be well and the President's warmth toward the new King and Queen would quickly heal whatever wounds there were.

But beneath the relaxed surface, there were fears. Churchill's words of the past year still echoed in the London streets; they were repeated in the New York clubs; translated in the Deux Magots and the Café de la Paix. "Britain and France had to choose between war and dishonor. They chose dishonor. They will have war."

2

Even for those who knew what was coming there was nothing to do but go about their daily business. The point of no return had been passed, the waters had begun to swell and there was, in all the world, no Dutch boy to put his thumb in the dike. Even Hitler was carried on by the ground swell he had created and events now seemed to be out of human control.

No one's crystal ball was clearer than Elmer Davis's and no one was less given to wishful thinking. Not only the facts but the truth behind them was sharp in his mind. He had read and analyzed the Führer's blueprint; further, he had believed it. For, however much Hitler might admire the lie as a tool of diplomacy, he told the truth in *Mein Kampf:* the truth about himself and, more tragically, about the Germany Bismarck had evolved, which the war of 1914 had frustrated into a submerged madness that could easily be inflamed by a mad leader. For the moment Davis put the inevitable on a shelf, so to speak, and went about his variegated writing.

In *Harper's* for February, 1939, which contained an article by Henry C. Wolfe suggesting that it was unlikely that Hitler would immediately attack South America, Davis had a piece about the spot furthest from the war than any in the world: namely the state of Wisconsin. Specifically, "The Wisconsin Brothers: A Study in Partial Eclipse" was about the La Follettes, Phil and Bob. More important and far more in the ironic vein which delighted some and displeased others in the *Harper's* public was "Roosevelt, the Rich Man's Alibi" in the October issue. We have no record of the blood-pressure index along Park Avenue when this issue entered the quiet living rooms of the millionaires' cliff dwellings, but it must have been high.

150

To the leaders of industry, commerce, and finance Mr. Roosevelt has been such a godsend as they could not have dared to hope for in the dark days of 1932. . . .

In his mistakes, actual or alleged, the conservative rich have been able to find a sufficient cause not only for everything that goes wrong, but for everything that has stayed wrong since his first year as Governor of New York. They ought to be the most zealous third-termers in the country. So long as Roosevelt is in the White House they are spared the painful effort of trying to think, spared, it may be, the still more painful confession that even if they tried to think no thoughts would come.

This piece had evidently been brewing for some time. It had brewed through alternating phases of its author's thinking. Elmer Davis had by no means an undiluted admiration for the President —as, for example, Robert E. Sherwood had—nor did he hesitate to condemn, in print, Roosevelt's errors and weaknesses. But toward "Big Business," his attitude had been constant since the collapse of 1929, and when this was a reference point he wrote of Roosevelt with the oblique praise that was so effective. What, he asked, had Big Business suggested as an alternative to what Roosevelt had done to advance recovery?

It is now almost a decade since Big Business, encouraged by a succession of respectfully admiring Administrations, finished its joy ride by running violently down a steep place into the sea.

In the first third of that decade,

the ruling class could reflect on its mistakes, and try to think out some justification for its continuance in power.

In those three and a half years Big Business and its

151

friends in the Administration produced exactly two ideas. One was the sort of economic planning which eventually was more or less embodied in the NRA; the business class which was chiefly responsible for that scheme was at least smart enough to duck the blame for its failure, leaving persons vaguely designated as "professors and theorists" to hold the sack. The second idea was governmental interference with "natural economic processes" by advancing money to people in trouble. So long as money was advanced only to the rich it looked like a happy inspiration; but most business men lost faith in it when it was extended to the poor as well.

In conclusion, he wrote of Roosevelt:

Many people who have little faith in the things he is doing still have faith in him. Why? Perhaps because they know that even if he does not run the country very well, they can count on him not to run it solely or chiefly in the interest of Big Business.

Whether he chooses to run or not [in 1940], the rich and well born could profitably reflect on that. His popularity may not tell much about him; but it tells a good deal about the former ruling class—the class which between 1921 and 1933 had unhampered opportunity to show what it could do, and showed it.

3

A professional writer always has work to do; always there is something unfinished; even when a deadline is met and passed, another like a buoy looms out of the fog ahead.

Wherever I go [wrote Elmer Davis in his article "Broadcasting the Outbreak of War" in *Harper's* for November,

152

1939], my ordinary business of writing goes with me; and this summer [of 1939], when the annual crisis began to simmer—the crisis that had been forecast a year ago by everybody on earth except the governments of Great Britain, France, and Poland—it looked like an anti-climax. . . . In any case, I had a job to do—a piece of writing which had kept me hard at work for some months and which, I computed as I got up on the morning of August 22nd, could be finished in about one more week of intensive and unremitting effort. Then, for the first time in months, I was going to take an equally intensive and unremitting rest.

Here is another buoy that is almost always on the writer's horizon—rest; a singing buoy this time rolling gently in the midst of a phosphorescent Gulf Stream where all is warmth and idleness and even the sea creatures have nothing to do but glow. We may imagine Davis lying in bed contemplating this, but then the postman came with the morning paper and that was the end of the dreams.

So Germany and Russia, swallowing their mutual hatred, had got together and signed the death warrant of the rest of the world. This, at least, was the implication of the banner head; but trained journalists skip the headlines and this one went at once to the details of the meeting of Stalin and Ribbentrop whose set smiles had masked the impulse to be at each other's throats and it was all quite familiar to a mind that had listened to the backstairs whispers of the past year.

Russia had once been the potential ally that could have stopped Hitler dead in his tracks. And as Churchill tells in *The Gathering Storm,* the master minds in Moscow had wanted to do precisely that. But when the Russian feelers reached Number 10 Downing Street, they found the door shut against them. The Prime Minister had listened long to the Cliveden set and others of London's rich and great whose recurrent nightmares pictured their fortunes lost and themselves hanging to Piccadilly lampposts. And Daladier in Paris, though he heard all the mocking voices that transliterated Chamberlain into *j'aime Berlin,* was committed to the Prime Minister. For however much the French voters might distrust Hitler and hate the Germany behind him, a rift with Britain was unthinkable. Furthermore, the Russian bear was growling, too, in the Place Vendôme.

It was pretty hard, then, for an ex-newspaperman who was fully aware of all this to put it out of his thought and concentrate on a job of irrelevant writing.

> The old firehorse turned out to pasture rears up his head and sniffs the breeze when he hears the alarm bell; big news was breaking, and I wanted to be in on the story. I went back to my typewriter—but that afternoon Paul White, who runs the news department of the Columbia Broadcasting System, called up from New York and told me that Kaltenborn was in Europe, where even before the war broke out no country was receiving anything like as much news as we get here. A news analyst was needed in the home office, and would I come down and help out?

For the journalist, the medium was unfamiliar. Yet Davis was not a total stranger to the microphone (though to the end of his days he protested he had chronic "mike-fright"); he had done occasional newscasting. Sometimes he had even pinch-hit for an absent Kaltenborn, when the job was merely routine,

> but to fill in for him in such a crisis as this was a little like trying to play center-field in place of Joe DiMaggio.

Those who remember those first vocal moments know that it was nothing of the sort. From the first five minutes of that voice, Hans Kaltenborn's immense reputation began to fade. But the impact was curiously imponderable. The overtones carried nothing like the implications of cultural background that were in

**154**

Kaltenborn's speech. Yet when Kaltenborn spoke one never felt his immediate presence. He was always talking from afar: one could picture the environment: the soundproof studio, the controls, the meticulously prepared script. Elmer Davis was right in your room. You could almost see him, though the visual technics were then far in the future. He was telling you in the fewest possible words what you wanted to know. The why of it was partly in the words, partly in the inflection. In that flat, even voice, the impact of the faintest up and down was stunning. And, hearing it, you could almost see facial expressions: the slight raising of eyebrows, the slighter twist of the mouth toward the smile that never quite came.

## 4

It was true then, in the late summer of 1939, that Americans knew more—or had the opportunity of knowing more—about what was going on in Europe than Europeans. The knowledge depended, of course, on the will to know and the capacity for separating the wheat of truth from the chaff of wishful thinking. Already the great split had come to the American people, separating isolationists from interventionists—or rather the neutrals from those who took sides. Very few, at that time, were actual interventionists in the sense of wanting the country to go to war in any circumstances. And few were actually neutral, for the isolationists tended to oppose the Allies—those snakes in the grass who had hoodwinked us in 1917.

This feud broke into the open in the representative bodies. From Hitler's first moves, Roosevelt had been avowedly against him. He had watched him closely from the moment he came to power—coincident with Roosevelt's own inauguration. In October, 1937, he had antagonized the isolationists by his celebrated quarantine speech in Chicago in which he advocated collective security against the menace of aggression. He was called an

155

Anglophile, supposed to have secret agreements leading to "entangling alliances." He had declared repeatedly against the Neutrality Act of 1936 with its embargo on the sale of arms and munitions to any belligerent. In 1939, he brought every pressure he could on Congress to repeal that provision. To deny to Britain the means of defense in case war should break out was to favor Germany. Roosevelt knew enough about the power of the British navy to know that Germany would be blockaded from importing the material of war. But while war was still only a threat, the bill for repeal was defeated by the followers of Borah and Wheeler.

According to his public words, Roosevelt, like almost everyone else in the United States, was opposed to armed intervention. He enjoined neutrality upon the people but he exempted "neutrality of thought." And Elmer Davis too, despite the strong feelings shown in his writings and, later, in some of the overtones of his broadcasts, was against American involvement.

From the time the news of the Russo-German pact, events moved so fast that even the radio could scarcely keep up with them.

On the first of September, Hitler invaded Poland and seized Danzig. The British and French governments delivered ultimatums to their ambassadors from Germany and on the third, Neville Chamberlain announced that "peace in our time" had come to an end. At the end of the month, Russia carved out her slice of unhappy Poland.

In the article "Broadcasting the Outbreak of War" in the November *Harper's*—from which quotation has already been made—Davis wrote of his first days at the studio:

> For me, and most people in the news side of radio, these nineteen days have been nothing but an endlessly unrolling strip of time, punctuated at irregular and unpredictable intervals by brief blank spots of sleep. The broadcasting systems used to close up for several hours in the early morning; but for four or five nights running at the beginning of

156

September they stayed open all night, to furnish whatever news there was to anybody who was up late enough to get it. Few of us who stayed with the story could tell you now, without looking it up, what day anything happened. But even if you lose track of the days, even if you are put on the air at odd hours, and cannot remember at the end of a day whether you have been on three times or six, you must never lose track of the minutes, nor even of the seconds toward the end of a broadcast when you are racing against a stop watch.

The broadcaster has, to be sure, a script which, given time, he has carefully prepared before he speaks; he knows precisely how long its reading will take. But he does not know about the late bulletins that may be put before him while he is talking, causing him to interrupt or even to revise a part of his broadcast. So it takes a state of mind that is always ready for split-second interpretation, and that was what Elmer Davis predominantly had. On a table, so to speak, in his brain lay the tools of his interpretation: tools of knowledge and above all of memory for there was no chance—a chance the newspaper writer always has—to look anything up. Davis's scripts had, therefore, always that fourth dimension of time: the clock ticked out the words. But he had learned, further, from his writing, economy of expression without sacrificing meaning. One word did for six in the mouth of anyone else; he had not only a flair but a great fondness for paring down a sentence. He hated waste. If elegant language failed to say what he meant he did not hesitate to employ slang or any colloquial expression, and he used no alibi in the form of oral quotation marks to apologize for any inelegance that clarified.

The *Harper's* piece that told about his beginnings is, besides being a documentary record of events, a useful exposition of radio techniques of the time. In this way it is a historical pinpoint. We find that many of the devices and devisings that we attribute to television had their inception with radio. One was the four-way telephone talks "between Ed Murrow in London, Grandin in

Paris, Albert L. Warner in Washington and Trout or me in New York." Although he is not sure he can explain exactly how this was done, he nevertheless makes a good try and adds:

At any rate it sounded to listeners, and to us, as if we were all sitting in the same room. (But you wear earphones clamped over your head; and while the sound of your own voice trickles in past them from the studio where you are talking, some engineering gadget keeps you from hearing yourself *over the phone*. If you did, its sound in the studio would only be an interfering echo.)

The sensational—"magic"—aspect of this technique greatly impressed the listening public. But it was also

a marked improvement over a simple transatlantic broadcast, especially in the early days of the crisis; Warner in Washington, or whoever was talking in New York, could ask the London and Paris men questions that were bothering people here, which might not have occurred to them, and thus get a point cleared up promptly. As actual war came nearer we had to be more careful about our questions, asking only the sort of thing that the censor was likely to let them answer.

There is much more in this piece about the details of broadcasting and the mind of the commentator. We must regard this period as the transition in Davis's life from writing to speaking; yet this article is testimony to the fact that the literary impulse persisted and was only gradually crowded out. Even in that frenzied, sleepless time when other radio folk were giving it their undivided attention, he was able to prepare this exposition of the magic that was mystifying everyone and to turn out what is, perhaps, one of the most informative pieces of writing he ever did.

Those of us who remember that winter of 1939-1940 recall the bewildering lapses in the continuity of the news. The conflict between Germany and the Allies was called a "phony" war; the aggressors seemed to have been stopped by the Maginot Line and there were rumors that the hostile soldiers were fraternizing over tea and schnapps in no man's land. Diversion came when Russia attacked Finland and we were surprised and shocked when the British navy failed to thwart the Norway invasion. Yet that, too, seemed irrelevant to the "man in the street"; it was not the way wars had always been fought—there was madness in it. Today when it is possible to put the pieces of the puzzle together the brilliant method is evident and it seems that if the master mind that planned it had continued in full sanity to the end the prediction shouted in the Nuremberg streets might have been fulfilled: *"Morgen die ganze Welt!"*

# 11 )))))

## 1

"THIS," said Edward R. Murrow on the second of September, 1939, "is London. The cabinet met fifteen minutes ago and is still in session. Well, where stands Britain tonight? . . . For the second time this country has expected the declaration of war and for the second time it hasn't come. Britain is still at peace."

Thus in that tense hour spoke the voice that was to bring England's bitterest nights into millions of safe American living rooms. In the years to come, the words "This is London" were to be familiar all over our land: the persistent reassurance that the world was still intact. In the dark days of 1941, one almost expected the ghostly echo of that voice to say, "This is London no more," but by then the three words had been reinforced by the angry defiance of Churchill:

> We shall go on to the end . . . we shall defend our Island whatever the cost may be, we shall fight on the beaches, we shall fight on the landing grounds, we shall fight in the fields and in the streets, we shall fight in the hills; we shall never surrender. . . .

But in that breathless moment in September, 1939, only one question hung in the air: would England keep her pledge to Poland; would the minister who had loved peace too much, move

160

to atone for the betrayal of the Czechs one year ago; would he now in this late day salvage what honor was left even at this greater cost?

The next day the question was answered.

Forty-five minutes ago [said the voice] the Prime Minister stated that a state of war existed between Britain and Germany. Air-raid instructions were immediately broadcast, and almost directly following that broadcast the air-raid warning siren screamed through the quiet calm of this Sabbath morning. . . . Now we're sitting quite comfortably underground. . . .

In a few minutes we shall hope to go up into the sunlight and see what happened. It may have been only a rehearsal. London may not have been the objective—and may have been.

I have just been informed that upstairs in the sunlight everything is normal; that cars are traveling through the streets, there are people walking. . . .

The crowd outside Downing Street received the first news of war with a rousing cheer. . . .

Murrow was talking, then, underground. But when he was not broadcasting—then and in the hundreds of days and nights that followed—he was everywhere; apparently indifferent to danger.

The only objection [wrote Davis in his introduction to Murrow's book, *This Is London*] that can be offered to Murrow's technique of reporting is that when an air raid is on he has the habit of going up on the roof to see what is happening, or of driving around town in an open car to see what has been hit. That is a good way to get the news, but perhaps not the best way to make sure that you will go on getting it.

**161**

This view of Murrow's recklessness did not, however, inhibit Davis's own performance when, later, he too was in London. But war correspondents, whether they work for radio or press are, if they are true reporters, not likely to let fear dilute their efforts. The true reporter is so intent upon his search for news that there is not always room in his mind for awareness of danger. That among the vast horde of American correspondents only a handful were true reporters, was evident to anyone who later spent much time in the bar of the Hotel Scribe in Paris, where the majority of accredited press people got their news at second hand.

2

For several months after the outbreak of war in Europe, broadcasters of the news in the United States felt that their words fell on deaf or incredulous ears. Murrow had a public continuing from peace time in England, but it was the so-called "human interest" of his narrative rather than concern about the war as a threat to all mankind that held them. His war stories, when they came, were of a far-off land; of people deserving of pity to be sure, but English people, not Americans and, occasionally, of an English government that it was our duty to regard with suspicion. Wasn't it Chamberlain, in fact, who was partly, perhaps largely, responsible for the mess? Yet the evacuation of the children from London was tragic, and Murrow's account of it extremely moving and his tales of the first blackouts were thought "fascinating."

But of all sorts of dispatches about the progress of the war the public here was skeptical.

With the outbreak of war [wrote Raymond Gram Swing], many Americans set themselves deliberately not to believe most of what they read or were told about it. The memories of the World War were already blurred, but there could be no forgetting the propaganda of that period. Since then, propaganda had been polished to a new perfection by the totalitarian states. With the war came censorship, which necessarily meant suppression. . . . Newspapers reminded their readers that their own foreign dispatches were not to be trusted, radio stations, before the reading of news, repeated the reminders, and for the first part of the war, news was subjected to an initial welcome of incredulity.

We know now that one of the reasons for this in the first months was that very few persons—even the persons in high places; even the "experts"—knew for sure what was happening. Hitler knew. He had his accurate, carefully prepared timetable before him and events arrived on schedule. But Hitler and his ministers were, in those days, adept at deception and many were fooled. Even the Prime Minister of Britain said to General Montgomery in the winter of 1939: "I don't think the Germans have any intention of attacking us. Do you?"

There was, nevertheless, a hard core of readers, listeners, analysts, statesmen and military men who were never fooled. As recorded in his *Memoirs*, General Montgomery, for example, in reply to Chamberlain's wishful question,

made it quite clear that in my view the attack would come at the time of their own choosing; it was now winter and we must get ready for trouble to begin when the cold weather was over.

Sumner Welles, then Cordell Hull's Under Secretary, referring to the widespread American response to Senator Borah's catchphrase of "phony war," wrote in *The Time for Decision*:

Why any considerable segment of public opinion in the United States should have regarded the war as a "phony" war in view of constantly accumulating evidence of Hitler's military strength, and in view of the ruin which Poland had already suffered, must always remain a mystery. Moreover, many people appeared to feel, like Senator Borah, that the failure of Great Britain and France to undertake the offensive was somehow reprehensible. This feeling was almost sadistic. It had in it something of the "boos" howled out by the spectators at a prize ring when the two contestants are not putting on as bloody an exhibition as they have paid to witness.

Americans were soon diverted, however, from their disgust at inaction on the Western Front by the news of plenty of blood on the snow in Finland. Here was a double opportunity for the expression of definite American feeling. First, the Finns had long endeared themselves by the scrupulous payment of their war debts to the United States while other greater and richer European nations lagged far behind. Second, Russia, in the back of the normal American mind, is the permanent Enemy Number One. We were still smarting from the perfidy of the Soviet-German pact—at which American Communists dropped away from the party like, in the simile of Fisher Ames, "windfalls from an apple tree in September"—and this ruthless attack against the Finns made the Beast of Berlin, by comparison with the Russian bear, seem almost friendly.

This diversion, however, was short-lived. By mid-March, 1940, it was all over and then the British failures in Scandinavia swung opinion back to its former anglophobic isolationism. It was not until after heroic Dunkirk; after the Germans had marched triumphantly up the Champs Elysées, and after Hitler had danced his jig before the *wagon-lit* in the forest of Compiègne, that America, in spirit, entered the war. And it was after these events that the society that called itself "America First"—the would-be flying wedge of the isolationists—began to arm in earnest.

**164**

3

Early in 1940, however, before the *Wehrmacht* had begun to move in the West, Elmer Davis lashed out at the followers of Borah and Lindbergh. He was still opposed to American intervention but not for the reasons these persons gave. He thought it was still desirable for us to keep out of the war "(provided the war keeps out of us)" because "we have unfinished business of our own," and because it was "doubtful if we could do Europe much good." But the pot and kettle argument, the view that there were no moral issues between the antagonists, that our own sins were so heinous that we had no right to cast stones at the Nazis—this was anathema to him. It resulted either from inexcusable ignorance or the refusal to face facts.

As to the pot and the kettle [he wrote in his article "The War and America" in *Harper's* for April, 1940], there are plenty of black spots on the past record of England, and France, and the United States; Nazi propagandists gleefully emphasize them . . . and many of our isolationists give all their time to reiterating the sins of the Allies (and our own) as if no other nation had sinned comparably. You would have to go very far back indeed in British or French history to find anything comparable to the horrors of the German concentration camps; this country has never had anything like them. . . . In any case these things in our record, or England's, or France's are in the past; and the overwhelming majority of Americans and Englishmen and Frenchmen are ashamed of them. What is the logical implication of the doctrine that we mustn't worry about what the Germans do because other people did something like it forty, or a hundred, or four hundred years ago? Is it that there is no use in anybody's ever trying to reform . . .

165

But the Germans were neither ashamed nor repentant. On the contrary, the words of Hans Frank, Governor-General of Poland, were proof that they were, indeed, proud of their acts.

He told his fellow-jurists on December 3rd that the beginning of their legal work was "the maxim, Right is whatever profits a nation, wrong is whatever harms it." To underline the point, Dr. Frank added: "Pale phantoms of objective justice do not exist for us any more."

And Davis further cited the words of Robert Ley, head of the German Labor Trust, who

put it even more candidly two weeks later, in a speech to the conquered Poles: "We have the divine right to rule and we shall assure ourselves of that right. . . . We want to be hard in this war. We are going to forget the arch-evil, our good nature, and be hard and relentless in battling for our demands.

In the conclusion of this piece which must, at the latest, have been written in February before even the Norwegian invasion had begun to dim the illusion of the "phony war," Davis made one of those prophecies that so often came out of the clarity of his vision. He wrote of the conflict between our sympathies and our fear of "involvement" as demonstrated when "our hearts bled for Finland" and "the Finns naïvely expected us to do something about it."

We are going to get more of that conflict, and more intensively, when or if German bombers begin to abolish London and Paris; still more perhaps when or if the German army overflows the Netherlands.

166

4

It was formerly proverbial that once a newspaperman, always a newspaperman, but there came a time when, for many old-timers, the "news" part of that word remained and the "paper" vanished. For with the advent of the revolutionary medium of communication, the press was forced into another category. The radio lured many a veteran journalist away from his old vocation and the daily papers brought in writers of stories which probed beyond the spot news into its background and were awarded by-lines. For spot news the newspapers came to rely more on the news services than on individual reporters of the old school.

These men, captured by the broadcasting industry, formed the core of its news branch. Occasionally, to be sure, they were joined by a maverick—a sort of outlander—who was regarded with suspicion at least until he had proved his competence.

We who work with Murrow [wrote Elmer Davis in his introduction to Murrow's *This Is London*] are keenly aware of his excellence as a reporter of pure news; indeed some of us—having, like most radio newsmen, learned our trade in another medium—are perhaps faintly scandalized that such good reporting can be done by a man who never worked on a newspaper in his life. . . .

Davis himself, however, once he had been inducted into the magic environment of radio news, was anything but loyal to his old trade. No more than two months after he had begun to speak instead of writing, he berated the press in his article about broadcasting in *Harper's*, for undervaluing the potential of the air waves.

Day by day [he wrote] newspapers insisted, directly or by innuendo, that you get too much news on the radio, you can't

167

believe the news you get on the radio, even that you get nothing on the radio which the newspapers hadn't given you hours before. . . .

There are things the newspapers can do which radio cannot, and all radio news men admit it. There are things the radio can do that newspapers cannot; but if any newspaper admitted that, its grudging concession was lost among the cavilings of its neighbors. Yet newspapers hungry for a prompt and drastic censorship of radio should reflect that any such action might set precedents for a chiseling away of the protection afforded newspapers by the Bill of Rights; and when the papers say you can't believe what you hear on the radio they are simply fouling their own nests.

So here he is, this tyro in a completely novel trade defending it against the age-old institution he served for ten years in every branch from city room to editorial office! Yet in this brief microphonic interval, he had learned much about the economics as well as the practice and philosophy of news broadcasting. He had learned, for instance, that in a time of crisis like that of the moment in which he wrote, the newspaper could make, while the radio lost, money.

Newspapers, with a great unexpected flood of news, can always add more pages to carry the news and the advertising too, at relatively little extra cost; but broadcasters cannot add any more hours to the day. When important news comes in at a moment when no news broadcast is scheduled, they have to put it on, even if a valuable piece of advertising revenue has to be thrown out.

Space was now converted into time. Where the newspaperman had to compress his story into inches the broadcaster must do it into minutes and seconds. To achieve this without panic took an entirely different set of nerves. To Davis the performance at the studio was "newspaper work intensified, faster, more exciting." From the pages of his article his enthusiasm at this challenge leaps forth. He is a little surprised and not a little pleased that a man of fifty can meet it. No wonder, he thought, that the men about him were so young.

On the morning of September 1st I looked round the Columbia news room, remembering how I had heard of the outbreak of another war in *The New York Times* city room on August 1, 1914; and it struck me that of all the men in the room—with the single exception of one of the top executives of the system who had come down because he was an old newspaperman and couldn't keep away from the excitement —I was the only one who had worn long pants in 1914. Most of my present colleagues, then, had not even been born.

Davis did not tell, here, the idiosyncratic details of his technique—perhaps he was unaware that they were peculiar—but the men who worked with him remember them. He never tore the paper as other men did from the teletype machines to make his script from them. He would go to the machines with his ruled pad, make notes, then go away to construct the broadcast from his notes. He was able to see at a glance the high points of the message and by the act of writing them down in notes fix them in his memory. He left the teletyped messages for others to take away if they wished. In this way too, perhaps, he achieved his celebrated economy of words, for the first step of reduction was the conversion of a sentence into a sparse note. And economy was the essence of what colleagues call his genius. It was this that first endeared him to CBS: he was able to do in five minutes what no one before him had ever done in less than fifteen—to give the core of the day's news *with comment upon it*. To an enterprise to which each fraction of a second is precious, this was a priceless asset.

Naturally it was harder; the time that was compressed out of the script had to be expended in its construction. This recalls the time-worn story of the man who asked his friend to forgive him for such a long letter: his excuse was that he had not time for a short one. The technique required sharp focus of concentration. The odd thing was that Davis's writing habits had not prepared him for such discipline. His writing was often verbose, sometimes repetitive when he wanted to emphasize a point. But he was acutely aware of the distinction between writing and speaking. Being rather laconic than garrulous and prevented by his native modesty from infatuation with the sound of his own voice, he cut drastically when he spoke. Also he had the rare gift of supplying many words by the tone of his voice, so that it was said of him that he was the only commentator on the air who could editorialize by inflection.

In September, 1940, one year after he had begun to broadcast, *Movie and Radio Guide* said of him:

Coolest, emotionally, of the commentators, Elmer Davis also has achieved the most perfect mastery of microphone technique.

5

Through 1941, as the inevitable American entry into the war became month by month more imminent, the voices of the isolationists became shriller. In their incessant attacks, Britain was their main target. Britain, they said in the face of British suffering, was playing the same devious game she had played in the first war, working on American sympathies to lure us to intervention. The barbed darts of "America First" were shot, especially, at such radio commentators as Murrow, Shirer, Swing and Davis. All of these men received letters accusing them of being in the pay of the British government. These reached the apex of absurdity when Davis was accused by a listener of being an Englishman ("Limey") in disguise who had trained himself to speak with a "phony" Midwestern accent!

Parallel with this movement, however, was the overwhelming anti-Nazi sentiment that was penetrating every part of the land. The tragic events of 1940 had convinced the majority of intelligent Americans of Hitler's cynical ruthlessness. There was fear, moreover, in the Atlantic centers, that the United States might be next on the Nazi agenda. The retreat of the British from Dunkirk, the end of the Battle of France, and the Battle of Britain still not won in the first months of 1941, had left the American people with the uneasy realization that England stood alone between Hitler and us.

On the twenty-ninth of April, Elmer Davis went to join Ed Murrow in England. Murrow had been there since 1937: London had become his permanent war assignment. Most American correspondents felt that England was not the best place to be in this time of nightly attack from the air. But Davis went at his own request and Murrow was glad indeed to welcome him.

Soon after Davis arrived, he and Murrow dined together at a London restaurant that had once been famous for its cellar. Davis asked if they still had his favorite *Châteauneuf-du-Pape*. The waiter sent for the proprietor.

"We have two bottles left. God knows when we'll get any more. I expect the Germans down in the Rhône valley will finish the rest of it."

They ordered a bottle.

Through dinner Murrow told Davis of incidents of the blitz: of the ruin and the carnage, the terror and the heroism. He spoke of the question in many English minds—though they did not say it—Can England win? Certain it was that Hitler meant the blitz to be a prelude to invasion. Murrow's words were punctuated by the sound of sirens and anti-aircraft fire. As they finished dinner, the noises came close.

"You know, Ed," said Davis looking at the empty bottle, "I

**171**

have a suggestion. I have two reasons for it. One, our time may be short. Two, Jerry *may* cross the Channel and good wine should never fall into the hands of an unappreciative drinker. So my suggestion is that we order the last possible bottle of *Châteauneuf-du-Pape.*"

For *Harper's,* as usual, Davis wrote "A Journey to England," which was published three months after his return. In it he wrote modestly—too modestly—of the job he had set himself to do. Fortunately we have, for this record, the story, privately told, by Edward Murrow.

> By a freak of chance [Davis wrote], for which experienced persons tell me I was not properly grateful, I never saw or heard a bomb dropped, in twenty-five nights in England.

They were dropped, Davis was told, one night when he "happened to be working in the soundproof sub-basement of the British Broadcasting Corporation." But Murrow tells another story. Perhaps, like many persons inured to the explosions resulting from the incessant rebuildings of New York, Davis was deaf to the sound of exploding bombs. But he saw, later, the devastation they caused, and he listened to

> An Englishwoman—a woman and emotional, but she happens to be a first-rate reporter besides—argued with me that an air raid ought to be reported differently: in terms of bowels blown about the streets, and lovely women smashed into a bloody pulp, and men digging frantically into the ruins of their blazing homes, unable to reach their screaming children. I did not see this; but others have seen it and I pass it on.

Davis tells of his arrival after flying from Lisbon.

> I arrived in London late at night and had a hearty meal before I discovered that I had to have special permits to eat

**172**

and to be out of doors after dark. To get this later permission took ten days; meanwhile I had to broadcast, and owing to the time differential, to broadcast very late at night. For most of those ten nights I was out around town, sometimes till five in the morning, and nobody seemed to know or care that they had in their midst a scofflaw who had no right to be out after dark at all.

He and Murrow then drove through the country. Most of the time Ed did the driving and Elmer called it "demon-driving." He saw more different parts of England in one week in May than in the three years he lived there. Much of it seemed as quiet and peaceful as if there had never been a war. But Coventry and Plymouth, Bristol and Southampton showed the devastation the *Luftwaffe* had wrought. Faithfully he reported as much as he could in his compressed nightly broadcasts and thousands of new listeners tuned in to hear him. In that month in England he gained more followers than from all his broadcasting up to that point and he did as much as any single man with the possible exception of Churchill to arouse American sympathy for the suffering English.

His observation did not slide over the little things. There was, for instance, tobacco. The English liked their Virginia straight, Americans wanted it softened by Turkish in a blend. But the supply of everything was short, especially the kind Elmer liked. Murrow tells the poignant story of one of Elmer's heroic sacrifices. It seems that for one stretch they hired a chauffeur. At the end, Elmer wanted to reward the man and thought that of all things he would like, cigarettes would top the list. He had only two packs of Camels left. After a long discussion with Murrow, he parted with one of these as an expression of his gratitude to the driver. The chauffeur looked carefully at the pack, turned it round several times, smelled it and finally opened it.

"Well," he said as he reluctantly put a Camel into his mouth, "I expect it'll burn."

**173**

The connection between Davis and Murrow remained close after Davis came home. In September, Murrow wrote him:

> I'm proud to be working with you. I have hopes that broadcasting is to become an adult means of communication at last. I've spent a lot of time listening to broadcasts from many countries during the past month and yours stand out as the best example of fair, tough-minded, interesting talking I've heard.

These were good words from the veteran to the tyro, barely two years after he had started.

# 12 |||||

1

**W**AR," wrote Clausewitz, "is the continuation of politics by other means." This celebrated student of the philosophy of war could scarcely have visualized the "other means" employed by his countryman a century or so later. Yet even in 1939 a kind of politics—even a hint of diplomacy—was attempted almost up to the last moment. According to Hitler's political book, such as it was, there was little likelihood that England would keep her pledge to Poland. But after that there was no more diplomatic maneuvering, no advance threats: the rule was attack first, present your "alibis" afterward, if at all. In 1940, the whole character of war changed; by 1941, the sneak attack, the undeclared war was taken for granted.

Still, it surprised most people when, a month after Elmer Davis's return from England, Hitler attacked the nation with which he had a supposedly firm nonaggression pact—a pact which had astonished the Western world because of the traditional enmity between its signers. But in Hitler's politics, a nonaggression pact was simply a smoke screen behind which he could mobilize for aggression.

In the dawn of June 22, 1941, CBS picked out of the air the announcement by Herr Goebbels that a German invasion of Russia was under way.

Before he had finished [recorded CBS in one of its histories] the network was broadcasting to sleepy or sleeping Ameri-

175

can homes—and all through the night top newsmen—Edward Murrow, Elmer Davis, William L. Shirer, Albert Warner, Bill Henry, Major George Fielding Eliot were on the air, reading bulletins, estimating, speculating. . . .

A few American pundits said they had expected it. But the Russians did not expect it—not, at least, on June 22. According to the German General Blumentritt, as quoted in Michael Joseph's *Fatal Decisions:*

> The Russians were clearly taken by surprise on our front. Almost at once our signals intercept service listened in to a Russian message: "We are being fired on. What shall we do?" They heard the reply from the senior headquarters to whom this request for orders was addressed: "You must be insane. And why is your signal not in code?"

It was two hours later that the German ambassador in Moscow handed Molotov the note from the German government that declared war. It is recorded that Molotov took the note without speaking, spat on it, rang for his secretary and said to him, "Show this gentleman out through the back door."

At about the same moment, General Halder made an entry in his diary: "I have just described the plan for the Russian Campaign to the Führer; the Russian armies will be destroyed in six weeks."

As we look back on this day from a twenty-year distance it assumes a significance quite different from its importance at the time, for it seems to mark the moment of transfer of world dominance from Germany to Russia. But in the West, in 1941, there was a widespread opinion that this new move of Hitler's boded well for the future. Now, it was thought, Germany and Russia could destroy each other in the barren, snowy wastes:

**176**

Hitler had turned away from his terrifying western objectives and there would, perhaps, be a breathing spell.

The voice of Britain, however, did not say this. Before the day was over, the radio brought to America the words of Winston Churchill:

> At four o'clock this morning Hitler attacked and invaded Russia. All his usual formalities of perfidy were observed with scrupulous technique. A non-aggression treaty had been solemnly signed and was in force between the two countries. No complaint had been made by Germany of its non-fulfilment. Under its cloak of false confidence, the German armies drew up in immense strength along a line which stretches from the White Sea to the Black Sea; and their air fleets and armored divisions slowly and methodically took their stations. Then, suddenly, without declaration of war, without even an ultimatum, German bombs rained upon the Russian cities, the German troops violated the frontiers. . . .
>
> Any man or state who fights on against Nazism will have our aid. . . . That is our policy and that is our declaration. It follows, therefore, that we shall give whatever help we can to Russia and the Russian people. We shall appeal to all our friends and allies in every part of the world to take the same course and pursue it. . . .

Churchill said he had seen it coming. He had warned Stalin. No doubt Stalin had been aware of the German design. Probably the *Wehrmacht* staff knew that Stalin knew—that was the reason for their suddenness, that was the reason for their deceit, their assurances of friendship up to the very night of June 21. What the confident German staff did not know was that every step their soldiers would take through the snow would be dogged by the ghost of Napoleon Bonaparte.

Churchill's change of front, offering aid to his former foe, was exploited by American isolationists, but it had an immediate

**177**

effect upon the mass of the people and with the paradoxical flexibility that comes when attention is focused upon a single patriotic aim, they forgot about Finland and the Moscow trials and a dozen other provocations and embraced Russia as a new ally.

Through the summer of 1941, the focus grew sharper and soon the disciples of Lindbergh and Wheeler found themselves not only isolated from Europe but from the bulk of their fellow citizens as well. As in 1916, the sinking of American ships by German submarines during the summer increased the pro-Allies sentiment. There was even a society or league which advocated immediate declaration of war against Germany. The majority of its membership was, to be sure, in the East and it was unusual for any of these folk—except a few businessmen whose operations crossed the Pacific—to turn their eyes westward to California and the Hawaiian outpost beyond.

So when winter came and we began to watch with satisfaction the plight of the German armies in the Russian cold, it was a surprise when a sneak attack came from another, largely forgotten, quarter.

2

It was a dull, quiet afternoon in New York when the news came. In the news room of the Columbia Broadcasting System, however, the men were alert; the teletype machines were closely watched. It was known that two Japanese envoys would probably call on Secretary of State Hull to continue a series of talks during which these persons had carried angry and provocative messages from Tokyo. There would probably be news of some sort; many guesses had been made that the Japanese were expected to launch an attack somewhere in southeast Asia.

Through the nation, there were relatively few radio listeners who were interested in the news that afternoon. There was jazz as usual and the New York Philharmonic Orchestra was giving a concert. Many people in the East were having a post-prandial nap or plowing through the pages of the Sunday *Times*. There was not a great deal of news there but Japan was not ignored. There was a piece by Otto Tolischus which said that "all Japanese eyes are glued on Washington in the hope that a big war may be averted. . . ." and an article by the military expert Hanson Baldwin showing that United States forces in the Pacific were definitely superior to the Japanese.

At 2:31 P.M. those whose sets were tuned in to CBS, heard John Daly say:

The Japanese have attacked Pearl Harbor, Hawaii, by air, President Roosevelt has just announced. The attack was also made on naval and military activities on the principal island of Oahu.

Voices then came through in breathless succession. Commentators, in the absence of immediate follow-up news, told their theories, most of which were wide of the mark. One was that the attack was due to an outburst of Japanese impatience—that Imperial Headquarters would presently repudiate it. There was general agreement that the Japanese had been foolhardy and reckless.

At 2:46, the military expert George Fielding Eliot said that "the appearance of any Japanese force in the neighborhood is likely to suffer very severely as soon as they can be located." Two minutes later contact was made with Fred Wilkins in Manila, who had not heard of the attack, but while he was talking, he was cut off the air.

At one minute and forty-five seconds after three, Elmer Davis came in. He spoke of the political background, explaining that

the argument when General Tojo came in [to power] was that now at last we had one of the ruling clique in control

179

of the government, and an agreement made with him was something that would stick. But it appears that this particular ruling clique had no idea of making any agreement at all; that the sole purpose of their negotiations at Washington was to gain time and to endeavor to throw American military and naval forces off guard, an endeavor which we hope has not been successful, so that they might make their attack.

We hope, indeed! For most of the afternoon, the tone was hopeful. There was incorrigible optimism. The thing was a flash in the pan. It would be all over in a month, six months at most. The Japanese planes were obsolete, their ships outmoded. Everyone was confident that the great United States Navy was invincible.

Then the calm, rather sad voice of Eric Severeid shattered all illusion. Severeid and Davis consistently refused to sugar-coat bad news if they believed it to be true. It was this that built the confidence of the American people in wartime radio news; that turned them away from bombast and oratory and dramatics and pontifical statement. And these men and a few others—but only a handful—were interested in the whole truth no matter how hard it was to get. "Truth has three dimensions," said Davis and, remembering Einstein, added, parenthetically, "(or maybe more)"; objectivity, factual reporting was not enough. He reached into the dimension of depth on that feverish afternoon when he said of the Pearl Harbor attack that "This was the technique that the Japanese followed in 1904, in the war with Russia, when they attacked the Russian fleet at Port Arthur before the declaration of war"—a preview of the new kind of war, which very few remembered.

But it was the broadcast of Eric Severeid in the evening that really set the wheels turning in American factories. For the first time, he told the grim truth about Pearl Harbor: that the damage to the American fleet had been disastrous, that it would be impossible to exaggerate it—that indeed the very core of naval

180

defense in the Pacific had been wiped out. They were terrible words, yet his listeners felt an odd sense of relief as they heard them knowing that the uncertainty was gone, knowing that it was plain now what all of us must do. How long we must do it no one could know but after Severeid's report on the harbor of Oahu, there could be no further illusion that the job was easy. For the first time since the early battles of the Civil War, the United States had been badly licked in combat.

3

When war comes the single desire to "do something" dominates every other impulse and, often, balanced judgment as well. Although there had been an elaborate plan called "M-day" designed between the wars, all of it went by the board in '42. For most unattached young men there was no problem; they either volunteered for the armed forces or, having registered with the draft board, waited till their number came up. Much of this routine had been prepared before the crisis. But for men above the draft age impatience for some sort of service for the "war effort" resulted in many misfits. In the American system war is fought both in the field and on the home front largely by amateurs. As there was no card index to show what special talents our citizens had or to record experience in both vocations and avocations, men and women found themselves with odd bedfellows. Persons rushed into economic bureaus who knew nothing of economics, or production boards in total innocence of production. We would do anything to be working, however ill-equipped for the job, so long as there was a vacancy, and the result in bureaucratic Washington —already elephantine—was cumbersome chaos.

On the periphery of all this earnest but undirected effort were those who stood to get something for themselves out of it. They were the wartime profiteers in building trades and industries and

181

those who saw ways open to power and position. There were those who wanted Congress to take advantage of the emergency by passing labor legislation that would force long hours without pay increases, and there were Senators and Representatives who were quite willing to oblige.

In a broadcast on the twenty-second of March, 1942, Elmer Davis had something to say about the fight in Congress over the forty-hour week, comparing it with the two-front war against Germany and Japan into which the nation had entered some three months before. There seemed, he said, to be an interval of pause in that war, though the Army and Navy had been laying the foundations that would one day win it.

> But if the war outside . . . appears to be in a lull at the moment, another war is going on more briskly than ever. That is the war of certain businessmen's associations and groups and of their friends in Congress against the labor unions and against an Administration which is friendly to labor unions. This is called the campaign against the forty-hour week, but that is not much more than a slogan. If it were really, as advertised, a campaign for more production, we all ought to be for it but the slogan attempts to disguise as a campaign for more production what is really a campaign for lower wages. And there is no doubt who most of the people are shooting at in the background. The other day a representative of the Associated Industries of Florida said to a Jacksonville Civic Club—"we are fighting two men, Franklin D. Roosevelt and John L. Lewis." If he said anything about fighting Hitler and Hirohito, it seems to have escaped the notice of the reporters covering the meeting.

Davis cited briefly a report of scientists at Princeton who had proved that at a certain point, worker fatigue slows down production—a fact later recognized by management itself—but he went back, then, to his main theme.

182

These domestic battles [he said] are one of the luxuries of democracy. France enjoyed them as long as there was a France and they are one of the principal reasons why there is at the moment a France no longer. England enjoyed them, too, but England had sense enough to drop them when the enemy was only twenty miles away. It might make sense if we dropped them before the enemy is off Ambrose and Bonita Lights. . . .

Obviously these remarks and others which recurred in broadcast after broadcast in these first months of our war were not calculated to endear Davis to certain of the legislators. In this time when he won the favor of millions of citizens whose only interest was in victory, he laid the foundations for bitter antagonism in high places.

Well [he went on in this broadcast], you may not like Mr. Roosevelt, but if he loses the war we all lose it with him.

Hitler has had a lot of help in all countries from people who thought they could concentrate on beating their domestic, political enemies, and then get rid of Hitler when they got around to it. . . . It might be a little safer if we all got together to get rid of Hitler first.

But for some of the men on Capitol Hill, Hitler was too far away for their imaginations to reach. It was easier to fight somebody nearer at hand. So when the President drew him into the government, these persons turned their fire upon Elmer Davis, and for them he seemed to embody Hitler, Hirohito and Mussolini all rolled into one. Such an array would have scared many a man who found himself, suddenly, in a position of responsibility such as he could never have dreamed.

It did not scare Elmer Davis.

183

4

Even before America's war began, there was a huge and sprawl-
ing bureaucracy in Washington. It was known as Roosevelt's
alphabet. As agencies, committees and offices were rarely called by
their full name but only by the initials thereof run together without periods, it required special mnemonic equipment to keep up
with the references. It was said that some absent-minded bureau-
crats had to resort to a code book before they could telephone
their colleagues. Some of the bureaus seemed to contain repro-
ductive equipment so that one agency might spawn a half-dozen
others in the night-time and the multiplying army of workers had
already glutted the Capital by December 7, 1941. That the be-
getting after that date was still more rapid goes without saying.
Pertinent to our story were twenty-six "defense" information
offices operated at a cost of twenty-million dollars a year and
employing more than three thousand workers. The departments of
War, Navy, Treasury and State plus the Office of Emergency
Management (OEM) and the Selective Service System all had
their own costly defense information services for domestic purposes. The offices of Co-ordinator of Information (OCI or COI),
and the Co-ordinator of Inter-American Affairs (CIAA) were
engaged in international news operations. There was also the
Office of Government Reports (OGR) with sixty field offices. In
October, 1941, the President set up an agency intended to coordinate domestic information called the Office of Facts and
Figures (OFF). It was thought curious that to head this bureau
with its cold, statistical name the President appointed a poet
whose background was anything but cold and statistical but who,
nevertheless, had had his feet on the ground sufficiently to occupy
the position of Librarian of Congress. There can be no doubt that
Archibald MacLeish immediately injected warmth into the office,
but his authority was limited. In the offing, but gaining impor-

tance with the rising heat of the war was the Foreign Information Service directed, oddly enough, by a writer of comedies, Robert Emmet Sherwood.

It was a strange galaxy. Furthermore, some of the offices were mutually hostile and when war came, they not only stepped on one another's toes but often on the highly sensitive toes of the Army, the Navy and the censor as well. The whole pattern, if it can be called that, was attacked with withering sarcasm by the anti-New Deal press and Republican legislators filled the *Congressional Record* with bitter "remarks."

For some four months in 1942, all this seems to have made no dent in the President's thinking. Perhaps he had other things on his mind. In the months following the outbreak of war, any Commander-in-Chief of the Armed Forces is likely to be much occupied. The sweep of the Japanese through the Pacific while what survived of the United States fleet limped into drydock; the sinking of the great British ships and the fall of Singapore were events which disturbed a President's sleep. In May, however, his eyes turned back to Washington—somewhat reluctantly it is said—and he took the chaos in hand.

The result was Executive Order Number 9182, effective June 13, 1942. It established a central authority which should channelize the flow of public information. The new agency was to be called the Office of War Information. It was to carry out the functions previously scattered among OGR, OFF, the information division of OEM and the Co-ordinator of Information (now known as COI). It was not to assume the powers of the Office of Censorship, which was to remain separate and intact, nor was it to have any part in the operations of the Co-ordinator of Inter-American Affairs. Executive Order Number 9182 was a large order indeed.

The President, according to those who knew him best, never liked to sign an order until he had made up his mind about the person who was to carry out its terms. Some say that the reason for his long delay in putting the nation's information house in order was that he could not decide this vital question. Perhaps he had listened to a CBS broadcast in which a voice already familiar to twelve and a half million people said:

> The whole government publicity situation has everybody in the news business almost in despair, with half a dozen different agencies following different lines. . . . Under one head, with real power, they might get somewhere. . . . Objection has been made that it might be hard to pick the man to head them. But almost anybody would be better than half a dozen heads.

Assuredly Elmer Davis was not thinking of himself as he spoke. He knew that he was doing a good job where he was and that the fifty-three thousand dollars CBS was paying him was adequate pay. Nor were there any headaches connected with his work—at least nothing to compare with those of his acquaintances in government work. Even the angry letters he had received from Anglophobes, savage Republicans and various partisans of the extreme Right had not disturbed him; on the contrary they were evidence that he was getting under their skins. No, that he might one day be the "almost anybody" who would be better than the diverse "heads," was remote from his most errant dreams.

Whether or not the President listened to Davis's "almost anyone" broadcast, it was attentively listened to by E. B. ("Andy") White of *The New Yorker* and commented on in that magazine in White's "Talk of the Town" pages, March 14, 1942, with a recommendation.

> Of the twelve steps [the editorial read] we would like to see taken in this war without further delay, the first is the unification of the information bureaus and the appointment of Elmer Davis to head them up. As a surtaxpayer, a registree, a bond buyer, and a son of freedom, we are discouraged and dissatisfied with the kind of news which has been handed us

186

since Pearl Harbor. The news has undulated in the murmurous region somewhere between the mysterious silence of the censor and the lyrical scream of the propagandist. It has been baffling, contradictory, and tentative. Mr. Davis, on the air the other night, presented the best case for unification and the strongest indictment of the present mess. In our opinion not only is he right but he is the man to sit at the desk.

Our eleven other recommendations for winning the war will be presented as soon as the government acts on the first one.

In any case, some two months later, Roosevelt reached his decision and invited Davis to the White House.

It was Roosevelt's habit after deciding about individuals to regard their acquiescence as an accomplished fact. It did not occur to him that someone might say no. In wartime perhaps this was logical thinking. There was a general feeling in those years that, like a soldier, when the Commander-in-Chief tapped you you did not question his judgment. To do so would have been thought unpatriotic. The result was that many persons later found that they were round pegs in square holes whereas if they had asked questions—as one in peacetime would do—about details and given the whole matter some careful thought they might have declined. But Elmer Davis was not requested to become Director of the new Office; he was so ordered—or at least that is how it seemed to him. A few days later, he said over the air: "This is my last broadcast, as I have been called into government service."

Some of his closest friends believe that Davis was not the man for the job. His whole career had been that of a lone wolf. He had no experience of administration. He had, to be sure, analyzed and appraised the work of other administrators but that is a theoretical, not a practical exercise. To direct the activities of three or four thousand men is a job for a trained executive, not a reporter or a commentator. As an editor under a trained executive Elmer Davis would, his friends say, have been ideal. But a failure to

187

penetrate such distinctions led Roosevelt into more than one mistake.

In this case the choice was not easy because of the uncertain borderland between the main functions of this news agency. Here the news aspect dominated all others. Administration seemed incidental. If the Director could give to the public through any mediums he might choose an accurate picture of how the war was going on, the control of personal conflicts, jealousies, internal politics and the large physical job of consolidating the agencies could be managed by others under his direction. The President did, in fact, appoint a deputy director to handle much of the administrative detail. The deputy was the general's brother, Milton Eisenhower.

But neither Davis nor Eisenhower could foresee the obstacles and frustrations in the road ahead. It was difficult to understand, for instance, how certain men would give up highly paid positions to work for virtually nothing on a "patriotic" impulse and then practice every sort of intrigue, deceit and throat-cutting to gain a personal power that would compensate him for the money loss. It was difficult to foresee, for another example, why it would be necessary to fight continuously against partisan members of Congress who could not forget politics, or why the armed services should turn from their traditional battle with each other to a concerted conflict with the Office of War Information.

It was inevitable that Davis should make mistakes. Yet he was never forced into error by intimidation. With persistent courage and a bulldog stubbornness he fought all his opponents. In the cases where an attempt was made to obscure the truth—and there were many such instances—he won. He never took his troubles to the President, though he had every right to do so, except when all else failed. But he had one solid rock which the President himself furnished that he stood on consistently. From this position nothing could budge him. Again and again he referred his attackers to the statement Roosevelt had issued along with his executive order:

188

The director [read this guaranty] of the new Office of War Information will have authority, subject to powers held directly by the President, to issue directions to all departments and agencies of the government with respect to their information services. He will have full authority to eliminate all overlapping and duplication and to discontinue in any department any information activity which is not necessary or useful to the war effort.

Once Davis was armed with this document neither generals nor admirals, neither cabinet members nor Senators could scare him. What his inner feelings may have been during the three and a half years of incessant abuse, smear, innuendo and frontal attack he never recorded even in intimate family letters. Such evidence as there is shows that he handled these things hardily, often with ridicule that set his opponents back on their heels, sometimes with good-natured humor, but always with the sort of logic which stemmed so obviously from horse sense that he left many a red face.

"We hated his guts," a partisan critic still remembers.

It is a precise statement.

189

# 13 ))))))

1

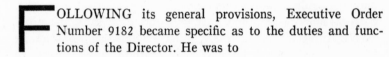

F OLLOWING its general provisions, Executive Order Number 9182 became specific as to the duties and functions of the Director. He was to

a. Formulate and carry out, through the use of press, radio, motion picture, and other facilities, information programs designed to facilitate the development of an informed and intelligent understanding, at home and abroad, of the status and progress of the war effort and of the war policies, activities and aims of the Government.

b. Coordinate the war informational activities of all Federal departments and agencies for the purpose of assuring an accurate and consistent flow of war information to the public and the world at large.

c. Obtain, study, and analyze information concerning the war effort and advise the agencies concerned with the dissemination of such information as to the most appropriate and effective means of keeping the public adequately and accurately informed.

d. Review, clear, and approve all proposed radio and motion picture programs sponsored by Federal departments and agencies; and serve as the central point of clearance and contact for the radio broadcasting and motion picture industries, respectively, in their relationships with Federal departments and agencies concerning such government programs.

e. Maintain liaison with the information agencies of the United Nations for the purpose of relating the Government's informational programs and facilities to those of such nations.

f. Perform such other functions and duties relating to war information as the President may from time to time determine.

This document, like most such directives, suggests a great abundance and complexity of duties. Yet there is nothing here that a trained journalist and news analyst need think is beyond his powers, given the assistance he is entitled to command. But it will be noted that many non-journalistic problems are not mentioned. The organization of departments, the appointment of department heads, the allocation of functions, the hiring of personnel, the ironing out of disagreements among them, the machinery for keeping in touch with diverse, separate and often remote operations—all these would be entirely manageable by the trained businessman—a top executive of some large corporation such as General Motors or Ford. But they were not easy for one who had spent his life either in the gathering and giving out of news or as a free lance in creative writing—a pointedly individualistic exercise.

Furthermore there was an implication in the order that not only factual information should be the material OWI was to work with but also news that would be in the interest of the "war effort." That meant propaganda. Now the great over-all directive and slogan of this agency was truth, nothing but the truth and as much of the whole truth as was consistent with national security. But when an imaginative writer, movie director, cartoonist or broadcaster starts to work with the material furnished by the news gatherer, he is almost certain to focus more on the war effort than

191

on the strict truth, and he ends up by coloring, fabricating or embroidering to the point at which a vivid but quite false picture emerges. For a director to keep a constant check on all these people is quite impossible, and this particular director was often shocked by distortions which came too late to his notice.

From the other organizations that were consolidated into OWI, Davis inherited several people who, like himself, had been or were, free-lance writers. Now a good writer is, above all things, independent of controls; the loneliness of his art makes him ignorant of the methods in use in a closely organized business corporation where group action is the rule. Such a person, when he is thrown into an organization in which the individual is anonymous and submerged, still retains the habit of doing things on his own without sharing the responsibility.

A story is told of Robert Sherwood who went from Foreign Information Service into OWI and became head of OWI's Overseas Branch which, apocryphal or not, is characteristic and illustrates the point. Sherwood, for years a free-lance playwright of international celebrity, received, one day, a directive outlining operations his branch was expected to perform. A businessman, on getting such a note, would have had it multigraphed and a copy placed on every desk. But not dramatist Sherwood. Bob read the memo, thought it a good idea and, writer-like, decided to keep it to himself and carry it out by himself when the time came. So he put it in his pocket but then forgot it. A week later when a note came asking why a specified operation had not been carried out, and a secretary went to Sherwood with it, saying that the directive had been intended not for an individual but for the whole branch, he answered, "Oh, yes, I do remember it. I put it in my pocket and I'm afraid that suit has gone to the cleaner."

Henry Pringle, a brilliant, Pulitzer-Prize-winning biographer, got in trouble with the Domestic Branch because he believed that his superiors were trying to sell the war to the American people by the methods used to sell Coca-Cola. He was a writer, he said, not a "copywriter" and he refused to treat legitimate news as sugar-coated propaganda. There was so much of this sort of thing that in his final report to the President, Elmer Davis wrote:

It might be pertinent to note one personal problem which came up again and again in both our domestic and our overseas branches, for which we never found a solution. . . . It is the problem of the brilliant and zealous individual who cannot work as part of a team. . . . Now an information agency, in a war which was in some of its aspects ideological, naturally attracted many free-lance writers and others who had been used to working by themselves and had always jealously cherished their personal integrity and freedom of expression. Such a man is very apt to insist that he must proclaim the truth as he sees it; if you tell him that so long as he works for the Government he must proclaim the truth as the President and the Secretary of State see it, he may feel that this is an intolerable limitation on his freedom of thought and speech.

It is obvious from the wording of this statement that even when it became necessary to fire or transfer one of these writers, Davis inwardly sympathized with his view. At the same time he was so sure of the need of teamwork that he must often have been torn between the two sides of the argument.

## 2

"As soon as they give me a chair to sit on in Washington," Davis told reporters when the announcement of his appointment was released, "I'll go to work." Giving anyone a chair to sit on in Washington was, in those days, a problem of considerable proportions. However, office space was presently cleared in Archibald MacLeish's Office of Facts and Figures in the old building of the Library of Congress, and there the new Director sat. Some of those who saw him on his first day wondered that he did nothing,

sitting at his desk with a bemused expression on his face and a
tapping of his fingers on the desk. He shuffled through the pile
of organizational charts and diagrams—the attempts to reduce
to graphic form the great conglomeration of agencies that was
about to fall into his lap. Then he pushed all the papers away
and his fingers tapped again on the desk. An embarrassed secretary came in and asked if he wanted to dictate. He looked up,
coming out of a kind of trance of troubled thought. "No," he said,
"I can't dictate. And I can't understand all this. I never could
understand charts. But look, do you suppose there's a typewriter
around? Could I have one?"

Instantly a machine was brought him and all day and far into
the night this incorrigible newspaperman wrote and wrote, immune to interruption.

A detailed account of his first day, however, is given in a letter
to his wife in New York. The fact that the letter is written in
longhand lends plausibility to the story about the typewriter:

*Wednesday 16 June 1942.*—My first day in office. Walked
over to OFF where they had an office for me, a temporary
secretary, and a ton of mail. (Still unread.) Assistants took
charge of me, showed me ropes, took much of the load off of
me—notably Allen Grover, late of Life. . . .

Newsreel men and photographers then took up ¾ hour—
last of that I hope. Nelson Rockefeller came along to take me
to lunch with the Vice President in the capitol. N. very
cordial and cooperative. [Milton] Eisenhower there too. The
V.P. and Nelson talked about Latin America; N. spoke of
relations with Mexicans in the Southwest, formerly under his
jurisdiction, now cut out of his budget. Maybe we could take
that over. A Committee on Interracial Relations (presidential) is down there holding hearings about how Mexicans
are treated in Texas and New Mexico; danger if bad publicity. . . .

Then to Budget Bureau (State War & Navy Bldg) to take

194

oath of office and meet a lot of budgeteers over our structural reorganization. Seems I have at most 2348 employees (not 30,000 as the Times said) and will probably spend $15-20 million next year. Really more since we need expansion abroad. Eisenhower produced a chart of the reorganized bureau; luckily I had engagements and got away before they discovered that I did not understand the chart.

I thought I had better set to work on my biggest job first, trying to get on better terms with army & navy. Grover saved me from a boner—I would have gone to the heads of public relations, he said no, I must call on the cabinet officers as a person of equal rank. Cannot say I got far. First to War Dept. to see Sec. Stimson. He sat under a portrait of Elihu Root looking very much like him (apparently intentional). Delivered a long lecture on difficulties of getting news from a modern naval battle—no ship ever saw an enemy ship at Midway—needs of military secrecy etc. Thought maybe he had been indoctrinated by whoever was there before me but heard later he is always that way. Specific question—why must we hear about Americans planes in the Near East solely from the enemy? Pretty good reasons, military and diplomatic; still all in all I got the polite brush-off. . . .

Then down to Navy to see Sec. Knox. He talked to me as one newspaperman to another—also about needs of military secrecy but he would like to help if he could. But he too knows only what they tell him. Adm. Hepburn out. They say King is the big obstacle to news there. All in all I don't think I got more than .0001 of a millimeter ahead. But will have to keep on trying; confidence of the men in the news business is my biggest asset and I won't keep it if I don't get results.

Walked back to the hotel—more letters, phone calls, etc. Letter from Tris Coffin . . . with good advice about finding my way around in the woods, warnings against unnamed wolves who would try to get me. Phone call from Linton Wells, warning me of a man in another dept. (I knew him and disliked him . . . seven years ago) who is already organizing an anti-Davis plot. Thanks for that; I'd forgotten all about that fellow.

Got down to dinner, alone. On way out met Herb Swope with Mr. (and Mrs.) Justice Frankfurter. F. said he didn't think my job would be very hard; turned out that he also thought the public would have less news, not more. Told him that was not what I was hired for. It wouldn't be hard if I followed his theory. . . .

Well, that's one day. I didn't step into any wide-open pitfalls but who can tell what poisoned thorns may have brushed my sleeve. Now to draft a letter for the President to sign, brushing off an ex-Senator who is willing to devote his talents to helping me out. Might step into something there if I'm not careful.

No more than a week after he had started, Davis had an interview with Winston Churchill which suggested that he had not yet acquired a wholly diplomatic approach on the highest level. In his *Hinge of Fate,* Churchill tells about it. It was in June soon after the fall of Tobruk.

On the 22nd Hopkins and I were at lunch with the President in his room. Presently Mr. Elmer Davis, the head of the Office of War Information, arrived with a bunch of New York newspapers, showing flaring headlines about "ANGER IN ENGLAND," "TOBRUK FALL MAY BRING CHANGE OF GOVERNMENT," "CHURCHILL TO BE CENSURED," etc. I had been invited by General Marshall to visit one of the American Army camps in South Carolina. We were to start by train with him and Mr. Stimson on the night of June 23. Mr. Davis asked me seriously whether, in view of the political situation at home, I thought it wise to carry out the programme, which of course had been elaborately arranged. Might it not be misinterpreted if I were inspecting troops in America when matters of such vital consequence were taking place both in Africa and London? I replied that I would certainly carry out the inspections as planned, and that I doubted whether I should be able to provoke twenty members into the Lobby against the Government on an issue of confidence. This was in fact about the number which the malcontents eventually obtained. The Vote of Censure was to be defeated in Parliament by 475 votes to 25.

Basically, however, Davis had a lucid understanding of what his office was supposed to do. Again and again in phrases and sentences of almost biblical simplicity he told this to reporters and in hearings before Congressional committees, certain members of which seem to have had twelve-year-old minds. The Office, he said, had two principal duties: to the armed forces and to the people on the home fronts. In a statement to the House Appropriations Committee some three months after his appointment he said:

The war is going to be won primarily by fighting, but history, both recent and remote, proves that victory of the fighting forces can be made easier by what is called psychological or political warfare, the prosecution of which has been entrusted primarily to this office. We are in a sense an auxiliary to the armed forces—an organization whose operations can pave the way for their operations and make their success easier.

Davis referred to this statement as "The most important literary work of my life. I hope to get the biggest price for this of anything I've ever written. I expect to get $25,000,000 for this piece." It was the opening gun of Davis's long war with this committee and with its chairman, Representative John Taber. He did not get what he asked for on this first try—not quite—and, as the war continued, much of Davis's time and energy were used

197

in getting enough money to cope with the President's large order. This, too, the order ignored.

Davis wrote of OWI's other duty in an article in the *Saturday Review of Literature* published in December, 1942.

> Our job at home is to give the American people the fullest possible understanding of what this war is about . . . not only to tell the American people how the war is going, but where it is going and where it came from—its nature and origins, how our Government is conducting it, and what (besides national survival) our Government hopes to get out of victory.

Here again is his insistence on what he called "three-dimensional truth":

> not merely the news that is immediate enough to get into the newspapers or on the radio but the background information that will help them understand what the news is about— through radio, movies, magazines, pamphlets, posters, speeches, discussion groups, and any other means that we think will promote the public understanding.

It was a high aim, and public opinion—less confused then than it later became—approved, and there was a prevalent belief in that second winter of our war that the ideal person to attain it was Elmer Davis. Yet even then, he had met frustration. Less than two weeks after he had taken office the War and Navy departments turned aside from their fight against the Nazis for a battle with the Director of the Office of War Information.

3

On a foggy night in mid-June, 1942, four men emerged from a U-boat, paddled ashore in a collapsible rubber boat and landed on a beach near Amagansett, Long Island. A few days later, four others, also from a German submarine, landed on a beach near Jacksonville, Florida. After landing, both groups behaved in identical manner. They buried wooden boxes they had brought in their boats as well as the boats themselves in the sand. Then both foursomes headed for a common meeting place.

The discovery of the caches by the FBI was one of that organization's prodigious wartime feats. The capture of the eight men within two weeks was another. The boxes contained the instruments of sabotage with instructions where and how to use them against key factories, railroads, canals and bridges. There was enough destructive material, J. Edgar Hoover said, for a two-year campaign of sabotage.

The news broke in the first week of July and, naturally, caused immediate and widespread excitement. Everywhere the question was asked: What would happen to these Germans, every one of whom had lived in the United States, spoke fluent English and was experienced in American ways? Who would try them? Well, the Army would try them. The public looked forward eagerly to the detailed news of the trials. At that point, however, there descended a curtain of silence.

Davis knew at once that here was war information to which the people were entitled. But when he asked the army commission which had the matter in charge, the commission's head, Brigadier General F. R. McCoy, refused any releases, nor would the general permit representatives of the news services or of OWI to attend any sessions of the trial. To the first meeting of the commission, nevertheless, Davis sent Henry Paynter, a former AP man. Paynter waited in an anteroom for an hour at the end of which a junior officer appeared and said: "The general does not wish to see the gentleman. The gentleman need not wait."

Davis then went, personally, to protest to the Secretary of War but Mr. Stimson shook his head. There remained but one resort and one which Davis was reluctant to turn to. The best he could get from the President was a compromise but at least he made a dent in the Army's strange armor of secrecy. From then on, General McCoy issued to the press two daily communiqués on the progress of the trials and eventually permitted the admission of reporters. Later, full press coverage was allowed of the trial of the American confederates of the saboteurs. The press conceded a first victory for OWI against the armed services and Davis was praised for his stubborn courage.

But it was obvious to him that there were other hurdles ahead: obstacles to the people's understanding of what he insisted was the people's war—not the Army's war or the Navy's war as generals and admirals seemed to think, with the public kept in the dark about losses on the land, sea and air fronts. Davis turned his searchlight into the shadows and saw some shocking things. The people, he knew, were not fighting as they should because they could not see the grim facts.

> We could lose this war [he said in one of his most famous declarations]. We have never lost a war; but it has been remarked that this means only that our ancestors never lost a war; and our ancestors were never up against a war like this. To win a total war we must fight it totally, and we are not yet fighting it that hard. Many individual Americans have made great sacrifices but as a nation we are not yet more than ankle deep in the war.

Ever since Pearl Harbor, the Navy had hidden the full extent of these first losses. At the same time the Japanese broadcasts told the truth and the public came more and more to distrust the official American communiqués issued by the services. These broadcasts told, for instance, of the capture of some of the American air men who had raided Tokyo—a fact the Army had concealed. There was wide public indignation when, months after the battle of the Coral Sea, naval communiqués told of the losses it must have known about long before. Nor was this indignation lessened when the Navy, after an argument with Davis, released, on October 12, the information that the cruisers *Astoria, Quincy* and *Vincennes* had been lost sixty-five days before.

> Both the Army and the Navy [wrote Ernest K. Lindley in *Newsweek*, November 2] are under suspicion of recent violations [of the rules on communiqués]; and the evidence in some instances seems sufficient to convict. . . . On the whole, however, Secretary Stimson, General Marshall and the public relations officers of the War Department have tried to adhere to the rules.
>
> The case against the Navy is more serious although it cannot be fully documented. . . . But the Navy has toned down, withheld or delayed disclosure of so much bad news that it rests under the heavy suspicion of trying to protect itself from public examination and criticism. The fault is not with the public relations officers. . . . It goes higher, to Admiral King, who has kept a tight control over Navy Department communiqués.

## 4

That Davis had already discovered that he must go higher up and that, eventually, unless he found a change of mood there, he would have to go still higher was not known in any detail to Mr. Lindley when he wrote this piece. Perhaps the details and, especially, Davis's own private feelings at this time, have never been known and can only now be revealed through excerpts from intimate letters to his wife written in the fall of 1942.

> Things [he wrote on October 9] get crowdeder and crowdeder . . . we have a major row on with the navy; I had a long argument this afternoon with Admiral King which got very acrimonious yet somehow remained friendly. He runs the navy so thoroughly that they are all afraid of him, and maybe it was something of a relief to him to find someone

who wasn't. This is a very serious matter, however, and will have to be resumed next week and taken right up to the top if they do not come around. (All this is very secret of course.)

Between the writing of this letter and October 28, Davis had exacted a promise from King that losses would be promptly reported unless security should be involved. In the case of immediate sinkings, secrecy would obviously be unnecessary as the enemy must know the fact. So Davis was confident enough to say in a public speech on October 28:

I can assure you that up to noon today when I last talked to Navy representatives, all sinkings of major United States vessels have been reported.

But then a curious thing happened that shook the public confidence not only in the Navy but in OWI as well. The following week a naval communiqué told of the sinking of a carrier on October 26—two days before Davis gave his assurance. Instantly, his office was besieged by newsmen. As usual, the Director remained calm but the background of the events with a revelation of his inner feelings is told in a letter to Florence Davis on November first.

He began the letter by saying that there was to be a celebration of the anniversary of the Russian Revolution during the weekend and suggests that she might join him for that in Washington.

That is [he went on] if I am here next week end. I probably shall be in spite of the rumors of my resignation which have been zealously spread in New York, Washington and Chicago this last week. However, I was almost mad enough to do it yesterday afternoon (though of course I'd have to put it off till after election) when the President, Knox and King fixed up the form of this communiqué about the carrier loss without consulting me and, originally, a very bad form. (It was still bad when they put it out in that they did not mention the name of the carrier; but not so bad as the first version). I couldn't reach any of them by phone but did issue an order to hold it up—the first order I've ever given any department I think—and was gratified to observe that even the admirals obeyed it. Though whether King would have obeyed it if he had been there is somewhat less certain. Then Knox got me on the phone about six o'clock and said that he had represented my views to the President, which I do not doubt, so that I at least got into the argument at second hand. And since something or other had to be got out for the morning papers and I hadn't been able to reach the President by seven, we finally let it go with some modifications. Very foolish, however, not to name the carrier; it makes the relatives of the crews of all carriers worry.

Davis then told his wife how it had all come out and in telling it revealed that he had won the argument and that, never again could the Navy's brass underestimate his authority. That the harassed public would accept the explanation—especially that part of the public which was opposed to the administration—and that the people in general would retain their confidence in OWI, was still doubtful. He was writing, of course, on the eve of the Congressional election and his words reflect the feverish state of Washington, torn as it was between the war and politics.

Well [he wrote] maybe that is the sort of teapot tempest that looks a lot bigger in Washington than it does on the outside; though it certainly makes it harder for me to do the job I am paid for. However, there may be a more serious angle. Last night the AP and UP called me up and asked me how this squared with the statement I made Wednesday [October 28] that all ship losses had been reported. I told them the truth, viz. that as the navy announced on Tuesday,

**203**

this carrier had been badly damaged, but that they thought they might bring her in, and that whenever she actually sank, I knew nothing about it on Wednesday night nor indeed till yesterday afternoon. I added that communications are slow from down there and I didn't think the navy knew about it till very lately.

All true; for Admiral King gave me his personal word of honor . . . that he would keep me informed of everything that goes on and I cannot presume that he has broken it by not letting me know till Saturday of something that he knew earlier. However, there remains the question of whether the newspapers and the public will believe me. I hope they will but it is always possible that some Republicans, between now and Tuesday [Election Day], will denounce me as a hired liar for the administration; and if enough people believe them my usefulness will be at an end. I don't think this is probable but it is a possibility that can't be overlooked. Nor can I afford to defend myself . . . by anything that might undermine confidence in King: for his job is to fight the war and as I said the other night, he should not be judged by his shortcomings in any other capacity. . . .

Meanwhile don't tell anybody I ever even thought of resigning, as the idea never occurred to me till four o'clock yesterday afternoon and I do not want to give any encouragement to rumors that may just ooze up from the ground or may be spread by somebody who sees an advantage in getting me out. And if I'm still here next week end I'd be most happy to have company if you find it practicable.

## 5

The reason Davis had to write thus to his wife instead of talking to her about his skirmishes with the War and Navy departments was that there was another frustration for which an elderly gentleman named General Grey (not in the Army) was largely responsible. General Grey was a large and extremely handsome Persian cat.

Since June, Davis had tried, in whatever spare time his exigent work might leave him, to find an apartment in which he and his wife might live in such comfort as wartime Washington could afford. In this effort many important people including at least one major general had assisted him. Under pressure of this prestige several realtors had offered apartments. But when the landlords heard about General Grey they shook their heads. No pets, they said—no, not even if the President himself should ask them.

Actually, Davis mentioned General Grey to Mr. Roosevelt and, as he wrote "Fliss": "Lunch with the Pr today, and . . . he was quite scandalized at the idea of an apartment house that wouldn't take cats. . . ."

That, however, was the grim fact and as neither he nor Fliss would think of abandoning the elderly general, they remained apart: Elmer in Washington's Carlton Hotel; Fliss and General Grey on West 116th Street in New York. What happened to the Persian gentleman when Fliss occasionally spent the weekend in Washington is, in the record at least, not clear. That he was well cared for by some cat-sitter is certain, for next to his family, General Grey had Elmer Davis's top consideration.

The apartment did, indeed, finally turn up just before Christmas, in Crescent Place, a pleasant street with many gardens, and there the landlord not only admitted the Persian but teletype machines as well. In this place the Davises lived for the rest of Elmer's life.

Fortunately his frugality, the absence of any luxurious or expensive desires, had made it possible for him to save up for a rainy day. He had, to be sure, made at one time what was known as big money by his writing. So when he left CBS and saw his annual income cut from fifty-three to twelve thousand dollars, the least of his troubles was financial.

But in 1943 in other ways the "rainy day" began in earnest.

205

# 14 ]]]]]]

I N THE PACIFIC, 1942 was a bad year for the Allies. The fall of Singapore in February was followed by a Japanese sweep through Thailand and Burma. In April, the long, stubborn hold on the Philippines was abandoned and General MacArthur left Bataan for Australia—a move that, at the time, disheartened Americans on the home front but would turn out to bring salvation in the long run. By June, Japan held the whole of the Malay peninsula, the Philippines, the Netherlands Indies, New Guinea, the Solomon and Ellice Islands, Guam and Wake. Her forces had operated from the bases in the Marianas, the Marshalls and the Carolines—those gifts of the League of Nations after the first World War—as well as from home ports. The only rays of hope came from Australian and American defensive operations: the thwarting, in the Coral Sea, of a Japanese attack on Port Moresby in May and the battle of Midway Island, which prevented the enemy from capturing that important outpost and, for the time being at least, assured the safety of Hawaii.

Then, in November, from across the Atlantic came a startling surprise. No one but the principals had known of the preparations for a British-American landing in North Africa. "Operation Torch" as it was called had been planned four months before by Roosevelt and Churchill and kept top secret since. It was intended to take the whole of Northwest Africa from the Vichy French who occupied it but halfheartedly, and thus not only protect the Mediterranean lifeline to Suez but provide a base for later operations against what Churchill called "the soft underbelly of Europe."

History offered no precedent for the magnitude of this effort. The American armada sailed from Hampton Roads, Virginia, three thousand miles away. It was an amphibious force: Army and Navy cooperated toward its success. The rendezvous with the British was at Gibraltar; the objectives were Casablanca, Oran and Algiers. The entire operation was under the command of the American general, Dwight D. Eisenhower. Though the major part in the invasion was American, the British made contributions without which the expedition would have failed; moreover, the undertaking was geared to the victorious desert sweep of the British Eighth Army consequent upon the rout of Rommel.

In all the annals of war it would be hard to find a more elaborately planned and precisely executed maneuver carried out by the cooperating forces of two nations. In long preparation the ground had been explored, centers of resistance softened and French sympathizers primed to assist the invading force. Even so, the French army, neutralized by the armistice of 1940, placed unexpected obstacles in the way; the navy, here and there, offered open, shooting violence against the landings.

The people at home in both England and America followed the news with mounting excitement. But then, as political activity ran parallel to the invading march, there was bitter criticism in both countries of what was thought a compromise with the enemy by inviting the aid of the Vichy-sponsored Admiral Darlan and rejecting de Gaulle and his Free French. This criticism, in the concerted view of Churchill, Roosevelt and Eisenhower, ignored the "realities of war." To those on the spot, finding to their surprise that the French armed services in Africa, being strict professionals and obeying only the duly constituted authority, would take orders from no one but Darlan, by-passed the moral dilemma in the interest of necessary speed; otherwise, as Eisenhower later explained in his *Crusade in Europe,* the entire operation faced failure with the sacrifice of lives, morale, and the first step toward victory over the Nazis.

The situation was complicated by the fact that the cables to Europe had been cut and the only information the OWI outpost men had came from the radio station at Rabat. As this station was in the hands of the Free French, the news it gave out was highly prejudicial to American negotiation with Darlan.

It became, therefore, the task of OWI at home to calm the moralists. The outpost men in Africa were recalled and replaced. Then the OWI gave what clarity it could to the promise that the first turning of the tide had arrived. And, after a time, when, as so often happens in the conduct of a war, the end had exculpated if not justified the means, the home-front public swallowed its moral disappointment and looked eagerly toward the dawn of a new day.

This precarious sailing between the Scylla of the whole truth and the Charybdis of war expedience was one of the necessities that made the operation of the Office of War Information difficult. To Elmer Davis, always a realist, it was clear that there was not time enough to debate the niceties of conduct of an army in so colossal a field. To win a war the generals and admirals must use the tools at hand and the people at home must have faith in their immediate judgment.

With the decisive victory of Torch and the triumphs that followed it, the whole of North and Northwest Africa from El Alamein to Dakar came into allied hands. Rommel, the "desert fox," was eliminated, the colonial French were moved out of the Axis shadow, and it was evident that the days were numbered for Mussolini—till now Hilter's Achilles' heel, yet at the same time a nuisance to the Allies in the Mediterranean. The trumpets of victory drowned out the complaints of the doubters and even the angry American supporters of the Cross of Lorraine held their fire.

There was hard fighting in Tunisia. The green, untried American troops had their ordeal of fire in the Kasserine Pass. With more training time there would have been fewer casualties, but the neophyte Americans were, after all, the tools at hand and no GI died in vain. The infuriated Nazis moved down to harden the underbelly and take possession of the whole of France, but this was a defensive position as were the strongholds in Italy. And even such bitter tragedies as Anzio were incidents of a turned tide.

## 2

At home in the early months of 1943, there was a more troublesome story. Americans in the hinterland or in the industrial fringes were unsure of the ideology of a war that was disrupting their lives. Interviews and questionnaires among these folk revealed a bewilderment that a year of war had not dissolved. Some of these were quoted in an incisive article in *Harper's* in February, 1943, by Michael Darrock and Joseph P. Dorn called "Davis and Goliath."

A war worker in a vital shipyard: How the hell can I make my plans? One day I'm going to be drafted, next day I'm going to be froze to my job. I don't know what to expect.

A corn-belt farmer: When a government runs around like a chicken with its head cut off and doesn't know what it wants to do, then the farmers will get disgusted and quit. They want you to produce more and they won't give you anything to handle the crop with. . . .

A young draftee: Why don't those labor boys sacrifice? Here they won't even work more than forty hours a week, and they're raking in money so it's a scandal, while I'm offering my life for my country.

A Boston woman, secretary in a small company: They all say they're fighting for freedom, but how can England say that when she still denies it to India?

209

A Chicago housewife: After the war we should keep our finger on world problems and be a big brother. . . . On the other hand maybe we should keep out entirely. It only gets us in trouble.

A Georgia Negro, a World War veteran: I cain't understand. Freedom. They say they's fightin' for Freedom. . . . Whose freedom? . . . There ought to be freedom for everybody.

These vague, uneasy questions could only be answered by the dissemination of "three-dimensional truth": telling the people "not only how the war is going but where it is going and where it came from—its nature and origin, how our government is conducting it, and what (besides national survival) our government hopes to get out of victory."

To do this, Elmer Davis had a large body of workers—the Domestic Branch of OWI—with headquarters in Washington. Being composed largely of artists of various sorts but mostly highly individualistic, it was subject to sporadic tangential movements. Each worker had his own idea of the most persuasive propaganda and exploited it in a pamphlet or press release: often this ran counter to the persuasions that were being beamed to Europe. Again it brought controversy from the War Production Board, jealous of its priorities of food and raw material.

It was natural for persons whose purpose was to clarify governmental acts to go overboard in praise of some aspect of the administration: this was a red rag to the Roosevelt-haters who sincerely believed that the continuing power of the Democrats augured the death of the Republic—war or no war. As the word Democrat in the view of these people was synonymous with the word Communist, it was soon being proclaimed that OWI had been infiltrated by heavy fifth columns of "pinks" and fellow travelers.

To keep his outfit in line and at the same time persuade the doubters among the people was Davis's most intricate job. In addition to other inherent difficulties was the fact that the Domestic Branch had many diverse legacies or hangovers from the outfits it had absorbed. Of this he later wrote in his final report to the President:

The Domestic Branch of OWI was a cocktail shaken up out of three very dissimilar ingredients—predecessor organizations which differed widely in their objectives as well as their techniques. It took almost a year to create a blend that was reasonably satisfactory to the executives of the agency; and about the time that this was accomplished Congress poured most of the contents of the shaker down the drain.

Already, in the early spring of 1943, there were evidences that the blend desired by the executives was beginning to take form. Some pamphlets created by the writers of OFF and officially published by OWI had been widely distributed and were doing much to answer the questions of puzzled citizens. Following memoranda from the President and the Department of State, attempts were made to satisfy doubts about what we were fighting for by citing the Four Freedoms, the Atlantic Charter and the Declaration of the United Nations. In its propaganda, OWI called the war "a crusade." The Domestic Branch made a systematic analysis of rumors and how they are spread and concluded that many of them were ultimately rejected or disbelieved.

The American people [stated the report on this analysis] are justly famed for their skepticism. If any people on earth is endowed with the natural talents for handling rumors it is the people of the United States.

"I'm from Missouri," the report added, was "a national trademark."

Other pamphlets were *The Unconquered People*, the exciting story of the European undergrounds; *Your War and Your Wages*,

*The Doctor Shortage and Medical Care of Civilians in Wartime, Toward New Horizons: the World Beyond the War,* a symposium with a foreword by Elmer Davis, and a manual on *Design and Operation of United States Combat Aircraft.* There were such inspirational publications as *The United Nations' Fight for the Four Freedoms, Tale of a City: the Story of Warsaw, The Thousand Million,* about the members of the United Nations in whose countries a billion friends of the United States worked and fought, and *The War and Human Freedom* by Cordell Hull.

Some of the propaganda was highly controversial. There was *Negroes and the War,* a picture book which caused explosions among southern members of Congress. There was *Battle Stations for All: the Story of the Fight to Control Living Costs* which Ralph Robey, writing in *Newsweek,* described as:

> one of the most barefaced pieces of prejudiced propaganda that has ever been directed at the American public by a presumably nonpartisan government bureau. . . .
>
> On almost every subject which is controversial the discussion is one-sided, incomplete, and prejudiced. And the prejudice is always on the side of the Administration and the bureaucrats. . . . Everything the Administration and the bureaucrats have done has been correct, and by implication at least everything on which they have been turned down by Congress has been unfortunate and has hindered the effort to keep down living costs.
>
> The OWI is supposed to present facts and information without bias. By no stretch of the imagination does this pamphlet come within those limits.

From the Republican point of view, grounds for this criticism could undoubtedly be found, and Mr. Robey's violence reflects strong partisan feelings.

From May, 1943, until the end of the war, the agency was to become a political football. The Roosevelt-haters became the

Davis-haters. A month later, a venomous attack came in the column entitled "Good Morning" conducted by Malcolm W. Bingay in the Detroit *Free Press*.

> Elmer's popping off again [wrote the elegant Mr. Bingay]. Yeah, Elmer Davis. Elmer, the dead-pan study in chiaroscuroistic physiognomy with white hair, gray face, bootblack eyebrows and long black bow tie to synchronize the movements of his Adam's apple with his thought processes. Yeah, boy! Elmer was born to be an actor and that is the role he is playing now—with plenty of ham.
>
> Elmer, as you know, is the chief of that weird, hydra-headed monstrosity of government mismanagement known as Office of War Information. . . .

This philippic so impressed Representative Roy O. Woodruff, Republican, of Michigan that he had the whole column reprinted in the Appendix of the *Congressional Record*. This was done a year and three days after the same Mr. Woodruff had welcomed the appointment of Davis, "known to the American public as an able, honest, and fearless analyst and commentator." The mood in Congress had begun to change; its members were becoming restive after the first flush of patriotism when, for a brief interval, the President, as Commander-in-Chief, had bipartisan support.

These blasts did not greatly disturb Elmer Davis. But in April, 1943, there was an internal ruction which did disturb him.

## 3

In the long backward view, the explosion in April, 1943, in the offices of OWI's Domestic Branch looks like the sort of teapot tempest that often occurred in government bureaus when sensitive personalities clashed. And so it would have appeared at the time, had the outburst been confined within the organization. Un-

213

happily it could not be so confined. Neither Congress nor the partisan press was in the mood to ignore an eruption that could be exploited to the hurt of any part of the Roosevelt bureaucracy. Even this, however, Elmer Davis could have answered blow for blow but for one Congressional weapon against which he had no final defense. Congress could cut off his funds and thus cripple his Office in mid-career and this, some two months later, they proceeded to do.

The trouble started in the group of writers and publishers who had produced the practical and inspirational pamphlets in an attempt to show the reasons for the war. They were able, talented men and women who shared Davis's insistence on three-dimensional truth, but who felt that this was being distorted by what we would call Madison Avenue techniques. Such devices, they believed, were introduced by executives who stood between them and the Director.

All had been well as long as they were accountable only to Gardner Cowles, Jr., who had been appointed by Davis to direct the Domestic Branch. But Mr. Cowles had called in two men to assist him and these had become the new bosses of the writer-publisher group. Furthermore the new bosses had brought along with them persons whose experience had been in the writing and commercial art of advertising. Now there is no greater antagonism than that between the writer and the copywriter—the independent artist or reporter and the committed advertising man who is grinding someone else's axe. That this axe should be Uncle Sam's was repugnant to the creative patriots. The American people were fed enough ballyhoo, they said, about toothpaste and cigarettes without being "sold" the war by the same methods.

The people, they insisted, must be given the facts so that they could make up their own minds. It was inevitable that advertising men, whose whole impulse was persuasion, should sugar-coat the facts. To demonstrate this, they produced a poster alleged to be the work of a copywriter done in the interest of saving gasoline. The poster showed a pretty girl with provocative legs and a long stride. It was entitled "Walk and Be Beautiful." Whether or not this was a genuine product of the Madison Avenue boys, it is reasonably certain that the poster that followed it—a drawing of the Statue of Liberty holding four bottles of Coca-Cola and labeled "The Four Delicious Freedoms"—was executed within the insurgent group. In any case, this was what the writers meant.

So, one morning in the second week of April, Elmer Davis found on his desk the resignation of Henry Pringle, a distinguished author, as we have seen, and winner of the Pulitzer Prize for biography. This was followed in the course of a week by thirteen others—among them Milton MacKaye, Arthur Schlesinger, Jr., Della Tuhn, W. McNeil Lowry, Katharine Douglass and Louise Baker. It was a hard blow. Many of these people were Davis's personal friends, all were trusted and respected employees. He called them in to talk to them, to ask them to reconsider. Yes, they said, they would if they could be allowed to work directly under him and be responsible only to him. For him they had nothing but respect.

But, said Davis, they had gone over Cowles's head. They had presented their resignations to him instead of to Cowles. Now he could not go over Cowles's head in transferring them from his jurisdiction. It was a course that any honest executive must follow. Otherwise all loyalty in the organization would be undermined.

Furthermore, Davis denied their premises. At his press conference, he said he believed in the sincerity of those who had resigned but he was convinced that they were wrong. The OWI had never swerved from its dedication to the truth and no such change was in prospect. And there in a deadlock of opposing statements the controversy rested. It was a simple matter of agreement to disagree and, under normal circumstances this should have been the end of it. But circumstances were not normal and the ripples caused by the internal conflict became, as they spread out, large waves of great destructive power.

215

Repercussions in the press and in Congress began immediately. Ignoring Davis's side of the argument, *Time*, "the weekly newsmagazine," took the part of the writers.

> From now on [it stated in its issue of April 19] U.S. citizens will get their news well washed and perfumed—that is, if the Office of War Information has its way. This depressing intelligence was confirmed last week when OWI went through another shake-up. When the dust had settled, the men who had tried to be realists about the war were unhorsed, while the so-called soap salesmen were in the saddle. . . . The writers tried to tell the truth, however bitter. They were not notably successful. One reason, they felt, was that admen sifting into OWI had other ideas: take it easy, tone it down, deodorize it. . . .

In the Senate, the day after the full news of the ruction was published, Senator O'Mahoney of Wyoming introduced a resolution asking for an investigation of OWI. Actually O'Mahoney was one of Davis's stronger supporters, but he felt that these wholesale resignations called for an inquiry. The hearings dragged on for some two months during which Davis was forced to devote time that should have been spent running his agency in defending its existence.

On June 18, the House passed a resolution abolishing the Domestic Branch by a vote of 218 to 114—a formidable majority. The House Appropriations Committee under Representative Taber's prodding had already cut nearly thirteen million from the over-all OWI appropriation. Various other cuts had reduced the forty-seven odd millions recommended by the Budget Bureau to some twenty-nine millions left for OWI's operations in the following year.

On the twentieth Davis stated that if the Senate should sustain the House cut, it meant the end of OWI and, in his news conference, he talked about other occupational possibilities for himself.

On this same date columnist Frank C. Wardrop wrote in the Washington *Times-Herald*:

Well, Uncle Elmer, you're a flop. The House of Representatives says so. The public distaste of your services says so. Uncle Elmer, get going, now.

In the House, at about the same time, Representative Starnes compared Davis's propaganda with that of the Nazis. To this Davis replied:

I believe Representative Starnes of Alabama honored me by calling me the American Goebbels. There are quite a number of differences, as Mr. Starnes could discover by reading the record. The only difference I would like to point out is that Dr. Goebbels does not have to go to the Reichstag for his appropriation.

But on June 30, the Senate, in refusing to go along with the House vote to abolish the Domestic Branch, allowed it three million dollars for the coming year. This meant the end of publications, motion pictures and field operations. It forced the closing of regional offices throughout the United States. It provided for the continuance of radio broadcasting, the news bureau and other special services.

4

Though the resignation of the writer-publisher insurgents had much to do with the blow-up in Congress, it did not initiate the antagonism which Representative Taber had promoted since 1942. In those early experimental days when OWI was still clearing out some of the debris it had inherited, Mr. Taber found a few farfetched trial balloons of propaganda, which Davis stopped as soon as he learned of them, and on this basis made some broad guesses as to the devastation the Office was causing. On November 11, 1942 he wrote Davis that it was

> perfectly apparent that these activities are hampering and interfering with the war effort and have a very serious and bad effect upon the efforts that the government is making to sell bonds. . . .
>
> Is it not about time that your organization started to support the war effort and quit the monkey-work that is making it a menace to the war effort?

Two days later, Davis replied

> If any member of Congress thinks we are a menace to the war effort it is not only his right but his duty to get up and say so, as loud as he can; though he might be more convincing if he gave specifications and backed them up with evidence. If the majority of Congress decides that our office is not worth the money we are costing the taxpayers, it is not only their right but their duty to refuse to give us another nickel. Pending such action, however, we shall continue to do our job according to our best judgment, and we will not be bulldozed by threats of denunciatory speeches in Congress or anywhere else. . . .
>
> You say that our activities "are hampering and interfering with the war effort. . . ." I think I have a right to ask you for some evidence on that. If we are doing that, we ought to be abolished; if we are not doing it we should not be falsely accused. When you talk about forcing our outfit to support the war effort, I can only invite you to make that statement on the floor; and then see which one of us they laugh at. . . .

218

I hope this letter is plain enough to be understood.

Mr. Taber did not accept this invitation. Instead he replied saying, among other things:

Your tone and attitude indicate a high hat feeling which in a public official is almost unpardonable.

I doubt very much if it is desirable to attempt to deal with you on any other basis than at arm's length because you do not seem to appreciate any other approach, assuming that you do not intend to do the right thing.

Later this correspondence brought out the sort of venom that was characteristic of the period—a venom not only directed against the President but against all his works: his appointees and the offices he created.

An OWI publication that aroused Mr. Taber's ire was a picture biography of F.D.R. done in comic strip manner and intended exclusively for overseas use. Thus, no accusation could be made that it was meant to influence American voters. Nevertheless, Mr. Taber found a copy and launched a personal tirade, maintaining that Davis was carrying on a political campaign for Roosevelt and the New Deal. Actually the pamphlet was not very good and Davis admitted its defects. But it was Taber's way to seize gleefully on such an admission and to use it as an argument against the appropriation of funds to the Office. On March 11, 1943, he wrote to Davis:

On March the 4th you admitted that it [the biography] was a failure and then evidently on March the 6th, having forgotten what you said on the 4th, you attempted to justify it by the statement, "especially as both our enemies and our allies use the personalities of their leaders as symbols of their nations."

May I call to your attention, Mr. Davis, that we are now

219

engaged in a war against those enemies to overthrow that very principle of dictatorship—the deification of one man as the leader of a country. That, sir, is Fascism in its simplest form. A confession by you that you are copying one of the most hideous elements of Nazism and Fascism is a startling thing when we consider the power that you today exercise over free speech.

These letters—and there were many more—suggest the sort of attack that would have had little effect on Davis but for the consequences in dollars and cents. Other attacks, he thought, seemed to prove Hitler's philosophy. In his final report on the history of OWI, he wrote:

The attacks of crackpot Fascists and of the copperhead press were a badge of honor; but many more respectable persons for a variety of reasons joined in the attacks, and our enemies went a long way toward proving the truth that if you tell a lie long enough and loudly enough it will be generally believed.

On the whole, it is difficult today to appraise the benefits that accrued from the operations of the Domestic Branch of OWI. It is probable, however, that historians will find extremely tangible results from some of the jobs done by the Overseas Branch. Occasionally these were immediately apparent: evidence was presented by prisoners of war when the enemies began to crack.

# 15 |||||

## 1

FROM THE TIME of the Allied landings in North Africa through the fateful year of 1943, there was much for the Overseas Branch to do. For one thing there was fertile soil in Italy for the seeds of propaganda, and the British and American offices made the most of it. Whether the Italian morale would have declined less progressively without this assistance from abroad may be debatable, but we do know now that both the BBC and OWI's Voice of America gave comfort to many unhappy Italians and that these broadcasts, plus the printed material that infiltrated the country the Nazis had enslaved, may have encouraged the dissidents in high places to bring about the capitulation a little sooner than it would otherwise have come about. And, as Elmer Davis said, "If the OWI can help to shorten the war by only one day, it will have paid for itself several times over."

There is no doubt that her Nazi allies had more to do with Italy's decline than her enemies. The fact was that, in the hearts of the people, Italy's place was at the opposite extreme from her official position. From the start, in every town and village and farm, there was hatred of the Germans. Traditionally, the Germans were associated with Austria, which had oppressed Italy for centuries. In 1916, Italy had fought against the Kaiser's armies. It was, as Churchill said, one man and one only who, by signing the "Pact of Steel," had brought her into the late alliance.

The Duce had told them that the alliance would make secure the great "Roman Empire" that he had restored: that an Axis victory would raise the crowded little country into the concert of great nations. A few had believed what he told them; the rest had simply accepted it as they must accept everything—there was no alternative.

From the first, Hitler had adopted a master-servant attitude toward the Italians. This had infuriated the proud Duce. Arrogant for ten years toward everyone, including his own people (whom he privately despised), he had at last found someone to whom he must be yielding and obedient. If he had entered the war with a brave, efficient and loyal army, he might have stood up to the German Führer, but his forces met defeat from the start. A German detachment had to go to the rescue of a decimated Italian force in the Balkans and to pull the Italian chestnuts out of the Greek fire. Hitler, scenting the Roman ambitions in southern France, had kept the Duce's men away from the French Riviera, sending them instead into the desert warfare in Africa where Rommel treated them with nothing but contempt. When the Germans were forced by the British Eighth Army to retreat across Libya, Rommel commandeered the Italian trucks and supplies to aid him in his headlong flight, leaving his allies to starve. As the Germans departed, the enraged Italian soldiers fired on their Axis partners.

A considerable part of Italy itself was virtually occupied by German armies. They lived off the Italian land, reducing the crops to the point where the people had hardly enough to keep alive. Disaster had overtaken the Italian troops that had gone to the Russian front; the poor men, unaccustomed to cold and unequipped for it, had died of exposure and disease before they had begun to fight.

When the heavy bombing by the British R.A.F. on the northern industrial cities began, Italians blamed the Germans more than they blamed the British. The bombing had two vital effects: it

222

sent evacuees swarming into other Italian cities too poor or too crowded to receive them, thus causing internal conflict; it also convinced many of the top Italian industrialists—such as the pro-British Dino Grandi—that they must join with the dissident generals to make clandestine overtures to get their country out of the war. When, in January, 1943, the Allies entered Tripoli, thus pulling down the curtain on Libya's part in the Duce's Roman Empire, important army commanders such as Marshal Badoglio knew that the jig was up and that, somehow, a divorce from Germany must be achieved.

As we look back over this period in which the tide turned so surely in our favor, it seems as if Italian bitterness toward the Nazis had needed no aid from psychological (or as it was then called, "political") warfare. What good was it to beam angry word pictures of Mussolini to the ears of scared people who already despised him? What good to show Hitler's treachery? Why should we tell them stories of the predatory operations of the Germans on Italian agricultural production? Had they not eyes and stomachs? Why torment them more than they were already tortured with descriptions of the bitter Russian front? Were men and women going to risk their lives by secret listening to advice with which they were already in perfect accord but which they were utterly helpless to follow?

The answer is that a mere divorce of Italy from Germany was not the aim of the propaganda machine. Rather, the purpose was to attach the Italian people, when the time came, to us, so that they could join our cause against what would then be the common enemy. We were not trying to make Italy a neutral; we wanted her for an ally. It was not, however, that we counted on an exhausted Italian army to help us but rather that we wanted a loyal and effective underground to guide us in a country whose terrain was so difficult. That we were, in fact, so aided, later, by the Italians who called themselves "partisans" was proof of the pudding that was cooked in the spring and summer of 1943 by

223

the British Ministry of Information and the Overseas Branch of
the OWI in the United States.

2

The Italian operation was only a fraction of the work done by
the OWI in these pregnant months. In all the areas of the world,
eastern and western, it had its outposts, and from them and from
the headquarters in New York and San Francisco, the Voice of
America spoke twenty-four hours a day from more than a score
of transmitters. The bulk of radio time was given to France and
Germany, but Italy was third on the list, and there were times
when nothing seemed so important as the Italian broadcasts. Yet
no operation was as controversial.

Italians are highly individualistic and argumentative; it is said
that if you put three Italians, picked at random, into a room
together there will be, within ten minutes, a vigorous three-sided
argument. An Italian once explained that this is why they needed
a dictator; that enough citizens could never agree to the point of
forming a democratic party. They must have someone who will
whip them into line, who will say to them: "Agree—or else." As
the Italian Desk of the Overseas Branch was largely staffed either
by naturalized Italo-Americans or by recent refugees from the
Duce's dictatorship, there were some lively times there. While
these persons were all fanatic "partisans" in thought and temper,
they differed pugnaciously on propaganda methods and content.

Almost none of the foreign nationals in the Overseas Branch
could understand why the propaganda sent to their fatherlands
should be tailored to fit American foreign policy, and the Italians
were the most recalcitrant. They insisted that they and not the
American "planners" knew what their fellow countrymen wanted
to hear; many of them would, indeed, be mortally offended by
some of the Americanized "nonsense" they were forced to listen
to. One example out of many was a statement in the broadcast

224

of Henry Wallace's speech about the "Common Man" that each person in the world should have a quart of milk to drink every day. Citing the Italian loathing of milk as a beverage, one staff member told his chief that every good Italian would "puke" as he listened.

But in good Italian fashion, these persons disputed among themselves. One group would describe a radio script as "sick-making" while another called it magnificent. The staff members in the Radio Bureau were always calling one another Communists. There would be angry conflicts between members of opposing political factions; there were fights between recent refugees and persons long Americanized, and there were sharp differences between the government insiders and groups independent of OWI that were propagandizing on their own—such as the Italian Socialist party in the United States and the Italian-American Labor Council. Also Mayor Fiorello La Guardia of New York was delivering frequent broadcasts to Italy in Italian, many of which diverged sharply from OWI policy.

Luigi Antonini, one of the zealots on the Italian staff of the Overseas Branch, took his complaint to Elmer Davis, and the ensuing correspondence between them reveals the limitations under which the propaganda office was obliged to work.

It is not the first time [wrote Antonini in July 1943] that your attention has been called to what I define as the mess in the short-wave programs to Italy.

The letter went on to complain that its writer's radio scripts intended to be sent over OWI transmitters were repeatedly censored in the organization. It said also that he had

received through government channels from the underground movement in Italy informations about their amazement of the way the OWI was suppressing the truth about the real character of discontent and dissatisfaction in Italy.

225

To this Davis replied:

> The Office of War Information is a part of the United States
> government, and programs broadcast through its facilities
> to Italy or any other foreign country, whether they are of
> government or private origin, must serve the policies of that
> government. We do not make those policies; in foreign affairs
> they are made by the White House and the Joint Chiefs of
> Staff; and the directives which determine their expression in
> propaganda are drawn by our planning board, on which the
> State, War and Navy Departments are represented.

This Overseas Planning Board was, indeed, an institution
whose broad operation sometimes prevented the delicate finesse
with which subtle propaganda is supposed to attain its maximum
effectiveness. On it sat, as Davis explained, the department representatives. Its chairman was Robert Sherwood, who had, so to
speak, a key to the back door of the White House and who
drafted many of the President's speeches. Therefore, Sherwood's
insight into the mind of Roosevelt was supposed to be accurate
enough to keep the words that flowed out of OWI from departing
too far from the Chief's views.

But the directives that emanated from the board were expected
to cover all "target areas"; they were to be broken down into
regional directives and then "implemented" by the various desks
and bureaus. Obviously such a scheme appeared to men like
Antonini to oversimplify what they thought was a complex
problem and to apply broad general principles to what they
believed to be a unique situation to be dealt with exclusively by
Italian "experts" and not by a group of "ignorant" Americans.

But what, in Antonini's letter, got most under Davis's skin was
the old, hackneyed implication that everything that went wrong
had a Communist origin. The letter stated that Antonini's superior in the Overseas Branch had threatened to replace him with
someone else.

In such frame of mind [he concluded] I would not be surprised if that someone else were a totalitarian fellow-traveler.

We see here a foretaste of the undocumented accusations that would haunt Elmer Davis for the rest of his life against which he fought his most effective fight.

I am getting a little tired [he replied to Antonini] of this constant innuendo about Communists in the Office of War Information, which is never supported by any evidence that will stand up. To you, as to all others who talk this way, I renew my invitation to show some evidence; if you can convince us that we have any Communists, we shall get rid of them. Till we have evidence, this sort of talk only provides ammunition for such men as Taber and Starnes.

So, in spite of Mr. Antonini and other insurgents, the Planning Board continued its sway and propaganda was made to conform to the secret plans of Uncle Sam to divide and conquer in his own devious way. But then, on one critical day in July, 1943, unbeknownst to Davis, the Planning Board and, apparently, Sherwood, the New York office of the Overseas Branch overrode the controls and, in the fevered time that followed, there was hell to pay. It was the beginning of that split between New York and Washington which, as we shall see, was to have formidable consequences.

### 3

Because, in the more mysterious purlieus of the State and War departments, it was known that overtures for peace had long been made by persons high in Italian office, there had been a search into the questions of who was who and why. Among other things, nine Italian generals captured by the American army, had been brought to the United States and induced to talk. Swiss listening posts had heard reverberations of an anti-fascist movement. The British had some definite information of the attitude in Italian industry and finance. There seemed to be indications that there was opposition between King Victor Emmanuel and old-guard Fascists, and that Italy's greatest general, Marshal Pietro Badoglio, had broken with fascism. All this new information had emphasized the established policy of not personally attacking the King because some day we might use him, and of not calling everyone in the Italian army a Fascist until it was proved that he was one.

But then, in the last week of July, 1943, when Italy fell apart, it turned out that the New York office of the Overseas Branch had a different policy. The "experts" there thought—or so they said—that the way to keep Hitler at bay was to treat all Italian governments as eternal enemies and to deny that the catastrophic events taking place in Rome had any revolutionary significance. Thus, when the King demanded and received Mussolini's resignation and then put the rebel Badoglio at the head of the government, a Voice of America broadcast said, in effect, Don't you believe that anything has changed: the King is still fascist and so is Badoglio.

Seen from this distance across a space that has been filled with precise historical detail, there seems to have been little excuse for the broadcast. Its wording was hedged by subterfuge. It quoted from a newspaper column and its writers later contended that the quotation did not necessarily reflect the views of OWI. It also quoted from a "John Durfee" who turned out to be a mythical character fabricated by the office. But its most damning paragraph was by Samuel Grafton who, writing in the New York *Post* said:

The moronic little King, who has stood behind Mussolini's shoulder for twenty-one years, has moved forward one pace. This is a political minuet and not the revolution we have been waiting for. It changes nothing; for nothing can change in Italy until democracy is restored.

And the imaginary "Mr. Durfee" was quoted as saying that the United States would continue the war irrespective of whether Signor Mussolini or Marshal Badoglio or "the Fascist King himself" ruled Italy. Yet only a few hours before this broadcast went out, the announcer on the Italian radio had triumphantly proclaimed:

With the fall of Mussolini and his band, Italy has taken the first step toward peace. Finished is the shame of fascism. Long live peace. Long live the King!

The two top men in the New York office, James Warburg and Joseph Barnes, assumed responsibility for the broadcast, but said it had not been beamed in Italian to Italy but in English to England. It was clear to Elmer Davis, however, that the Radio Bureau of the Overseas Branch in New York was getting out of hand, and events that followed in its train led to one of the unhappy upheavals in the organization.

The President lost no time in rebuking OWI for its indiscretion. Then the old theme was played again in a highly slanted news story by the perennially cantankerous Arthur Krock who wrote that it was

the high official view here [in Washington] that the New York Office of the OWI deliberately and consistently borrows from these sources [i.e., Grafton] to discredit the authorized foreign policy of the United States Government, or to reshape it according to the personal and ideological preferences of Communists and their fellow travelers in this country.

So Mr. Krock, who might well have known better, joined the persecution gang with his undocumented "high official view."

229

Why the *Times* permitted him to put his editorializing into the middle of a news story instead of in his column on the editorial page is not clear, but newspaper practice had changed a good deal since Davis's day when neither personal opinions nor by-lines characterized the news columns. It was true, to be sure, that the New York office of OWI had been out of line, but not because of Communist penchant.

## 4

It was the indiscretions, not the effective world-wide work of the Overseas Branch that drew the headlines. This was partly because the mistakes were easier to spot. The work of the outposts was remote and often classified. Leaflets prepared in the outposts and dropped over enemy lines seldom got into the news; the broadcasts to Europe from powerful foreign-based transmitters like the one in North Africa were not picked up in America as were the short-wave emanations from home-front senders. Little was known here of the prisoner interviews, the gathering and appraisal of information from refugees, the contacts with underground workers in enemy countries that were outpost operations.

By the spring of 1943, OWI had twenty-six of these outposts. These were in Rekjavik, Stockholm, London, Dublin, Berne, Madrid, Algiers, Oran, Casablanca, Accra, Lagos, Brazzaville, Asmara, Beirut, Cairo, Ankara, Teheran, Karachi, Bombay, Calcutta, Delhi, Johannesburg, Chungking, Honolulu, Canberra and Anchorage. But as the war progressed, the outpost situation changed.

As offensive military action [Davis explained in June] brings new territory over to the United Nations we shall put men on the ground operating printing presses, disseminating news, helping the Army carry on combat propaganda, and hitting

the enemy behind the lines with everything we can to in-
crease the tempo of his demoralization as has been done
successfully in Tunisia.

When the invasion of Italy began, OWI men accompanied the
invasion.

Propaganda [wrote Davis in his final report to the Presi-
dent] is only an auxiliary weapon; it never won a war by
itself but, properly used, it can powerfully reinforce the
effect of military operations. That OWI and its British
colleagues served this purpose in Sicily and Italy, where
their combat teams landed with the armies while their radio
was steadily continuing its strategic campaign, was acknowledged by the enemy himself; after the Italian government's
surrender in September, 1943, Japanese government spokes-
men warned their people that this could partly be ascribed
to "British and American propaganda aimed at the disintegration of the home front." It was added that intensified
propaganda might be expected "against the solidarity of the
Japanese nation"—a prediction which OWI soon fulfilled.

These campaigns were greatly assisted by the new 50,000-watt
transmitter that had been set up in North Africa and began
operation in mid-June. From this, long- and medium-wave broadcasts were beamed all over the European war area and these
were now loud and clear unlike the faint signals that had come
by short-wave from American stations. There were four languages: French, German, Italian and English. Because OWI was
determined to establish in enemy and occupied nations an American reputation for honesty, it used a technique directly opposite
to that of the Axis. There was no bombast, no attempt to excite
listeners, no indulgence in superlatives. Factual news made the
bulk of the broadcasts; the descriptions of Allied victories were
simple with understatement the rule. There was a deliberate

231

policy of telling the unfavorable news along with the favorable—there was even a description of the coal strike in America. The Axis leaders were never vilified, but as an OWI man told a reporter, "We let them vilify themselves by recalling in connection with current news their claims of the past." The only approach to editorializing was in the warnings to Italian civilians to keep away from war factories and other bomber targets.

The most important outpost was in London. Though the propaganda here was, in the beginning, intended mainly for the British, the London office eventually prepared most of the European material. It had the advantage of not being dependent on Congressional appropriations, for the bulk of its expenses were covered by "reverse lend-lease"—paid, that is, by the British in return for American material sent them on the lend-lease plan. Eventually the London office became a branch rather than an outpost and in the war's last year it was the headquarters for all the operations in northern Europe.

5

Though psychological warfare was the most sensational of the operations of the Overseas Branch and the one about which the press was most curious, it was not the largest overseas activity. A huge quantity of material went to neutrals, to Allies, to friendly people under enemy occupation such as the French, the Norwegians, the Filipinos and, of course, in the last year, the Italians. There were motion pictures, radiophotos, magazines, newspapers and "novelties." The movie reels penetrated to remote villages in Poland and China. Radiophotos showing the immense American industrial operations were greatly heartening to people discouraged by Axis propaganda about "degenerate" America; others, such as that showing the Japanese fleet limping away from the Midway battle, stiffened the Chinese will to resist.

A series of little goodwill tokens were dropped by plane and

232

gave the sense of American friendliness. In places where the steel that once went into needles had been taken for munitions, thousands of sewing kits with encouraging messages delighted the women. Cakes of soap were dropped on soapless France "from your American friends." From *"Les Enfants des Etats Unis aux Enfants Français"* went games and picture puzzles.

Not all of the publications were successful in design. In the New York office there were too many workers whose policy was to thrust America down the throats of Europeans. It was hardly politic to show the luxury in which Americans—unharmed by enemy attack—lived through the war. Large, costly publications, printed in color on the most expensive paper, did not suggest sacrifice. The old urgency to show that the United States had the biggest, the best and the richest of everything resulted in much that was nauseating to foreigners.

Chronic Congressional critics were quick to attack one of these publications—a magazine called *Victory*—and Arthur Krock with his customary eagerness to exploit such targets paraphrased the comment of Senator Rufus C. Holman, Republican of Oregon:

It will not win friends for the United States abroad though this is its purpose, because it is "smug, self-glorifying" and a "vulgar display" of American might and luxury to peoples living in hardship.

And Mr. Krock added a quotation from a letter he had received about "the lavishness of *Victory* with its photographs in color of well-stocked grocery stores and tables groaning with plenty":

What would your feelings be if you were an inhabitant of Africa and saw the United States as the editors of this magazine want them to see us? All this display is beautifully calculated to confirm the worst things said about us by our enemies. Only last night a friend of mine who lived most of her life in impoverished lands said that these pictures would

233

seem to the poor and undernourished in the rest of the world like a display of luxury set forth behind a plate-glass window for beggars to contemplate hungrily. *Victory* is a disaster for its own stated purpose: to gain friends for us abroad and help us win the war.

The justice of the criticisms is hard to dispute. That this sort of operation was allowed to continue in the Overseas Branch without interruption was an indication that too much was escaping the attention of Elmer Davis and his assistants in Washington. It is true that Davis was constantly harassed by persons who were his enemies because they were enemies of the New Deal—one of the non sequiturs consistently accepted by the right-wing Republicans of the time. It is true that he had to fight for appropriations when he should have been fighting the war. It is true that he was sometimes betrayed or deceived by his subordinates. But it was irrefutable testimony of his lack of administrative experience that the right hand in Washington knew so little about what the left hand in New York was doing.

In the first months of 1944, he found out how far astray the New York office had gone and then acted—suddenly and ruthlessly—with consequences which took him into the inner sanctum of the White House itself.

# 16 )))))

## 1

ROBERT EMMET SHERWOOD, director, under Elmer Davis, of OWI's Overseas Branch, was one of the most talented authors of his time. His comedies, *The Road to Rome* and *Reunion in Vienna,* had delighted huge Broadway audiences for long seasons and his later more somber plays, *Idiot's Delight, The Petrified Forest* and *There Shall Be No Night,* interpreted complex and tragic events of a changing world with ironic penetration. When war came, in 1939, or even when, in the shadows of Munich and Mukden, it threatened, he could think of nothing else and became wholly absorbed in the hope of victory over the tyranny and the enslavement of mankind which he saw, in the war years, close on the horizon.

He had fought once, in Canada's Black Watch before the United States entered the first World War; now in the second, he was beyond the age of combat and devoted his energies to such work with the government as he thought would advance the cause. In 1940, he was special assistant to the Secretary of War; as he was President Roosevelt's constant supporter and friend, he became an intimate of the White House, where he was the master mind of the team that assisted the President in the drafting of his speeches. At the same time, he made such an incisive study of propaganda and whatever means of psychological warfare were in accord with his concept of truth that he seemed to Colonel William J. Donovan the natural choice as chief of the Foreign

235

Information Service in the office of Co-ordinator of Information. And FIS was one of the legacies that Elmer Davis inherited when the Office of War Information was formed. That was how Sherwood came to be the director of OWI's Overseas Branch.

It was one of the typical wartime accidents that put such a man in an administrative position. That Davis should have to concern himself with management was bad enough; to put such a task in the hands of Bob Sherwood was far worse. Intensely creative, pugnaciously individualistic, uncompromising and wholly inexperienced in office routine, his mind had no place for the daily details of a business employing some three thousand persons. But above and beyond all this, he was continually on call from the White House for the exercise of his more apt talents, so that his absence from the New York office was more usual than his presence there. And as he had no gift for the delegation of authority, it was natural that a group of his subordinates who wanted action should assume it. Thus the Overseas Branch drew more and more into autonomy; such episodes as the notorious "moronic little King" affair became symptomatic of its independence from the centralized control for which Elmer Davis was responsible.

The key figures in this undeclared but effective independence were Edd Johnson, chief of the Overseas Editorial Board, James P. Warburg, deputy director of the Propaganda Warfare Policy, and Joseph Barnes, deputy director of Atlantic Operations. All were distinguished men on leaves of absence from important careers. They were powerful individuals in their own rights, accustomed to command acquiescence among their subordinates and more experienced than their superiors in organization.

But when complaints came from various sources that this group had "taken over" the Overseas Branch, Davis instigated an investigation. This was conducted by his new associate director, Edward Klauber, whose appointment had followed the resignation of Milton Eisenhower in the summer of 1943 to accept the presidency of Kansas State University. The results of the inquiry were alarming, to say the least, and Davis put the blame on Sherwood who, as chief of the branch, must be held responsible.

## 2

With his customary quick action once he was convinced that a situation required it, he ordered Sherwood to reorganize the Overseas Branch, eliminating Johnson, Warburg and Barnes. Sherwood refused. According to the strict interpretation of Executive Order 9182, it was a simple case of insubordination. Davis had every right to fire Sherwood and any other employees who might buck his authority. Instead, because he always leaned over backwards in the effort to be fair, he permitted Sherwood to take the matter to the President.

In the second week in January, 1944, he received from the President, the following letter:

> The White House
> Washington
> January 8, 1944

Dear Elmer:

Bob Sherwood has shown me your draft of a staff order for reorganization of the Overseas Branch. He explains that he does so with your full knowledge.

Perhaps you have facts concerning the work of the Overseas Branch which are unknown to me. If so, you should submit them to me at once.

Until and unless I receive such specific information, I do not feel that you should take any steps toward the proposed reorganization.

> Very truly yours,
> *Franklin D. Roosevelt.*

Evidently the President had not got round to reading a letter Davis had sent him four days earlier. In it, among other things he had written:

Bob Sherwood is an able propagandist, but his administration has led to confusion and ineffectiveness, of which the recent troubles in our London office are the most conspicuous example. I have therefore decided to relieve him of all operating duties, while retaining him as director of propaganda policy, so that he can devote all his energy to the thing he does well. I have also concluded that the office would benefit by the removal of three men—James P. Warburg, Edd Johnson and Joseph F. Barnes—whose activities are, in my judgment, directed more to getting and keeping power for themselves than to furthering the purposes of the organization.

Mr. Sherwood disagrees with my conclusions, denies my right to insist on any personal changes and has informed me that he is appealing to you. He threatens further that if he cannot induce you to revoke my authority to direct this organization, he will endeavor to persuade you to split it up, and set up the Overseas Branch as a separate entity. Ordinarily I should of course dismiss an executive who adopted such tactics; it is pretty hard to sail my craft when the first mate permits himself to be put at the head of a mutiny against the skipper. However, since Sherwood says he will accept any redefinitions of his functions if you so instruct him, I feel that I should let you know that I am willing to keep him on provided, and so long as, he recognizes the full authority of the head of this office and behaves accordingly.

After getting the President's letter of January 8, Davis again wrote—this time more than three pages, single-spaced, of specifications. He stated that the chaos and confusion caused by Sherwood's mismanagement and the control of the "clique" had

238

caused the resignation of key figures from the London office, that Sherwood's slowness in answering communications was evidence of bad administration, that there was a specific complaint from the Norwegian government that an Overseas Branch magazine had contained eighty-two errors in sixty-six pages, and many other matters. For a reply to this letter he waited ten days and wrote again. Finally, the President arranged a meeting for February second with both Davis and Sherwood with the purpose, as it turned out, of knocking their heads together.

Davis kept these notes on the conversation:

Sherwood and I were called to the White House today. The President told us that he wished he had a good long ruler, the kind that school boys' hands used to be slapped with when he was in school; that he was good and God-damned mad at both of us for letting a thing like this arise and get into the papers at a time when he had a war to think about. He said he did not want to lose either of us, both because he was fond of us both and because it would take too much of his time to find someone to take our places. He said it must be clear that I was the head of the Agency and responsible for the operations but that he did not want Sherwood sent to Guam, as they used to say in the Navy. Regarding personalities he said that Warburg was the only one he knew . . . but that he wanted us to go out in the Cabinet Room and get together.

We went out into the Cabinet Room and after considerable discussion failed to get together. I suggested that we talk it over again tomorrow.

Later we talked with Steve [Early] and Sam Rosenman. When Sam and Bob left I asked Steve to tell the President that I would make every effort to come to an agreement with Sherwood but that if this proved impossible I would have to go ahead even if it meant that he would resign.

239

Three days later, the agreement was signed by both Davis and Sherwood in the interest of "harmony of operation and to avoid misunderstanding." It acknowledged that:

> The Director of OWI, being responsible for both the policies and the operations of the Overseas Branch, has complete authority over both. . . . The authority of the Director of OWI over the Overseas Branch will be exercised through the Director of the Branch. The Director of OWI has the right to initiate any policies or operations that he may consider desirable, instructing the Director of the Overseas Branch to carry them out. . . .
>
> The Director of the Overseas Branch will keep the Director of OWI fully informed of the policies and intended operations of the Branch. He will submit all proposed appointments or transfers of bureau chiefs, outpost heads, or other important personnel to the Director of OWI, without whose approval such appointments shall not be valid.

Davis then sent for Edward W. Barrett to come home from North Africa to become executive director of the Overseas Branch. Sherwood, who still retained the title of director, went to London and took charge of the vital psychological warfare that would accompany the Normandy invasion. For Sherwood it was a superb opportunity and a task for which he was supremely fitted. Davis then wrote to the three controversial executives and asked for their resignations. They were at a loss, they told the press, to understand why. But they resigned.

It was a clear-cut victory for Elmer Davis and one that he believed saved the Overseas Branch. But it presented an opportunity for bitter comment by the Republican *New York Herald Tribune*. Its editorial on February 11, 1944, was entitled "Inviting the Wreckers" and stated, in its conclusion that when Mr. Davis tore his agency to pieces for no explainable reason, he was tending only to destroy the support it has enjoyed and to invite in the wreckers, who have been prompt to accept the invitation.

It was not Davis's custom to reply to editorial criticism but in this case he wrote Geoffrey Parsons, then the *Herald Tribune*'s chief editorial writer.

My reasons [he wrote] for making the changes were not, as your editorial of the 11th calls them, "obscure and unexplained"; still less "unexplainable." They were explained at length, six weeks ago, to the immediate superior of the men involved, who I presume transmitted the explanation to them; and further explanations were given by letter last week. . . . The story that no explanations were given is as romantically fictitious as the earlier story heard by many people in New York, that I got rid of these men to "appease the Fascists."

Naturally there is some resentment. I find that a great many people in the New York office have felt that they were working not for the government of the United States but for Joe Barnes. This feeling, which I am sure was not at all of his deliberate creation, is a testimonial to his personal charm; but I don't think it contributed to the effective functioning of a war agency.

Then, when this most sensational of all the internal news of his Office and one of the few that was carried into the White House was over, Elmer Davis turned his personal attention to the vital overseas campaigns that, in this last year of the war, were to liberate occupied lands in both East and West.

241

## 3

No one knew when D-day would come on the beaches of Normandy. But everyone knew that it was coming. The preparations were the most prodigious in the history of the world: they included military plans, propaganda plans, psychological warfare plans, engineering plans and logistic plans. From the crews of ships to the drivers of trucks the training through the spring of '44 was constant, the rehearsals were daily. Every potential detail of triumph or disaster had to be foreseen; the landings must be covered by fire from ships and planes, the route inward from the beaches must be explored, liaison must be established—cautiously with the Russians, clandestinely with Free and Occupied French.

OWI's task was manifold. For the European phase, London became the headquarters. In his final report to the President, Davis told specifically of the work done by the 1,200 men and women in London.

Of these [he stated] 279 eventually went into the Psychological Warfare Division of General Eisenhower's forces; the remainder (under the executive direction of Philip S. Hamblet but with Mr. Sherwood on the spot and exercising a general supervision) were engaged by all means possible in propaganda to confuse and discourage the enemy, to hearten the populations of the allied countries, and to prepare the underground forces to assist in the liberation. They transmitted news to the neutral capitals of Europe; they prepared newspapers and leaflets dropped from American airplanes on the occupied nations and on Germany, and books, pamphlets and magazines to be distributed among the liberated populations; they sent newsreels and documentary pictures to all parts of Europe where they could be shown; and they intensified the radio broadcasting which now, by long or medium wave, covered virtually all of Europe.

In the United States, the OWI sponsored a mission intended to get word of the advance preparations for the invasion into the neutral press and so to the enemy. Nineteen foreign newspapermen, Swiss, Australian, Chinese, Swedish, British and Free French and representatives of British and other news services were invited to take a plane trip to army camps and air bases to watch maneuvers in rehearsal for the invasion. Under the personal supervision of OWI's Armitage Watkins and with the cooperation of the War Department, these men were given front-row seats at some of the most impressive shows.

At Camp Polk, Louisiana, they saw a demonstration and firing of armored-division weapons and a simulated attack by a combat team of such a division with preliminary air and artillery preparation. In the night firing exercises, live ammunition was used, thoroughly scaring everyone except the army officers. At Camp Siebert, Alabama, the correspondents saw demonstrations by Chemical Warfare Service groups showing the use of smoke for signaling, of smoke screens and of flame throwers. At Hendricks Field, Florida, there was a show of precision and formation flying; at Laurinburg-Maxton Army Air Base, North Carolina, there were parachute jumps and glider exercises, and at Fort Bragg, North Carolina, the men, by this time exhausted by astonishment, saw a simulated infantry attack on a fortified position.

The correspondents went home loaded with photographs, technical data and memories—with everything but information about the date of the invasion—and wrote stories for their home papers —full or understated stories according to the temperaments of the writers—and even the most objective and unemotional accounts of what they had seen must have thrown alarm into the headquarters of the German High Command as soon as the

243

papers filtered through. This was one of the most ingenious devices designed by the OWI for psychological effect in the war's final phase.

4

A function of OWI that Davis felt must parallel the propaganda campaign in Europe was that of getting the invasion news promptly, accurately and fully back to the American people. As his personal representative he sent George H. Lyon to work from February on in close cooperation with General Eisenhower at Supreme Headquarters of the Allied Expeditionary Force (SHAEF) in London.

> At my request [Lyon reported to Davis] General Eisenhower's views on press relations were supplemented by official orders, in conversations with the chiefs of the Public Relations Division of SHAEF and in staff conferences. Long before D-Day I believe all the Allied Expeditionary Force had caught the idea that this—the greatest of all military stories—was to be reported as no military story had ever been reported before.

> No one, of course, knew when D-day was to be. It might come in May; it might come in September—so a great many bets were possible. The certainty that it was coming, overhung by the mystery as to when and where, created the war of nerves that Eisenhower was waging against the enemy through the spring.

> My principal work during those months [wrote Lyon] consisted of impressing SHAEF PRD [Public Relations Division] with the magnitude of the story to be covered, of arguing with them that they should demand a maximum of facilities from other groups in the armies—not minimum—I

244

wanted a fully adequate number of reporters and photographers with radio transmission facilities on the beachheads, plenty of airplanes to report the story from the sky, sufficient and large enough boats to ferry copy across the channel, a a fool-proof wire network to carry copy from the channel ports into London and an adequate motorcycle courier service to act as backstop in case enemy action destroyed wire communications. Eventually, all these facilities were made available—including carrier pigeons to be released from the beachheads. On D-minus-7 day the last detail had been worked out—correspondents had been assigned to their posts and we were ready for business.

Still, the date was unknown, except to a handful of officers in the top brass. German intelligence figured that it would have to be after mid-April. But even in the highest military echelons there was doubt until, after a long examination of the weather reports, Eisenhower gave the order for the four thousand ships to sail on the night of June the fifth. To repeat here the story of the events that followed would be superfluous and irrelevant, but *the story of the story* is pertinent to the Life and Times of Elmer Davis. Here it is, in the words of George Lyon, who wrote:

Thus when the D-day story broke in General Eisenhower's communiqué at 0932 hours on June 6 we were in this position as regards news coverage:

1. A carefully selected team of Allied news correspondents, broadcasters and photographers . . . was in strategic positions on the beachheads, in boats in the channel and in airplanes. . . .

2. All means of fast communications—radio, speedboats, airplanes, teletype and cyclist-couriers were being effectively employed to bring the story from Normandy into the Ministry of Information in London. Here a copy receiving room, a large news room, censorship and filing facilities had

245

been set up on a single floor. Fifty women on another floor cut stencils for mimeographing pooled copy for the Allied press of the world.

3. A well-trained censorship division was reading and clearing stories on an 11-minute average, copy was flowing smoothly to the United States, Signal Corps transmitters were speeding both voice broadcasts to the American networks and radiophotos to the U.S. picture pool and the War Department Air Transport Command and flying motion picture footage to the United States.

For the first five days of the invasion, all pooled material was transmitted to OWI in Washington, thence to be distributed to American news agencies, newspapers and news weeklies. On the fifth day, the pool was no longer believed necessary and after that, the coverage was on a competitive basis—each correspondent out for himself, free to make what scoops he might.

In Lyon's recapitulation, it appeared that on June 6, 571,744 words of press matter passed through SHAEF copy-control room, of which 313,581 went to the United States. In the first six days— to June 12—there were 2,666 pieces of copy, films and film recordings. To the United States, 754 photographs were sent plus 360 telephotos. The daily dispatch of motion picture films averaged 20,000 feet.

The whole operation was one for which the American press gave little credit to OWI, and very little of the story of the news has yet got into the history books.

5

A month after D-day in Europe, Elmer Davis went with President Roosevelt to Honolulu. In the Pacific, OWI had been handicapped by a recurrence of the Navy's security scare. It had been refused permission to prepare psychological warfare material for the invasion of the islands. But Admiral Nimitz was Davis's personal friend and in the course of direct, face-to-face conversations, Davis was able to convince the admiral that the value of propaganda accompaniment to military attack overrode any possible damage from information leaks. By this time, of course, Davis had the testimony of the European operation of June to buttress his arguments.

From this time on to the end of the war, the Navy cooperated fully with the psychological warfare organization that Davis set up in Hawaii—later extended to Saipan.

> Our magazine, *The Free Philippines* [Davis told in his later report], was sent in by submarines and widely distributed by Filipino guerillas; our combat propaganda teams landed with the army on Leyte and went with it right on up to the capture of Manila; and our . . . broadcasts to Japan were being conducted from Manila, in preparation for further operations, when the atomic bomb put an end to the war.

Meanwhile, when he got back from his fruitful trip, he made, on August 15, 1944, over the Columbia Broadcasting System, one of the best broadcasts of his career. It is doubtful whether, in all the literature of the war, any story has been told more clearly and simply yet with a high, true color that makes it seem that the scenes are moving before our eyes. They still jump from the pages of the typed script from which, into the microphone, he read, still sharp in focus undimmed by the distance of the years.

> I came with the President's party as far as Honolulu and then went west—as far west as Saipan and Guam which today are our westernmost frontiers, though they will not long remain so. Of General MacArthur's brilliant campaign in the Southwest Pacific . . . I can speak only from hearsay. . . . But I can give something of an eye-witness report of what is going on in the central and western Pacific—a war as differ-

247

ent as possible from that which was fought in Africa, and is now being fought in Europe. . . .

The fighting in this theater has been amply and brilliantly reported. . . . But much less has been said—because it is a less picturesque aspect of the war—of the enormous logistical job, the job of transportation and construction, that has to be done before our men and material can be got out to where they can fight at all. What makes this a stupendous job is of course the vast distances of the Pacific. . . . Pearl Harbor is the base and headquarters for this war in the Pacific Ocean areas—Pearl Harbor, which in volume of traffic is now the fourth seaport in the United States . . . and which has become one of America's great industrial cities as well. But Pearl Harbor must draw its materials from the factories and mines and farms of mainland America; and it is as far west of the California coast as Denver is west of New York. Then go on west—the Johnston Islands, Kwajalein, Eniwetok, and so on to Saipan and Guam; and when you get there you are farther from Pearl Harbor than is Seattle from Boston. Every man who fought in the Marianas, every cartridge he fired and every ration he ate, had to be transported anywhere from five thousand to eight thousand miles. This is one reason why this war is tough.

He explained that, though the Pearl Harbor base was a *sine qua non* of the whole Pacific war, yet in the thirty-five hundred miles to Guam, there had to be intermediate bases such as those established on the great atolls of the Marshall group,

each of them capable of giving secure anchorage to the whole navy; but they too had to be fought for; and after they had been taken, and considerably knocked about in the process, they had to be rebuilt from the ground up—or even farther. To make a base you must have dock facilities—you generally have to build them, for what was there was smashed in the

preliminary bombardment; you have to build a town, first
of tents and then of Quonset huts—all brought in by ship,
of course—and sometimes you have even had to build an
island for the town to stand on. We have elaborate and busy
air and shipping bases in the Pacific that were created out of
coral reefs—scooping up the bottom of the shallow sea along-
side to make land out of it as Miami realtors used to do in
the days of the boom.

The Seabees, he told, deserved much of the credit but they were
followed by aviation and army engineers. Then, to make the details more clear and vivid:

Let me tell you what happens on such an island, as I saw it
on Saipan only four weeks after the heavy fighting had
ended, as I saw it on Guam while the fighting was still going
on. Take Saipan, for instance—an island community of some
fifty thousand people—half of them military, half civilians—
with plantations, factories, a port with docks and ware-
houses, and a couple of flourishing towns. Suddenly the attack hits—first the air bombardment, then the naval bombardment, then the landings. Some of you have lived through
hurricanes . . . and remember how the landscape looked the
morning after. So do I; and I can tell you that one of our
amphibious attacks hits as hard as a dozen hurricanes.
Saipan was one of our great battles; taking the island cost
us more than sixteen thousand casualties. . . .

A battle like that does things to improved real estate.
When it is over the towns have been flattened to smoking
rubble; the palm groves have been stripped of their fronds
or simply knocked to pieces; the whole landscape is a mess
of pulverized coral lumps, filth, mud, smashed guns, wrecked
trucks, disabled tanks, punctured and flattened gasoline
drums, and all the multifarious and unappetizing trash and

249

garbage of war. There are civilian enemy dead to bury, too—plenty of them; and there are thousands of refugees to care for—friends as they were on Guam, enemies as on Saipan; but in either case helpless human beings, men, women and children, who need food, medical care and, when you can get it, shelter. And instantly the work of reconstruction begins. The men who have destroyed hardly have a chance to catch a little sleep before they have to begin building—cleaning up the wreckage, widening roads or building new ones; seeing that the refugees get fed, and improving their own living conditions as they go from fox holes to tents and from tents to barracks. Even in the two days I was on Saipan I could see the vast improvements; give the engineers time—and not too much time, at that—and the place will look better than it has ever looked before. . . .

Well, all this is a long way from the dark days of two years ago last winter, when we were still staggering from the great disaster of Pearl Harbor. . . . Today the bulletin board at the naval air transport station on Saipan lists arrivals and departures for Guam and Eniwetok and Kwajalein and Pearl Harbor, as the bulletin board at the Chicago airport lists arrivals and departures from New York and San Francisco and Miami; clearest proof of all that in those areas, neither the Japanese navy nor the Japanese air force is any longer any cause for worry, is this—between Saipan and Eniwetok transport planes (unarmed, of course) fly at night with their lights on. So far have we got, in two and a half years.

Even with all this good news, Davis said, we could not be complacent. The end was still distant. Though Guam was five thousand miles from San Francisco, it was still twelve hundred from Tokyo. The Japanese were stubborn and desperate. It was true that Tojo's government fell when Saipan fell,

250

But more Tokyo governments will have to fall before they are ready for the unconditional surrender we shall demand. If this were an old-fashioned war, the kind of polite chessboard war people used to fight in the eighteenth century, the Japs might give up, acknowledge that they had lost the decision on points, give up some of their loot and immediately start planning the next war. But this is a war for world security—an objective that demands that all the conquests of Japan for half a century past be disgorged, and that the power of Japan to commit aggression be broken utterly. It will be some time before the Japs are ready for that.

It was, in fact, almost exactly a year. It was the OWI, in 1945, that told the people of Japan of the secret surrender offer their government had made, in three million leaflets dropped from B-29s. Meanwhile the corpse of Mussolini had hung upside down in the streets of Milan to be defiled by a bitter crowd; Hitler had shot himself in a Berlin bunker and his gasoline-soaked body had been burned to flakes of cinder; and unconditional surrender had been demanded and given in Germany. There, too, the door had been opened to admit a new, future enemy and through its opening blew the first blasts of a cold war that Elmer Davis would live to see.

251

# 17 ]]]]]]

## 1

I F, AFTER THE WAR was over and the Office of War Information was properly liquidated, there was a sigh of relief from Elmer Davis, it was not audible except, perhaps, to his friends. For three and a half years he had endured more than most men are expected ever to endure. Open accusations and thinly veiled innuendos made him out to be a Communist or a crook: acting on instructions from Moscow or secretly receiving a stipend from some broadcasting company. At the same time he was said to be in an inner circle of the Democratic party in which his primary job was to promote Roosevelt and the New Deal.

When Roosevelt died in April, 1945, Davis received an unusual assignment. Immediately on receiving the news of Truman's succession the Madame Tussaud wax works in London lost no time in starting a figure of the new President. To do this accurately, a representative of the gallery called up the London office of the OWI to ask for Truman's collar size, the width of the back of his head and other measurements, all of which they must have in an unprecedented hurry. So Victor Weybright who took the message cabled it direct to Elmer Davis personally and got a response within the hour giving all the information requested.

It would be pleasant to report that, after his arduous war work, Davis took a long rest, perhaps in his beloved Key West where he and Paul Kieffer went at least once a year on a vacation from

252

both work and families. In former days, there was many a gay evening "when you started out [as Davis later wrote] after dark with no idea of where you were going or where you would go from there; but sure that wherever it was it would be a good evening." In that time Key West was

> still largely a Cuban town . . . walk down Duval Street in the evening and you heard nothing much but radios tuned in to Havana stations and Spanish conversation from cafés where men were drinking Cuban coffee. . . . There were dances downtown by the Club Juventad Latina. . . . There were fight programs at the Athletic Club on Friday night with a 99 cent top. . . . And then a whirl at Pena's to finish up, where you drank tropical beer and occasionally Jimmy the Tenor Guitar or some other wandering minstrel dropped in and played soft music; and then a walk back home in the moonlight, with no sound except the swish of the surf and the rustle of palms.

But between the effective date of OWI's liquidation, September 15, and the postwar broadcasts in the first week of December there was little time for rest—what with the cleaning up in Washington and the arrangements for going again to the radio studios.

He did not go back to CBS. It has often been said that the American Broadcasting Company offered him more money, but this would scarcely be a consideration with Elmer Davis. It is more likely that he believed he would feel freer in the new post. In Columbia, there was a rule that news commentators must always be wholly "objective" in their news reporting—an adjective which Davis hated and which he always insisted did not mean what it said. To him, there must be a kind of slant in absolute objectivity—it inevitably omitted an element of depth which kept it from telling the whole, three-dimensional truth. Now none of Davis's broadcasts was ever wholly objective in the sense

253

that there was no human appraisal of events; yet he tried to be fair in giving the opinions on both sides and was usually successful except in the cases where his own vigorous emotions were involved. He could not tolerate injustice and he said so in sharp terms; nor could he allow a lie to go on propagating if any word of his could castrate it. Nor could he allow the highly slanted diatribes of such commentators as Fulton Lewis, Jr., to go unchallenged.

In the first postwar session of Congress, there was a rash of investigations: of Pearl Harbor, of communism at home—though we were still officially friendly with Russia—and of the constant conflict in China between the Communists and Chiang Kai-shek's Kuomintang. Now that the war was over, the isolationists came trooping back and tried to show that the war had been unnecessary and that President Roosevelt had brought the United States into it in order to divert public attention from his own subversive behavior.

In his first ABC broadcast on December 2, Davis referred to the many legislative proposals President Truman had laid before Congress:

> Maybe [he said] they ought to be passed, maybe they should be beaten; but whichever way a man votes on them he might make some enemies. It's a good deal easier to put them off while you conduct investigations—especially if you're investigating such a juicy subject as communism in the State Department. If your alleged Communist sympathizers are also accused of simultaneously supporting British imperialism that makes it all the juicier.

This was a charge, he said, made by the Ambassador to China, Pat Hurley, that State Department officials supported both communism and British, French and Dutch colonial imperialism—a symptom of the postwar chaotic thinking. Commenting on the Pearl Harbor investigation, Davis cited certain Republicans as

254

"trying to prove that a peaceful Japan had been pushed into war by an American ultimatum." A week later, he told of General Marshall's appearance before the Pearl Harbor investigating committee.

Two things stood out in General Marshall's testimony this last week. The first was the poise and self-possession of the man who had raised, trained, equipped and commanded in victory the greatest army in American history; who was not afraid to admit that he . . . could not remember every detail of what had happened in his six years' service as chief of staff.

In mid-December, Charles Lindbergh, hero of the isolationists, came back into the news, after several years of silence, with a statement condemning the Nuremberg trials.

If Lindbergh is shocked [commented Davis] not by the crimes but by the trials, maybe he hasn't been reading the papers lately. Back in June, 'forty-one, his explanation of the war was very simple; England and France had beguiled Poland into a futile war, and when Germany turned east they attacked her in the west. It would all have been better, he thought, in those days, if they had done a little more negotiating with Hitler. More negotiations like Munich. . . .
Again and again, in nineteen forty-one, he insisted that we could not win a war. In May, he knew—he said he knew—that England couldn't win even with our help. In June he said you could never base enough air squadrons in the British isles to match the German air force. An invasion of Europe, he said, would mean the loss of millions of American lives—actually our total killed on all fronts in the whole war was little more than a quarter of a million; and if we could win at all he said it might be in ten or twenty or thirty years. Finally in October 'forty-one he said that that might be his

255

last speech because maybe the administration was about to abolish free speech, and he suggested that the administration might not permit Congressional elections to be held in forty-two. There is the record—part of the record. All of us who talked about public affairs in those days made mistakes in our estimate of what was coming, but Lindbergh's mistakes all fell into a pattern.

Two days before Christmas, Davis attacked that portion of the press which had come to be known as the Patterson-McCormick Axis.

The isolationist inquiry [into Pearl Harbor] proposed to prove that President Roosevelt not only was responsible for the war, but left the fleet at Pearl Harbor so as to tempt the Japs to commit the overt act that would make the American people willing to fight. It is interesting to note that this line of argument was spearheaded by the two newspapers—the Chicago *Tribune* and the Washington *Times-Herald*—which three days before Pearl Harbor published to the world the complete plans by which our Army and Navy proposed to fight. The men who published that did not know, of course, that Japanese carriers were even then drawing near Oahu; but they were; and there was our plan exposed to the enemy.

In his review at the end of December of the year 1945 which he said was perhaps the greatest in human history, he paid tribute to the President whom in twelve years he had come to believe in and support:

A truly great man died this year, wearing himself out in winning the war and trying to win the peace. The best proof of Franklin D. Roosevelt's stature is the continuing venomous endeavor of his enemies to smear his memory. Like all statesmen, he met with honest opposition on principle; but beyond that he was hated more viciously than any other of our Presidents except Thomas Jefferson. Both men were hated for various reasons; but basically they were hated because they tried to give the average man a break. They both diminished the power of the rich. Men like them will always be hated—and loved—so long as private property carries private power with it.

There was something new this year, he said in the same broadcast, in world history: America had emerged as the first of military powers.

Our primacy was a thing that some foreigners feared, but it was not a thing that many Americans wanted; it was forced on us in self-defense; and no sooner had the war been won than we began throwing it away. If international affairs should take a bad turn, it might prove that the biggest news of the past four months had been the headlong demobilization of the American army and navy, a demobilization amounting to disintegration. It was natural enough; with the war won, our soldiers and sailors wanted to come home; we their families wanted to have them home . . . but from the viewpoint of national interest it is impossible to feel too comfortable about this sudden melting away of our armed forces, in a world where we cannot yet be too sure that the moral influence of a nation is effective without force to back it.

2

In the three years of his hibernation, while the Russians fought to save their homeland, the Bear that Walks Like a Man seemed to have slept. Many of us thought, perhaps, that he was dead; in our admiration of the last-ditch stand at Stalingrad and of the offensive that followed, forcing the Germans back to Germany, we even forgot about him. A reborn Russia, chastened by suffering, purged through its ordeal by fire of its old evil, must emerge from our alliance against Hitler. This seemed to be indicated by the greetings of Russian and American soldiers when they met on the Elbe; by Stalin's amicable speeches and by the friendliness of "Uncle Joe" (as Truman called him) in the first postwar conferences. Those who shook their heads were thought to be only the old die-hard "red baiters," the incorrigible anti-Soviets, blinded by prejudice against seeing the change in communism, black pessimists in this dawn of a new era. Such, at least, were the views of those wishful thinkers who are always vocal in the American crises and who, because they were wishful, because they were vocal, and because they espoused the hope of "Soviet-American friendship," were headed for trouble.

Winston Churchill was one of the first alert watchers who saw the Bear walk out of his cave and recognized him for the same old Bear. Churchill was visiting us when, in March, 1946, he first revealed this. He was traveling through the country, receiving honorary degrees at American educational institutions, and it was at one of these—Westminster College in Fulton, Missouri—that he warned the wishful thinkers in one of the most significant addresses of his career.

We welcome Russia [said Churchill] to her rightful place among the leading nations of the world. We welcome her flag upon the seas. Above all we welcome, or should welcome, constant and growing contacts between the Russian people and our own peoples on both sides of the Atlantic.

It is my duty, however, and I am sure you would not want me not to state the facts as I see them to you, it is my duty to place before you certain facts about the present position in Europe.

From Stettin in the Baltic to Trieste in the Adriatic an iron curtain has descended across the Continent. Behind that line lie all the capitals of the ancient states of central and

258

eastern Europe, Warsaw, Berlin, Prague, Vienna, Budapest, Belgrade, Bucharest and Sofia, all these famous cities and the populations around them lie in what I might call the Soviet sphere, and all are subject, in one form or another, not only to Soviet influence but to a very high and in some cases increasing measure of control from Moscow. . . .

The Communist parties which were very small in all these eastern states of Europe, have been raised to pre-eminence and power far beyond their numbers and are seeking everywhere to obtain totalitarian control.

Police governments are prevailing in nearly every case. . . .

However, in a great number of countries, far from the Russian frontiers and throughout the world, Communist fifth columns are established and work in absolute obedience to directions they receive from the Communist centre. Except in the British Commonwealth and in the United States, where communism is in its infancy, the Communist parties or fifth columns constitute a growing peril to Christian civilization. These are sombre facts for anyone to have to recite on the morrow of a victory gained by so much splendid comradeship in arms and in the cause of freedom and democracy, but we should be most unwise not to face them squarely while time remains. . . .

As the address gained publicity, "Iron Curtain" became part of the language. But the words which accelerated the hysteria that would one day threaten our democracy were those about the "fifth columns" outside Russia. The more ignorant or crackpot leaders of what they supposed to be an anti-Communist movement, discounted Churchill's exceptions of Britain and the United States; how, indeed, they said, could he speak of communism being in its infancy in the Commonwealth after the exposure of the Canadian spy-ring a month before he spoke? And, obviously, he could not know of the situation here—as the crackpots knew it—where there was an American Communist under every American bed fully equipped with the means of overthrowing the government of the United States.

We know now that the prime mover in the ensuing wave of terror which lasted well into the 1950's was the isolationist group that was holding post-mortems on our entrance into the war. Being isolationist, they had no interest in going outside America to defeat the Communist menace; no understanding of the evil that was deep rooted in Russia except as it might manifest itself in the behavior of Americans. They did their best, indeed, to prevent any such understanding by persecuting teachers who taught Soviet history in the schools and colleges. The enemy, they believed, was not in Russia but here in America; the war, therefore, that they were fomenting was not foreign war but civil war.

Already, in 1946, Elmer Davis was fully aware of the embryonic existence of this movement and of its portents for the future. In all the land there was no more vigorous anti-Communist than he. Again and again, he had written and spoken against both the theory and the practice of communism. He knew what it was. He had studied its origins and its causes, not its symptoms. He knew that the disease could not be cured by trying to clear away its rash with violent skin treatments. He knew, too, that infection could best be resisted by maintaining a healthy body and that the body of the Republic would be weakened by panic.

All this was maturing in Davis's mind as he watched the investigations in the Congress; the beginnings of the suspicions that would come to hang like millstones round the necks of such persons as his former employee, Owen Lattimore, and the haloes that were beginning to glow round the heads of reformed and breast-beating ex-Communists. At the same time he was painfully aware of the sincerity with which otherwise sane and decent American men and women were becoming disciples of the agitators.

Through the spring and summer of 1946, Davis, in his broadcasts, talked so much about the Russians that a listener wrote and said she wished he would change the subject. Another berated him for scolding the Communists.

September 2 was the first anniversary of the Japanese surrender, and that night Davis said:

> There is no better measure of the deterioration of the world's hopes than a comparison of MacArthur's eloquent speech at the surrender ceremonies with his anniversary statement. . . . "Today," he said a year ago, "freedom is on the offensive, democracy on the march." But this morning he says over all things and all men hangs the dread uncertainty arising from impinging ideologies—that is to say, democracy and communism.

### 3

In much of 1946, American attention had been held by the struggle in China. The public had been greatly confused not only by the sequence of happenings in a land which, relieved of Japanese oppression, should have blossomed into freedom and prosperity. It was even more confused by the vague experimental Far Eastern policy of the American State Department. The combination gave ammunition to the promoters of the American anti-Communist panic who, somehow, always found an American responsible for most of the ills of the postwar world and led to reckless accusations of "treason" against some of our most patriotic statesmen.

General George C. Marshall had gone to China as the President's personal representative late in 1945, and he had gone with high hopes. A unified China was the American aim; it was thought feasible to heal the split between Communist and Nationalist factions and establish a coalition which could work efficiently in the evacuation of the Japanese from Chinese territory and the restoration of Manchuria to Chinese control. To assist in these operations American marines were sent to North China and very large sums of money and quantities of supplies of all kinds were furnished to Chiang Kai-shek.

Unfortunately, little was known in the State Department about the Chinese background. The gulf between rich and poor was enormous. The corruption among the Nationalists was deeper rooted than any but the most knowledgeable Americans could understand. The Nationalist government was a dictatorship of absolute proportions and the hope of a new constitution with a democratic regime established upon it—such as General Mac-Arthur was promoting in Japan—was one of the rose-colored postwar dreams that were so common in the first sunrise of victory.

Yet Marshall was encouraged in his first meetings with both Nationalists and Communists. He found liberals as well as radicals in the Communist group; men who seemed to want unity and even democracy. He believed that if he could get the liberal, moderate elements of both sides together he could accomplish his mission—especially as he sensed a strong desire on both sides for the coalition. Early in the negotiations there was agreement— *provided* certain conditions were met.

All summer, the negotiations dragged on: the parties would come again and again to a point of compromise—then split apart over some issue. Meanwhile fighting was going on between the forces of the Communists and those of Chiang Kai-shek—the Kuomintang—and, in Manchuria, there was much bloodshed. In September, there was a last agreement followed by a final split and, at the moment of suspense, an attempt at an explanation was given by Elmer Davis which, though some of it is debatable in the light of subsequent developments, showed that he had a better idea than most Americans of the background of events.

Both sides have agreed [he told in a broadcast] to General Marshall's proposal of a five-man committee—two from the Kuomintang, two Communists, and the American ambassa-

262

dor [Leighton Stuart] as chairman—to carry out the creation of the coalition government that they all agreed on months ago; but there are strings to the Communist acceptance. They want Chiang Kai-shek to halt his armies first; and there are no signs that he is going to do that so long as they keep rolling forward.

It may seem illogical that we keep on trying to promote a coalition between the Kuomintang and the Communists in China, when we oppose the spread of communism in Japan. But there is a perfectly good reason for the difference. In the first place, the Chinese Communists are there, the effective rulers of many millions of people; the only way to get peace in China, which is our great objective in our own interest as well as in that of the Chinese, is to get the two factions together. Furthermore, the Chinese Communists get their popular support only from the desperation of the people, a desperation which the Kuomintang in recent years has done little to satisfy; it is support not for communism but for somebody who promises to do something—and does it—for the underdog. The Kuomintang could get that support—*if* the faction now in control would consent to give up the gravy, and earn its keep by giving decent government to the mass of the Chinese people.

But as Davis spoke, it was already too late. The extremists on both sides had got control and by December, 1946, all hope of coalition was ended. Chiang Kai-shek was determined to pursue civil war against the Communists and win victory for his Kuomintang by military force. But as General Albert Wedemeyer said, China was being invaded by an idea and the only way to combat the idea was to do so with another idea with stronger appeal. This the Nationalist government was unable, because of its corruption and incompetence, to do; the only recourse, then, that Chiang had was to arms.

263

Marshall saw this and came home. In January, 1947, he admitted the failure of his mission, saying that the first agreements were for

> a liberal and forward-looking charter which then offered China a basis for peace and reconstruction. However, irreconcilable groups within the Kuomintang Party, interested in their own feudal control of China, evidently had no real intention of implementing them.

But to a majority of Americans—or at least what Washington believed to be a majority—Chiang Kai-shek was an undisputed hero who could do no wrong. He was, after all, they said, leading a crusade against communism. Any lack of success in that crusade was due, they said, to the refusal of the United States to give him adequate backing. So, for two years more our government, under pressure of the popular infatuation, continued to send him money and supplies until, in 1949, he had withdrawn to Formosa leaving most of the mainland of China in the hands of the Communists. Then, in 1949, the State Department issued a White Paper stating that, since 1945, three billion dollars' worth of aid had been given the Nationalists and that a large part of this had been squandered by Chiang's regime or allowed to fall into Communist hands. The Nationalist government, the White Paper went on to say, was "so inept, selfish, purblind, and faithless, as to be beyond resurrection."

At the end of 1946, disillusionment was such that it had become fashionable to say that the victorious Allies had destroyed the two strongest bulwarks against communism—Germany and Japan! Such a view was, of course, a product of ignorance and a distortion of values resulting from a superficial study of the sequence of cause and effect. But it was inevitable that in a time like this, values should be awry: we had, after all, gone through some pretty violent mental adjustments since Munich. Now we must go from respect for our Russian ally back to the old hate—

264

and some Americans did so with a kind of relief after the orgy of hate against Germany and Japan. Davis lived to see the new enemy fully replace the old ones.

4

Beginning on January 6, 1947, Davis's time at the microphone was increased. Since his return to radio, he had given his news commentary on Monday and Tuesday evenings from 7:15 to 7:30. Raymond Swing filled in on Wednesdays, Thursdays and Fridays. But now Swing retired from the program to devote his time to writing and lecturing.

In March, President Truman, in a move toward what George Kennan had called the "containment" of Soviet expansion, asked Congress for aid to Greece and Turkey to save them from subjection to the Russian sphere. At the same time, he made a statement of principle, later called the "Truman Doctrine."

I believe [he said] that it must be the policy of the United States to support free peoples who are resisting attempted subjugation by armed minorities or by outside pressure. . . . The free peoples of the world look to us for support in maintaining their freedoms. If we falter in our leadership, we may endanger the peace of the world and we shall surely endanger the welfare of this nation.

Two months later Congress responded by passing a bill granting four hundred million dollars for the purpose and the resulting stabilization of the economics of Greece and Turkey was one of the major achievements of Truman's career.

In June, General Marshall, who had succeeded James Byrnes as Secretary of State, delivered an address at the Harvard commencement which contained by far the most extensive program for European rehabilitation and stabilization that had yet been imagined. It offered American cooperation (which meant financial aid) toward recovery to any European country that should ask for it.

> Our policy [Marshall said] is directed not against any country or doctrine, but against hunger, poverty, desperation and chaos. Its purpose should be the revival of a working economy in the world so as to permit the emergence of political and social conditions in which free institutions can exist. . . . Any government that is willing to assist in the task of recovery will find full cooperation, I am sure, on the part of the United States government.

American isolationists rushed to oppose the Marshall Plan on the old ground that any aid to a foreign nation was simply pouring money down a rat hole, but these objectors were soon embarrassed by finding themselves on the same side as the Russians. The Soviet Union and its satellites, though invited to participate, were antagonistic because the plan competed with their efforts to win friends. But other European powers welcomed the cooperation and Congress launched what it called the European Recovery Program, based on the Marshall Plan, and provided more than five billion dollars for the first year of its operation.

It seemed, then, that the United States was finally assuming the responsibilities that had devolved upon her as the strongest and wealthiest nation. But at home negative forces were at work. With the approach of an election year came the usual search for political issues and the inflation of political ambitions. A center of unrest was Henry Wallace, round whom there gathered a circle of vague dissidents and a good many left-wing agitators who hesitated, however, at the brink of communism. Wallace had lately visited Russia, Siberia and China and had acquired various ideas which seemed to be confused in his mind with the biology of corn and chickens.

Davis had taken issue with Wallace in his broadcasts, accusing him of indiscretions which dangerously embarrassed the State Department and of other obstructionism. The story is told that Wallace became extremely anxious to meet Davis to debate these questions, and made several approaches. A meeting was finally arranged at Davis's favorite Algonquin Hotel and a third person who came as moderator reports that nothing was mentioned but corn and chickens and that Davis became so fascinated by Wallace's truly expert descriptions of breeding methods that he too forgot about politics.

As the year closed, it appeared that the people were tired, at last, of the Democratic party and that there would be a landslide Republican victory in 1948. This, at least, was the opinion of what turned out to be the vocal fringe.

# 18 ]]]]]

## 1

EVERY SORT and condition of men, Bernard DeVoto once wrote to Elmer Davis, were in Davis's audience. DeVoto at the time was driving through the West on one of his extensive and intensive explorations of the country in preparation for one of his celebrated volumes. When he wrote he had just passed through Sangre de Cristo, the Tetons, the Wyoming badlands along the Yellowstone, and in the barrens of North Dakota. "Shoe drummers," he wrote, "gas station attendants, truck drivers, county farm agents—everybody was listening to you, learning from you, applying you."

Seven years later with the war in between and in the hot days of the cold war, a sign painter wrote

I approve your attitude towards those Kremlin gangsters, but it is a sad fact that so many of us who love our country do not write to commentators and our policy makers in Washington, whilst the traitors in our midst make it their business to exert pressure and noise on everyone who criticizes our Kremlin masters.

This letter interspersed, in 1947, among those that called Davis a "pink" and a fellow traveler, gives an indication of the undercurrent of perceptive understanding that ran below the vocal surface. It has since been proved to us more than once that there

268

is an inarticulate majority that thinks contrary to all the loud-speakers—even, sometimes, to the verdicts of pollsters and public-opinion computing machines.

Early in 1948, signs appeared of the quadrennial national madness that marked it as an election year. What was thought to be the maddest of all gestures came in January when Henry Wallace threw his hat into the ring.

All week long [reported *Time* the following week] the rush to stay clear of Henry Wallace gained momentum. In varying degrees of censure and regret, Socialist Norman Thomas, the Liberal Party's chairman Adolf Berle, Jr., the heads of the anti-Communist Americans for Democratic Action got out from under. Most of Big Labor, such leftist publications as Manhattan's *PM* and the *Nation* had already checked out. Last week a newspaper poll in the South showed that even Negro listeners who had loudly applauded Wallace as an itinerant foe of segregation—would not support him as a candidate.

Like it or not (and Wallace did not seem to mind), his only visible means of support seemed to be the Communists and the organizations the Reds controlled.

Davis had already expressed himself about Wallace: he referred to him again in the spring of 1948, recalling the impact one of his indiscreet speeches had had on Russian thinking:

The Russians really don't know much about us, and their system makes it hard for them to find out the facts even when they want to. After Henry Wallace's Madison Square Garden speech in September 'forty-six, attacking the foreign policy of the administration, Molotov told the late Jan Masaryk that there spoke the real voice of America; that this marked the beginning of repudiation of the Truman-Byrnes policy of resistance to Russian demands. In that case

269

Molotov soon found out that he was wrong; but he seems to be still getting the same kind of misinformation that then misled him.

But the foreign news that hit Davis the hardest came in February. His affection for Czechoslovakia and his belief in the democratic potential of that little republic had begun in the first years after the first World War when, under Thomas Masaryk, it got its start as an independent nation. As we have seen, Davis was particularly bitter about the tragedy of Munich because of the British and French betrayal of the Czech people. Now that unhappy country had come into the Soviet sphere. Yet in its first national election after the puppet government had taken over, it was evident, said Davis,

that the spirit of democracy has not been smothered in that country, even though its inhabitants are powerless against the dictatorship. The Communist Premier Gottwald had said beforehand that this election would be the freest in the world; which was very sour comedy to a people which had a really free election two years ago. This time there was only one ticket and the citizens were free to vote for that. They couldn't vote for anybody else but they could cast a blank ballot if they chose and God help them if they did. In most polling places the voting was open; the election officials —all Communists or pro-Communists—could see how a man voted; and if he cast a blank ballot he knew he risked losing his job, and perhaps even more serious reprisals. Yet in spite of that the government admits there were more than seven hundred and seventy-two thousand blank ballots— almost eleven per cent of the total.

The government admits that; almost certainly there were far more than that. Men assigned to counting the votes told American correspondents that in the early returns the blank ballots were running from twenty to thirty per cent, in some

270

cases fifty per cent. Whereupon the inspectors from the Communist Ministry of the Interior told the men who were counting to go home; they would finish the job themselves.

## 2

While the Iron Curtain closed down over the last true democracy in central Europe, the age of suspicion came on apace in the United States. With every move the Soviets made to stifle freedom abroad, the American agencies of distrust bored further into the private lives of American citizens. Especially active in this direction was the isolationist-named Un-American Activities Committee of the House of Representatives whose hearings were beginning to look more and more like trials in a court of law. These hearings and those of various investigating committees in the Congress differed, however, from legal trials in that the safeguards which normally protect a defendant against possible injustice were missing. The issues, however, were subversion—perhaps treason—and therefore many patriotic Americans overlooked these juridical defects.

For Elmer Davis, patriotism did not necessarily exclude justice. The exclusion of justice was one of the things that made a totalitarian state totalitarian and to him it was patriotic to defend the United States against the trend toward dictatorship. Yet, in his broadcasts in this dawn of the age of suspicion he made every effort to be fair—even to this suspicious committee—giving it credit for its occasional useful achievements.

The Un-American Activities Committee [he said in April] will bring in a bill requiring the Communist party to register with the Justice Department as an agency of a foreign government—which, on its record, it clearly is. . . . The Committee would also forbid any member of the party to hold an appointive Federal office, or run for an elective office unless

271

he announced that he was a Communist. There seems to be good reason for all these proposals; they must still pass Congress, but Congress in its present mood would probably pass any law aimed at Communists, even if it required them all to be painted red for purposes of identification.

But then he turned to the case of Dr. Edward U. Condon of the Bureau of Standards saying that that persecution

appears to be one more instance of the kind of tactics Mr. Thomas [chairman of the committee] has employed before. You smear a man in newspaper headlines, with a little direct allegation and a lot of innuendo; you promise him a chance to appear before a committee and at least give his side of the story; and then you give him the runaround. Some of us would like to believe that that sort of thing is an un-American activity.

In this election year, Davis wondered, as all thoughtful people must wonder in these periodic withdrawals of the United States from the rest of the world, what foreigners, especially Russians, must think of us. For it is customary in these years for American politicians to accuse each other, not of venial political offenses but of the darkest crimes. In 1948, it was fashionable for them to hint that an opponent is a Communist—an allegation that had a formidable impact upon the average American who had only the dimmest concept of what a Communist was. No more interchangeable word had been discovered by what Davis called the doublethinkers: its very imprecision gave to many frightened mentalities the occasion for hobgoblin fantasy. Thus when a politician in an election year hinted at the subversion of another politician or bureaucrat he was probing at the most vulnerable spot in the public fancy. Actually, he was often merely manipulating potential votes and once the election was over both accuser

272

and accused—knowing that the intent went no deeper—would forget.

Foreigners, however, were never able to get used to this sort of scrimmage and in election after election, they were astonished by these political methods. In midsummer, 1948, Davis broadcast an analysis of pre-election behavior in the light of efforts to come to an agreement in the Moscow conferences, then in progress. After reviewing some past difficulties, he went on:

But at present the symptoms, for what they are worth, seem to indicate that they are willing to explore the possibility of agreement, though it remains to be seen what kind of agreement—whether it is something the West can accept. And Russian decisions may depend largely on their estimate of both the resolution and the strength of the Western powers. On that point, it might be remarked that if Stalin believes all he hears from Washington these days, he might reasonably believe that the United States is coming apart at the seams and he can go as far as he likes. In the Senate today Mr. [Styles] Bridges of New Hampshire demanded the resignation of Federal Security Administrator Oscar Ewing and said he ought to be sent back where he came from—which happens to be Greensburg, Indiana—or deported to another country. The reason for that is that former Education Commissioner Studebaker, whose office has now been merged in the Security Agency . . . claims that the Agency's information section censored an anti-Communist speech he wanted to make; the agency says it was merely held up for a few days for clearance, that nobody told the commissioner he mustn't say anything, it was only suggested that it might be wiser not to say some things that he went ahead and said anyway. And this was the work of subordinates; Mr. Ewing knew nothing about it.

All this, to anybody with experience in government, is no more than a bureaucratic squabble of a familiar type. But to

Senator Bridges it is a betrayal of something or other which justifies deporting Mr. Ewing either to Greensburg or to Siberia; the fact that Mr. Ewing is vice-chairman of the Democratic National Committee is purely coincidental. Senator Eastland of Mississippi agreed with Senator Bridges about the iniquitousness of Mr. Ewing, but not about the cure; he said you couldn't get the Communists out of the government by electing Dewey because New York is for all practical purposes a Communist state. Now we know that all this means is that Senator Bridges is trying to elect Dewey, that Senator Eastland is trying to elect Thurmond, and that Senators have to kill time in a session which is not going to do anything but still has to drag on through this week. But if Stalin hears about it, and takes it seriously, he might think he's doing pretty well over here with New York State and the Federal Security Agency both under his control.

Davis thought—as did many of his supporters—that much of the ignorant anti-Communist activity in the United States was not only giving the men in the Kremlin an image of American weakness but was even helping Soviet espionage here by focusing on the alleged subversion of the wrong people. On August 5 he said:

The President said this morning that the current spy investigations were a red herring to divert public attention from what Congress ought to do; that they had brought out no information not known to grand juries and the FBI; that they are doing irreparable harm to certain persons, and undermining public confidence in government. That this is their effect is certainly true; but it seems doubtful if their purpose was to divert attention.

Davis's most useful words, however, gave the true figures on subversion within the government: a calm statement of the facts

274

beneath the ballyhoo and a revelation of the terrorists' inflation which must have convinced many listeners that the spy-hounds, red herring or no, were barking up the wrong trail.

Now the problem of loyalty and security is a serious one; but try to put it in perspective. The Loyalty Review Board reported yesterday that the FBI has checked more than two million Federal employees. In five thousand cases—one fourth of one per cent—they ran into derogatory information, true or false, that required full investigation. Twenty-six hundred of these investigations have been completed and only fifty-four people have been fired; though some five hundred others resigned during the investigation, in many cases no doubt for quite different reasons. Any disloyal employees are too many; but five hundred out of two million is a pretty small proportion.

3

As the summer drew toward its close, the pundits and guessers gave specific reasons for their certainty of Dewey's election apart from the one that the people were heartily sick of the Democrats. Even if, they said, there were still a good many normally Democratic votes, the party had been splintered by Wallace and the renegade southern group. The conductors of the "infallible" polls had announced Dewey majorities as a result of exhaustive "sampling" of opinion. Even Davis, whose fingers could be expected to be more firmly on the nation's pulse than those of other prophets, wrote a piece which was published in *Harper's* September number called "President Dewey's Strange Bedfellows." These he named: Joe Martin, Charlie Halleck, Leslie Arends, Harold Knutson, John Taber, Leo Allen, Jesse Wolcott, Ham Adams and Dewey Short. By the ancient machinery of seniority, Short was assured chairmanship of the Armed Services Committee but was "about as fit for that position as I am to replace Joe DiMaggio in center field."

In that article he made an unusual statement, in parentheses, of his own penchant:

(For the record, I have no political affiliation as becomes a voteless resident of Washington; if I still lived in New York I should belong to the Liberal party, to the left of the organization Democrats and to the right of the fellow-traveling Laborites.)

Davis got further assurance of the coming Republican triumph from one of his angry critics in a letter written in the first week of September:

Radical speakers [wrote this correspondent] rail against everyone and everything worth while and decent men uphold the props of the community, but you employ a rather unique style of seeming to talk equitably of all factors, whereas you constantly insert as vicious a procession of digs at the conservative element as ever came to the attention of the writer.

When this Election Day is over and this worthless gang has been thrown out of office in no uncertain terms, I do not believe your current efforts of discrediting the strength of the country are going to awaken very happy thoughts in your own breast.

On November first, Davis said in a broadcast that Dewey's election was practically certain and he spoke of some of the problems Dewey would face. But two days later, when, after an all-night session, following and interpreting the returns, he came on the air for his evening broadcast, he said:

Well, the most amazing election upset in the history of the republic may give Mr. Truman an even more decisive victory

276

than was foreseen this morning. . . . His popular vote so far reported is twenty-one million three hundred thousand—about sixteen hundred thousand ahead of Dewey; and very close to the total for Dewey, Thurmond and Wallace put together.

Davis spoke of the good sportsmanship shown by Dewey in his defeat and added:

A three-time loser deserves sympathy but the man who gets the presidency in times like these deserves some sympathy too, even though he let himself in for it. European problems have grown no better in the past few days, the Chinese problem has become much more acute; and the President will have to worry about them before he starts laying out the domestic programs to be presented to the Congress . . . which meets in January. . . .

In the day after an election that was "about as startling as if Spearfish had beaten Notre Dame by seven touchdowns—this victory of David over Goliath"—Davis came to the conclusion that there was somehow a logical explanation. Yet:

Any of us who analyze news on the radio or in the papers must hesitate to try to offer any explanation to a public which remembers too well the lucid and convincing explanations we all offered day before yesterday why Dewey had it in the bag—we have all beaten our breasts and heaped ashes on our heads since then but we probably still all look pretty foolish and had better not stick our necks out again. Our only consolation is that everybody else was mistaken too; foreign diplomats and the able correspondents of the foreign press in this country . . . and the United Press reports from London that diplomats are remarking with some

amusement that one of the most conspicuously wrong was
Stalin. In his attack on western policies last week he noted
that Winston Churhcill had been turned out of office by his
own people and predicted that the same fate would befall
the others whom he had called warmongers.

Through the summer and fall of 1948, Davis had not, however,
been preocupied with political guessing to the exclusion of other
national and international topics. He had talked about housing
bills, defecting Russian schoolteachers, the Taft-Hartley Act, the
latest French crisis, the Russian air maneuvers, the question
whether the Soviets had the atomic bomb, the Berlin airlift,
Eisenhower's memoirs and the early testimony in the Hiss-
Chambers case. About this last, he said on December 9:

Well, the point remains that somebody gave Chambers some
secret documents. From testimony at the hearing last night
it appears that the documents found in the famous pumpkin
never got to Russia at all; for ten years Chambers kept
them hidden out. There is no evidence that any member of
the [Un-American Activities] committee or of its staff knew
of their existence till last week; but it would be interesting
to know how many people besides Chambers did know about
them, and how they happened to turn up just at this
time. . . . This time, I repeat, the committee has got hold of
something of real importance; and at a time when there is
nothing particular going on which would seem to require the
dragging of a red herring across the trail. Last summer's
hearing, however intended, had the effect of a red herring
distracting attention from the special session of Congress;
though it turned out that it wasn't red enough.

On the fifteenth, he reported that the grand jury had indicted
Hiss

278

and it represents a distinct triumph for the Un-American Activities Committee, which had been afraid the grand jury would indict Chambers and not Hiss.

4

In this curious year when the divergence between the loud voices that were heard in the land and the silent voice of the people in the polling places, Davis got some bouquets along with the brickbats and there were some diversions from current events in the political realm. A letter in October from Harold Ickes said

> I did not happen to hear you the evening that you said something to the effect that my speeches were the only ones worth listening to in this campaign. But several people have told me about it and, if I could, I would kiss you on both cheeks. . . .
>
> You should know that my two youngsters, aged nine and seven and one-half respectively, quote you and speak your name frequently. I wish that I could say that this is because they are intellectuals of a high order, interested in public affairs, but I honestly cannot. They are addicts to "The Lone Ranger" and you precede him. In order not to miss him they tune in on you but I really think that is going to be a case of unconscious assimilation and I am looking forward to the day when they will have acquired the habit of listening to you after they have graduated from "The Lone Ranger."

In October, the *Saturday Review of Literature* published one of Davis's finest critical pieces in an essay-review of Robert Sherwood's *Roosevelt and Hopkins*. Here was final proof, if any were needed, that a hangover of rancor from the old OWI conflict between Davis and Sherwood could not blur Davis's literary

279

judgment. The piece was more than a review—it seemed like part of the book itself—a new contribution to the story of the times that Sherwood was writing about.

> For writing such a dual biography [Davis reported] Sherwood is admirably equipped. He was an unofficial member of the White House staff; he writes a book that is a pleasure to read, and not the least of his merits is that being a playwright, professionally concerned with exploring the complexities of character, he knows enough about it to know how much he does not know. . . . It is a rare biographer who faithfully chronicles not only the errors of his subject, but his own . . .
>
> This may be as near an approach as we shall ever get to a summary of the way things looked from the White House in those days. Sherwood makes no such claim; he deliberately refrained from consulting Mrs. Roosevelt . . . but unless she . . . some day tells us how it seemed to her, there is likely to be no report on better authority than this. It is also the best contribution so far to the history of the war— better even than the Stimson memoirs, since it incorporates a multitude of immensely valuable documents.

Davis went on out of his own thinking:

> It is probably true that as Wallace Carroll, Mr. Sherwood's late colleague and mine, has written in "Persuade or Perish," we fought the war too much for merely military victory with insufficient emphasis on political objectives. The chief reason for that in my judgment was that the country was by no means united on political objectives; by vigorous exercise of his leadership Roosevelt might have united it but he was too busy winning a war. He underestimated the duplicity of the Russians but it is hard to see how else he could have behaved at the time; the people who

280

now say that before we had finished licking the Germans and Japanese we ought to have taken on the Russians too would have been the first to denounce him for such criminal folly if he had done it. . . .

Well [he concluded] it is perhaps a Constitutional weakness that so much depends on one man; but when Congress is led by the Tabers, the Knutsons, the Martins, the Hallecks, what can you do but try to find a President endowed with exceptional qualities?

On New Year's Day, 1949, Davis had some fun about television—a medium he never got used to. Although he often said he had mike-fright in the radio studio, it is probable that television was the only thing that really scared him. This gay conclusion to the New Year's broadcast—probably a welcome diversion to those who had celebrated too late the night before— was also a kind of addendum to his talk of November 3.

During the early hours of election night [he said] the question that shook the nation from coast to coast—to judge from the phone calls that came into the ABC news room—was not who was going to spend the next four years in the White House. Everybody knew that Dewey had that in the bag. The issue that had roused the people's passion was whether or not Winchell should take off his hat. This was a question that would never have arisen in the old days of radio—a simple industry, but a nice one, in its time. Listeners would never have known whether Winchell had his hat on or not, or even his shoes. But television, which has changed so many things, has changed that too.

Winchell sat there with his hat pulled down over his eyes, and soon the switchboard was swamped with calls demanding that he take it off. Eventually he yielded to popular demand and took it off—but the switchboard stayed swamped, this time with demands that he put it back on. The

281

Klieg lights of television, glancing off his dome, made such a dazzle in the news room that televiewers complained they couldn't see the motions George Gallup was making with his fingers, to ward off the evil eye. So eventually there was a compromise; when Winchell's hat was on Pearson's was off, when Pearson's was on Winchell's was off, and everybody was satisfied. A fine example of bipartisan cooperation.

But by the time the question of Winchell's hat was settled and we had time to notice what was going on, it turned out that something very strange was going on; Truman was ahead. New York was going to Dewey as expected—thanks to Henry Wallace, who drained off half a million anti-Dewey votes; but Ohio, and Illinois, and Iowa, were going to Truman; and so was most of the Solid South in spite of Thurmond.

In January, 1949, President Truman settled down in the White House for four more years, glad no doubt, in spite of the tough problems he knew he must face, that he had a Congress that would probably back him in most of his attempted solutions. He was probably unaware that one problem would be presented by a Senator on the minority side of the aisle who, two years before, had defeated young Robert La Follette in a Wisconsin primary and, Wisconsin being a Republican state, had won his Senate seat easily from his Democratic opponent.

In two years, he had not especially distinguished himself. Several of his colleagues regarded him as a crackpot; those who were able to judge knew him as a vulgarian. But in 1948, it could hardly be predicted that in two years more this insignificant person would acquire a dictator's power and profoundly scare not only most of the Senate but a large part of the American people as well.

Even to Elmer Davis, the name, in 1948, of Joseph R. McCarthy meant little enough.

282

# 19 ]]]]]]

## 1

FROM THE LAST MONTHS of 1948 through the spring
and summer of 1949, the agencies of government which
were supposed to be concerned with intelligence were too
busy trying to expose American Communists to pay much attention to Russian ones or to those of Russia's more accessible
satellites. Most of the nation's press—though some papers were
critical of the recklessness of Congressional investigations—
devoted far more space and the blackest headlines to what Davis
called the "flamboyant trimmings" and "razzle-dazzle" of the
espionage case which involved Alger Hiss. It was, to be sure, an
opportunity for dramatic presentation and the star witness,
Whittaker Chambers, contributed plenty of color with his own
confessions as a reformed spy and the hollow pumpkin on his
lonely farm in which was found the startling evidence that so
elated the Un-American Activities Committee.

The evidence—papers and microfilms—had been produced by
Chambers because Hiss had sued him for slander.

What was in them? [asked Davis]—we don't know; the
committee yesterday consulted former Under Secretary of
State Sumner Welles—presumably because no present high
official of the State Department was in it ten or eleven years
ago—as to whether it was advisable to publish them. What
*he* said we don't know directly; but Congressman Nixon
[of the committee] said this afternoon that *he* would never

283

vote to publish the documents and implied that to publish some of them might impair the national interest, though he hinted also that the administration was trying to cover up some other things that would only embarrass the administration. Mr. Nixon of course is a Republican; there is no visible evidence of covering up, but the fact remains that the Un-American Activities Committee was alert enough to get hold of this material, and that the Department of Justice was not. . . .

Mr. Nixon's implication that the administration is covering mistakes of its members hardly stands up for none of the men who then directed our foreign policy are still in the government. But it is always possible that some of this material may bear directly or indirectly on current diplomatic disputes, or might embarrass friendly foreign governments. At any rate the crime was committed ten or eleven years ago; but it is important to find out who did it and how, and to make sure that State Department procedures have been tightened up so that it can't happen again.

What crime was it? Congressman John Rankin who thinks these documents were responsible for the Stalin-Hitler treaty, Pearl Harbor, and probably Noah's flood says the crime was treason. Technically it was not; treason can be committed in time of peace only by levying war on the United States; most of us will feel that the impulse was treasonable but it was not treason under the law. . . . The Justice Department advises me that the crime was a violation of sections . . . of the criminal code dealing with the willful and unlawful destruction, concealment or removal of public documents; for which the penalty may be three years in jail, or a fine.

The question, Davis added, of whether or not "the criminal might escape under the statute of limitations" ought not to "obscure the fact that this time the committee seems to have done a useful job."

284

The broadcast is an especially pointed example of Davis's skill in putting a matter on which public thinking was at fever pitch in calm perspective. His repetition of the phrase "ten or eleven years" was calculated to quiet the sudden anxieties roused by the headlines that the pumpkin papers had brought new secrets into hostile areas. His discounting of the sensational aspects of the revelations—played up by the majority of the newspapers—was likely to suggest to his listeners that they would do well to sleep on the facts rather than to spend the night looking under the bed for a spy. His reference to Rankin brought in the comic relief at an appropriate point.

An effect of the investigations and their tabloid publicity that deeply disturbed him, however, and kept him disturbed as long as he lived, was the suspicion of *guilt by association* they aroused. This, he believed, was not only a challenge to the age-old philosophy of jurisprudence; it was the bodily adoption in America of a familiar Soviet police practice. By creating community distrust of individuals, it not only brought ruin to innocent citizens but it spread the sort of fear that was prevalent in Russian cities where families waited in terror for the knock on the door of the secret police agent.

The tragic death of Lawrence Duggan [Davis said in a broadcast directly following the tragedy], former State Department official who either fell or jumped from his office window in New York, raises new questions about the Un-American Activities Committee. Who among its favored witnesses is to be believed when their testimony is in conflict? Acting Chairman Mundt of the committee, on hearing of Duggan's death last night [December 20, 1948], said that the committee had been told that Whittaker Chambers had named him as one of the State Department people who had handed him secret papers. Today Chambers said he never said it. The committee's information had come from Isaac Don Levine, editor of an extremely conservative magazine

285

and a mysterious figure in the background of this investigation; he couldn't be found today to comment on Chambers's denial and the committee isn't going to try to clear matters up; Mr. Mundt says the Duggan case is a closed book. So the committee closed the book on Harry White, whose heart gave out after he had defended himself in a long and exhausting examination; and whose loyalty was never questioned by the people who knew him best. That is true of Larry Duggan too; Sumner Welles, under whom he served as chief of the bureau of Latin-American affairs, called him one of the most brilliant, most devoted and most patriotic public servants he had ever known. That was the general opinion. Yet the FBI had talked to him ten days ago—what about, they wouldn't say; presumably on some information either from Chambers or from Levine. Mr. Levine is a violent anti-Communist; so is Mr. Chambers, now. Yet no Communist could ask for anything better than the atmosphere of general distrust and suspicion they have created. . . .

Meanwhile the Un-American Activities Committee, which has been properly critical of the lax security that once prevailed in the State Department, might look to its own security a little more carefully. Four of the stolen documents are still withheld, on the ground that their publication might damage the national interest. Yet the contents of the most important of these documents were leaked to certain newspapers—newspapers which in the late war seemed more hostile to the government of the United States than to our enemies. The committee is quite right in calling for more security; they might begin at home.

2

Yet with all his conviction of the violation of American principles of justice, Davis never became preoccupied with it to the point of neglecting other news or its interpretation. Nor did he confine his indignation to these curious performances on the Hill.

I seldom deal [he said in January, 1949] with crime news or trials. But there was a trial today in Lyons, Georgia, which is of more than local importance in view of its probable effect on Federal legislation. Two white men were charged with murder, as alleged participants in a masked mob which had lynched a Negro. One of them was acquitted in twenty minutes, the charge against the other was dismissed. Witnesses swore to an alibi for the accused; another witness said she had been told by another person—who was not called—that the murdered man had shot first. And two jurors stepped out of the box to appear as character witnesses for the defendant, and to say they wouldn't believe the victim's widow, the complaining witness, on oath. This appears to be perfectly correct under Georgia law, as it was for the defendant to deny the charges without being either sworn or cross-examined. I am one of the people who believe that a Federal anti-lynching law is unsound policy; but I must note that the citizens of Lyons, Georgia, have probably made more propaganda for it in one day, than the National Association for the Advancement of Colored People could make in a year.

To many small-minded persons in the radio audience which listened nightly with mixed feelings to Elmer Davis's broadcasts there was something suspicious in what they called his inconsistency. There was always a considerable sprinkling in his huge "fan mail" of letters which showed that their writers were congenitally unable to see beneath the superficial paradoxes to the basic issues—to the truths he saw so clearly. A case of this "inconsistency" occurred in Danbury, Connecticut, where a prominent organization was scared out of keeping an appointment which most of its members doubtless wanted it to keep. Here is Davis's appraisal, in mid-February, 1949, of the incident.

This morning's papers carry the news that the Lions Club of Danbury, Connecticut, which had invited Henry Wallace to speak at one of its luncheon meetings, had canceled the appointment on account of the protests of the six Catholic priests of that city, who said that Mr. Wallace would have a bad influence on the thinking of thousands of school children. Now listeners to these broadcasts know that I yield to none in my conviction that Henry Wallace is wrong. But wrong or not, he has just as much right to express his opinions as I have or anybody else. Free speech means free speech for everybody, not merely for those whom you happen to approve personally. It may be said that Mr. Wallace has no right to be heard by the Lions Club of Danbury if they don't want to hear him, and that is true; but evidently they did want to hear him till the heat was turned on. If the school children of Danbury have been so poorly instructed by the home, the school and the church that Mr. Wallace is likely to corrupt them, the only logical thing would be to forbid anybody to talk to the school children of Danbury till they are grown up and able to judge for themselves. It is poor business for the representatives of a church which has stood up, and properly stood up, for free speech in Hungary to put on the pressure to suppress free speech in Connecticut. If the principle is a good one, as most Americans believe, it is good here as well as there.

Then, on Washington's birthday, he looked again overseas to the unhappy life his Czech friends were living behind the Iron Curtain.

This is a double anniversary, one good and one bad. Washington's birthday had its customary celebration; and as

288

usual every speaker said in substance, If Washington were
living now he would agree with me. But if this is the birthday of the man who won us our liberty, it is also the
anniversary of the day the Czechoslovaks lost their liberty,
just a year ago. Their Communist government celebrated the
day by various measures which look as if it suspects that
many citizens would like to get their liberty back. Armed
Communists patrol the streets of Prague, police check up on
everybody in the city limits, and parliament passes a bill
permitting the dismissal of army officers who, as they put it,
fail to comprehend the principles of the people's democracy.
What they mean, of course, is officers who comprehend them
well enough, but don't like them.

## 3

In Europe the cold war was waged by the Soviets by an
ingenious technique of turning on the heat to a point at which
it looked as if the conflict would soon become a hot war and then
allowing it to lapse back into its normal cold state. In 1948 they
focused on Berlin, and, taking advantage of the anomalous conditions in that split city, brought about by Allied miscalculations
at the Yalta conference, tried to force the Allied occupation
troops to withdraw from their legal zones. The device they
adopted was a blockade of the supply routes to western Berlin
which would starve the inhabitants of the Allied zones. As
Berlin lay deep inside the Russian zone, this was easy enough.

So many years have elapsed since the failure of this experiment that the events in them have largely obscured our memory
of the heroic operation that answered the Soviet attempt. Even
at the time, a true appraisal of the performance was limited by
the spectacular efforts of Congressional committees to put Hiss
and others in jail. Yet in the whole of American history there is
no bolder piece of strategy than the Berlin airlift that broke the

Russian blockade. For nearly a year, a continuous flight of cargo planes over the Soviet zone brought supplies into the beleaguered sector of the city. Most of the planes were American. From July, 1948, to May, 1949, this great chapter of history was written by daring pilots who never knew when the Russians might decide to end this crusade against the starvation of our friends by shooting down their aircraft.

Through the year, Davis was never diverted even by the sensational happenings at home from this remarkable performance not only by the airmen but by the officers who directed the operation and by those who managed the supply organization. On May 11 he was able to report that the blockade had been lifted.

Through the year, the North Atlantic Treaty, signed in April, 1949, by twelve non-Communist nations which agreed to help one another's defense against armed attack was implemented by NATO, the treaty organization. The efforts to build the military strength of these peoples against the threat of Soviet aggression; NATO's internal conflict and Russia's hostility to it provided Davis with material remote from the work of isolationist committees.

But the event that will mark 1949 as the critical year of the cold war was announced by President Truman on the twenty-third of September. An explosion had been detected which showed, the President said, that the Russians shared with us the possession of the supposed "secret" of the atomic bomb.

The atomic story [said Davis that evening], overshadows all the rest of today's news which didn't amount to much anyway but while it is extremely important, it is not immediately so important, and certainly not immediately so dangerous, as might be supposed. . . .

Now this raises several questions. Are we sure of it? Is it a real bomb or an experiment that went wrong? How did we find out? And so what? Well, in the first place I am told by all informed government officials that we *are* absolutely

290

sure that there was an atomic explosion; and it seems to be the general view that it was the test of a bomb, and not an accidental explosion in a laboratory—though this latter is not beyond possibility.

Davis's broadcast reflected the mood of the government. The President's statement said that possession of the bomb outside the United States had been inevitable. Secretary of Defense Johnson warned reporters against "playing up" the news and most papers not in the Hearst empire heeded the warning. The scientists explained that there had really been no "secret" anyway, that the Smyth Report issued soon after the Hiroshima and Nagasaki explosions had told the atom story in a good deal of detail, that the potential of nuclear energy had been generally known for at least a decade, that the Germans at war's end were on the brink of exploiting it and had certainly carried their knowledge into Russia since the war.

The effect on the people, nevertheless, was profound. It increased as more thoughtful Americans induced reflection in those who, in their concentration on communism, had forgotten about Russia. Suddenly, Russia thrust itself into the foreground of their thought. It was not the Russia that they had believed: populated by dirty, ignorant, unlettered folk. It was a Russia that, overnight, had reached their own level—or nearly so—in understanding of science, in skill of engineering, in large industrial installation.

The illusion from which we were abruptly wakened was not surprising. To have thought of Russians as highly educated persons, men and women skilled and trained in the activities that we believed were uniquely ours, would have been "un-American." To have investigated Russian methods, Russian schools, Russian industrialization, was regarded as subversive. Any teaching of Russian history, government, philosophy or economics made the teacher suspect. To be one hundred per cent American one must

291

regard the citizens of the Soviet Union—if one regarded them at all—as dirty, ignorant, unlettered folk.

The revelation brought a curious mood in some quarters. The discovery of a scholarly trend in Russia made intellectual activity in America unfashionable. The word "egghead" came into the language as a designation of contempt; to be a member of the "intelligentsia" was almost synonymous with membership in the Party. Elmer Davis gave a striking illustration of this out of his own experience.

> A girl who had been a Wave during the war wanted to get back into the Navy as a civilian employee; she gave me as a reference, and a security officer of Naval Intelligence came around to check up on her. I gave her a glowing recommendation, as I conscientiously could; I spoke highly not only of her loyalty but of her intelligence— At which he frowned. "These intelligent people," he said, "are very likely to be attracted to communism."

Notwithstanding this occasional attitude the great body of thinking Americans—and these were far more numerous than the vocal minority would have had us believe—began to inquire seriously into the Soviet potential and became, eventually, so impressed with what they found, that the specter of the American fifth column came to fade out of focus. This awareness, the full extent of which Elmer Davis did not live to see, that the Soviet Union was a real competitor, not only in military strength but in education, in scientific research and in industrial achievement was one of the factors that brought a swing away from isolationism and the witch hunt at home. But we were a long way from that change in 1949 and in the early fifties.

For a short time after the news that Russia had the bomb, the Congressional investigators found some difficulty in getting their headlines on the front page. With the Hiss trial in October, however, and the noisy trial of the eleven Communists in New York

292

before the unhappy Judge Medina, these came back. And, in 1950, the rising star of Joe McCarthy provided a continuing sequence of news sensations.

## 4

"Subversion: The Old Story" was the title of a review by Davis in the *Saturday Review*, April 1, 1950. The book was Nathaniel Weyl's *Treason: the Story of Disloyalty and Betrayal in American History*. Like most of Davis's reviews it was, in addition to an account and appraisal of the volume, a vehicle for some of his own views. The subject was, of course, at the top of his mind and here as, so often, when current American behavior seemed to threaten the death of the Republic, he went back into history and found other even more reprehensible conduct that we had ultimately risen above.

The record shows [he wrote] that in every crisis of our history the United States has been simply sodden with treason—or with sedition and disloyalty which escaped being treason only because of the narrowness of the Constitutional definition. Yet the Republic has survived.

He then recalled to those many Americans who were using the word in 1950 with little understanding of its technical significance, the definition by the Founding Fathers:

Treason against the United States shall consist only in levying war against them, or in adhering to their enemies, giving them aid and comfort. No person shall be convicted of treason unless on the testimony of two witnesses to the same overt act, or on confession in open court.

No one had ever been put to death for treason in the United States though

293

Robert Best and Douglas Chandler, broadcasting from Germany in an attempt to undermine the morale of their fellow citizens in the interest of the enemy, got life imprisonment and certainly deserved it. Other men throughout the war were writing in American newspapers things not much less virulent than what Best and Chandler were saying but they were in the clear. They often gave aid and comfort to the enemy but they did not adhere to him. What made Best and Chandler traitors was that Goebbels paid them to say it. The distinction may seem illogical; more harm can be done by a widely circulated American newspaper than by short-wave broadcasts of known enemy origin, to which few people listen. But it was precisely to preserve that distinction that the Founding Fathers wrote their definition of treason, and to obliterate it would probably create far more evils than it would cure.

But it was in the early days that the real big-league traitors operated. While the men who had written the provision in the Constitution were thinking of Benedict Arnold or perhaps of the Butlers and Johnsons of the Mohawk Valley, "they never dreamed how many forms the essence of treason could assume."

Nor were all our traitors or near-traitors small fry. They include a former Vice-President of the United States, a former Secretary of State and a commanding general of the Army—though not the ones whose names may suggest themselves to students in the Pegler-Lewis-O'Donnell school of historiography.

In this piece, Davis had something to say about the Smith Act, described by author Weyl as "a frontal attack on the spirit and tradition of the Bill of Rights." This was the law under which eleven Communists were tried in New York and convicted "for advocating unpopular beliefs."

Its constitutionality and Judge Medina's substitution of the doctrine of "sufficient danger" for "clear and present danger" will ultimately [Davis believed] be passed on by the Supreme Court.

But totalitarian ideologies have, in Mr. Weyl's book, given new dimensions to the older concepts of treason.

If [said Davis] I may offer a couple of illustrations which Weyl would undoubtedly have offered, if they had occurred before his book went to press—the treacherous act which has recently done most harm to the United States, as well as to the nation to which he owes allegiance, was committed by a British subject, Klaus Emil Julius Fuchs. French Communists who try to stop shipment of American arms to France are giving aid and comfort to the undeclared enemies of the United States as well as of their own country. Treason nowadays is treason to the free world.

In conclusion:

This in any case is no new problem. . . . For the overall impression you get from this history of disloyalty is that ever since we became a nation against which treason could be committed treason has been one of the most popular, at times one of the most respectable, and certainly one of the safest of our national pastimes.

Yet the Republic has survived.

But in the next five years, Elmer Davis was to wonder if the Republic could truly survive—the old Republic, that is, that he and his contemporaries had learned to believe in; if it could survive the new kind of treason that was becoming a new pastime on the Hill: treason against the freedom of the mind.

# 20 ]]]]]]

## 1

SENATOR JOE McCARTHY began his rise out of obscurity on the ninth of February, 1950. On this day, in Wheeling, West Virginia, he made a speech. Wheeling was the springboard for a speaking tour which the Senator hoped would bring him into sufficient national prominence to impress the Wisconsin voters and persuade them to re-elect him when his term should expire two years later.

In Wheeling, his audience was the Ohio County Women's Republican Club. This was a respectable organization but not one calculated to spread immediate fame for its speakers. The speech, indeed, was scantily reported in the press: only the local newspaper and the Chicago *Tribune* carried stories on it at the time; it was three days before any mention of it came in the New York *Times* and *Time*, the alert "weekly newsmagazine," ignored it entirely.

> While I cannot take the time [the Wheeling *Intelligencer* reported McCarthy as saying] to name all of the men in the State Department who have been named as members of the Communist Party and members of a spy ring, I have here in my hand a list of two hundred and five that were known to the Secretary of State as being members of the Communist Party and who nevertheless are still working and shaping the policy of the State Department.

296

What McCarthy had there in his hand has never come to light, though he afterwards said it was a letter from former Secretary of State James Byrnes. But McCarthy was no longer in Wheeling when the State Department, on February 11, sent him a wire asking for the names on his supposed list, adding,

As a loyal American you owe it to your country to inform the officials responsible for any such characters existing in the government.

The *Times* story on the twelfth quoted Lincoln White, press officer at the State Department as saying:

If he [McCarthy] is correctly quoted, his allegation that the Secretary of State has a list of 205 Communist party members who are working and shaping policy in the State Department is entirely without foundation.

We know of no Communist party members in the department, and if we find any they will be summarily dismissed. We did not furnish Senator McCarthy with any such list, and we would be interested in seeing his list.

The Senator from Wisconsin, however, had already embarked upon his crusade and had begun managing it with the technique to which Elmer Davis called attention: "if yesterday's front-page story blows up today, there is always today's front-page story to bury the refutation." Without replying to the State Department's questions, McCarthy, having arrived in Reno on his speaking tour, revealed a letter he had just written to President Truman about the fifty-seven (no longer 205) Communists he knew were still in the State Department.

This list [he told the President] is available to you, but you can get an even longer list by ordering Secretary Acheson

297

to give you a list of those whom your board listed as being
disloyal and who are still working in the State Department.

Where McCarthy got the figure fifty-seven, unless as Richard Rovere suggests in his biography, it came from a study of
Heinz pickle advertisements, is as unclear as the source of the
eighty-one he presented to the Senate in a five-and-a-half-hour
speech on February 20. Of this *Time* took notice and called the
speech "a wild attempt to decapitate both Harry Truman and
Dean Acheson in one horrendous swing."

About the eighty-one, McCarthy went into particulars—some
of which would have done credit to the best of our whodunit
writers—but still mentioned no names. Of one, he said:

What do you suppose he is doing now? He's a speech writer
at the White House. I am doing President Truman a favor by
telling him this. He wouldn't have this individual there if he
knew it.

This statement was so sensational that the President's denial
could have little effect upon McCarthy's sensation-loving followers—of whom he was already collecting a sizable number. As
Joseph Alsop wrote in a column which Davis quoted:

One of [McCarthy's] great assets is that his supporters have
the true mark of the fanatic—they are not interested in
facts. The endless exposures of McCarthy's endless untruths
do not affect them.

The brief account in *Time* of the February 20 Senate session
concluded on an ominous note:

Two days later the Senate voted unanimously to investigate
McCarthy's charges. Republicans hoped they might turn up
another Alger Hiss case; Democrats felt that they didn't

dare stifle an inquiry—and besides, they said confidently, they weren't worried.

Was there any fire at all below Joe McCarthy's smoke signals? Maryland's thorough and careful Democratic Senator Millard E. Tydings, chairman of the investigating committee, promised "neither a witch hunt nor a whitewash."

Many Senators, including Tydings, did their best to keep panic out of the investigations that followed but the fanatics, powerfully supported by members of the Un-American Activities Committee at the other end of the Capitol, managed to put on a witch hunt that in unreason was only exceeded by the Massachusetts affair at the end of the seventeenth century.

Even in 1950, Davis was getting the fanatic repercussions. Later, he remembered that

when McCarthy was making his first attacks on the State Department, I ventured to suggest in a broadcast that these were merely accusations, so far; we had better wait and see if the evidence justified convictions. Whereupon an infuriated citizen, apparently a man of standing in his community, wrote me, "We cannot wait for convictions; what we want is confessions." But suppose there is nothing to confess? That is no problem in Russia or any other totalitarian country; they get the confessions anyway. But this republic has not been operated on that principle, so far.

But, from the very beginning of what Davis called the "perilous night," to the time when it seemed that McCarthy, through wholesale intimidation, was on his way to becoming a veritable dictator, there were anchors of sanity as well as crusaders, like Davis, against the subverters of freedom of the mind. One was the New York *Times*. Immediately after the speech in the Senate a *Times* editorial declared:

299

Senator McCarthy of Wisconsin has been giving a good imitation of a hit-and-run driver in his attacks on the State Department. He has made the damaging charge that there are "fifty-seven card-holding Communists" on the Department's rolls. . . . And when he has been called upon to account for these charges, either by the Department or by colleagues in the Senate, he has taken refuge in the explanation that he cannot name names because this might embarrass "the activities of investigating agencies."

The power of the lie, however, is, as Hitler discovered, greater as the lie grows bigger from other lies being added to it. In 1950, it was still small. But in the next few years it would receive many additions both from McCarthy and other politicians who found them highly profitable.

2

Today, a decade later, in our "agonizing reappraisal" of the early fifties, the career of McCarthy takes a subordinate place. That is not only because, in time, it was licked by such apostles of truth as Elmer Davis but, too, because communism outside America has exerted such distracting pressures that the under-the-bed American Communist has been almost forgotten. To the historian, what stands out in these years is Korea. In a broadcast on the twenty-sixth of June, 1950, Davis said:

All of us who are old enough to remember twelve or fifteen years back feel tonight as if we were hearing a familiar piece of music played over by a new orchestra, under a new conductor, but with the same interpretation. This is where we came in; not indeed in December '41 nor even in September '39; but say about 1938, when the pattern of totalitarian aggression had become clear; and the only questions were when—if ever—somebody would try to stop it; and if they did, whether they would not do too little and too late.

With regard to Korea those questions are still unanswered. It looks as if the South Koreans can't stop the invasion from the North. The Communists, with heavy artillery, tanks, and at least some planes against the light weapons of the defenders, broke through the southern lines about sixteen hours ago, and the government of President Syngman Rhee is evacuating Seoul and will set up a provisional capital farther south. The United States commission in Korea says that the country may be conquered in a matter of days; and the North Korean Communists are so confident that they have dropped the pretense that the Southerners attacked first, and now frankly say that they are going to smash the South because it is an American colony. In other words we are the real enemy they are attacking. . . .

The President said this morning that we will vigorously support the action of the United Nations, and American arms are being shipped from Japan to Korea; but Korean officials say this help is too little and too late.

Some people have suggested that a bolder policy might bring results. There are enough American troops in Japan to chase the Korean Communists right back home—unless the Russians joined the fighting in force, and so far there is no indication that any Russians were engaged. . . . It is probable that the President, under his own powers and in support of the United Nations, could order those troops into action; but he would hardly do so without assurance of popular and Congressional support—bipartisan if possible. Two Republican Congressmen, Eaton and Velde, did say that we ought to use arms if necessary (not just send them). But the Senate Republican conference this morning unanimously decided that while we have some moral commitments to help the Koreans help themselves the incident is not a provocation for

301

war. In other words, we should hang our clothes on a hickory limb but not go near the water.

Fortified by this resolution, Republican Senators had a good time castigating the administration—quite properly—for the failure of our political and military intelligence to foresee the attack; but they didn't say what we should have done if we had foreseen it. Senator Bridges did indeed insist that we take a calculated risk and call the Communist bluff; but he didn't say how. Senator Knowland issued a ringing demand that we do what we are doing already—that is, send arms. Senator Ferguson said we should have been in a position to act but he didn't say how we should have acted. Senator Taft, that incomparable second-guesser, blamed it all on the decisions made at Yalta but didn't say what we should do about it five years after Yalta. Only Senator Wiley said that there is no use constantly dwelling on past mistakes unless we can profit by them.

Senator Connally . . . said that nobody wants to act until we have all the facts. By the time we have them all it is not certain how much there will be left to act on.

The immediate sequence is in the history books. On the twenty-seventh, Davis was able to announce that

American planes and warships under General MacArthur's command have already begun combat operations against the North Korean Communists, carrying out the President's order issued last night and made public at noon today.

There was quick bipartisan support for the President's action. Even Senator Bridges said, "I approve completely what has been done," and Republican Representative Eaton said, "We've got a rattlesnake by the tail and the sooner we pound its damn head in, the better." Both houses of Congress quickly voted to

302

extend the peacetime draft and there was an appropriation of sixteen million additional dollars for South Korea and the Philippines. Nevertheless, the Korean War became a political football during the summer of 1950 in the campaigns for the Congressional elections in November. The goal post, so to speak, over which this was repeatedly kicked by the Republicans, was Secretary of State Dean Acheson.

This "Crusade Against Acheson," as an article by Davis in the March, 1951, *Harper's* was entitled, was, he believed,

> a vicious and sustained attack on a man of whom the President said, correctly, that "no official in our government has been more alive to communism's threat to freedom, or more forceful in resisting it."

Here, Joe McCarthy who had, at first, been pushed off the front pages by the Korean War, got back into the act.

> Senator McCarthy, of course [wrote Davis], began it. I shall not speculate on his motives, being neither a psychoanalyst nor an inspector of sewers; nor would it be charitable to comment on the many respectable men who were at first disgusted by McCarthyism, but eventually went along with it because they believed (in most cases correctly) that it would help them win an election. It was discovered in 1950 that it is less profitable, politically, to say you believe your opponents are mistaken than to call them Communists and perverts. . . .
>
> But why pick on Acheson? Well—last spring, before McCarthyism had conquered a party (or much of a party, for there were honorable holdouts to the last), John Duncan Miller of the London *Times* had interpreted it as essentially "a revolt of the primitives against intelligence." Acheson is intelligent; he also has the misfortune of being a

303

gentleman and what in his case proved to be the greater misfortune of being a Christian.

His origins are appallingly respectable—the son of a bishop, educated at Groton, Yale, and the Harvard Law School; an editor of the *Harvard Law Review*, followed by a term as secretary to Justice Brandeis before he went into the practice of law in Washington. He has, as one of his old friends remarked to me, "all the virtues that were considered estimable when you and I were boys." Also, he dresses well and speaks correct English; for which he has been sneered at by Mr. Fulton Lewis, who can also speak correct English and dresses well enough to impersonate a man of distinction in whiskey advertisements. All this makes Acheson an easy target for the Fascistoid elements in American society—the people from whom the Ku-Klux Klan and the Christian Front were recruited, the kind of people who gave Hitler his first mass support. But for all that, you would suppose there must be something in his official record to justify the holy crusade that was waged against him.

There is not.

After noting Acheson's work in support of the organization (NATO) "by which the free nations can make most effective use of their united powers to beat Communist imperialism," Davis wrote:

So McCarthy calls him the Red Dean of Washington; Jenner accuses him of a pro-Communist betrayal of the American people; and even decent men, who have repeated their story so often that they have come to believe it themselves, demand his dismissal on the ground that they have persuaded the people to lose confidence in him. The attack on Acheson, said John Dewey, after the election, was a victory for the Communist cause that the rulers of Russia could not have obtained by any activity of their own. Why should men who presumably want to stop the Russians have tried to destroy the man who has done more to stop the Russians than anybody else?

## 3

From start to finish, Davis reported the Korean War in his broadcasts with as much detail as was possible in the time allotted him. But this was never to the exclusion of the home hysteria which seemed at times to damage the very war effort. In October, 1950, he was shocked by a demonstration of this in the annual lunatic gathering of the American Legion in which resolutions were passed that would make the United States a grim laughingstock in the world outside. In a Columbus Day broadcast, he said:

When the State Department has succeeded in getting almost all the world to support us in Korea, when it stands on the verge of the greatest success American diplomacy has achieved in many years—obtaining the reorganization of the United Nations so that it can act in any future crisis—just then the American Legion demands that the men who have accomplished this be fired as unable to deal with communism. If there is any better way to discourage nations that are inclined to support us I don't know what it is. Such a resolution would be understandable from the Eighth Ward Political Club three weeks before election; but it is somewhat surprising from the national convention of a patriotic organization.

Another resolution at this convention demanded that all members of the Communist party be immediately interned and tried as traitors. After referring the Legion to the Constitution, Davis said:

305

It may be argued that the Founding Fathers never foresaw such an institution as the Communist party; but they probably never foresaw such an institution as the Legion's Americanism Committee either.

In this time when both Russia and the United States had atomic bombs, several writers indulged in fantasies about the next war. This was usually done in fiction as in George Orwell's *1984* with the writer standing upon some vantage point of the future and writing of a war already concluded. For Davis this kind of story presented an occasion for satire and he used a short piece, written for his favored *Saturday Review of Literature* as a vehicle for some of the barbed darts he liked to throw at the obstructionists on Capitol Hill. "Another View from 1960" (so-called because it followed a similar piece in the magazine) is readable today only for its satire—events have nullified its prophecy—which, indeed, Davis hardly intended to be taken seriously.

The war, he said, grew out of the Korean conflict in a manner unsuspected by the Soviet instigators and it was a world war. It ended in a Russian defeat because the Russians used what few atomic bombs they had with disregard of the factors of chance and efficiency. This, of course, makes little sense today but it was in his picture of how it all started that Davis made his point about the causes in Washington of Stalin's miscalculations.

The first and greatest blunder [he wrote] was Stalin's; he started the war too soon. To be sure he intended in 1950 only what the Austrians intended in 1914; a cheap little local war; but that precedent should have warned him. With his flock of satellites, his gaggle of Quislings in the democratic nations, he had too many plates in the air at once; when he spun a single one out of the circle it was inevitable that some of the others would crash. And it must have been an irresistible

306

temptation to the Politburo when they discovered that a number of men on Capitol Hill would insist that the United States must not win a war unless Chiang Kai-shek and General Franco could win it too. With Congress apparently determined to disrupt the antiaggression alliances that had been put together with such difficulty, it is no wonder that the men in the Kremlin felt that now was the time.

There was probably much truth in this description; but there was even more profound truth in the abstraction to be drawn from it that the American paradox is perennially misunderstood abroad, especially in undemocratic areas. The Russians, like the Germans in 1915 and in 1940, thought that the loud voices of isolationist members of Congress constituted the voice of America. So they were astounded when the real voice spoke in the guns in South Korea.

The reaction amazed them; they had failed to comprehend the virtues as well as the failings of democracy; they had made the calamitous error of suddenly starting up American rearmament at a time when they had, as yet so few atomic bombs that they had to concentrate on a campaign to outlaw the atomic bomb.

So this otherwise unimportant piece shows that even in the darker moments of "the perilous night" Davis kept a stern faith in the less articulate America that had so often subdued the vocalists in the great crises. There were times, it is true, when he so emphasized the lapses of freedom of the mind that he seemed to foresee its disappearance, but he kept coming back to the answer that was so plain to him.

I regret [he said once] that I have to mention McCarthy; I regret that he exists. But he does exist, and not to mention

307

him would be as if people in a malarial country refused to mention the anopheles mosquito. (There is a quinine that can neutralize his venom; it is called courage. . . .)

So don't—he would say when the voices were loudest—don't let them scare you.

# 21 ]]]]]]

"**M**OST IMAGINATIVE YET,**"** Davis wrote on the envelope of a letter he filed under "Personal Attacks." The letter was signed "X Gov't Agent" and postmarked Charleston, S.C., and stated that the "facts" it contained were documented in the files of the Central Intelligence Agency. The letter was addressed not to Davis but to the president of the American Broadcasting Company who, the writer hoped, would promptly fire the offender. The company's president promptly forwarded the letter to Davis, knowing that it would gratify him with the knowledge that he had got under the skin of a hostile listener and delight him with the picturesque quality of its vituperation.

> Davis [the letter read] is an atheist, a jew-baiter and Catholic hater. Yet he has the nerve of calling people Fascists. He is the propagandist for the wild radicals and Communists but as far as I know never joined the party. However, he is a close friend of many of them who founded the American labor party, a Commie front and later the ADA, another Commie front for "intellectuals." If Davis ever earned an honest dollar by working for it, it was when he worked for the Times. They let him go because he was a jew-baiter and hater. Then he took over OWI and filled that outfit with Reds. . . .

For very different reasons, he must have been gratified by a long appreciation from Los Angeles.

My wife and I are blind folks and we live out here in a little house. . . . Though it is humble, and without ostentation, it serves as a home for us and our dear German shepherd dogs that lead us any place we want to go to. . . . Every day around six-fifteen, P.M., I ease up close to our radio so I can hear you give out the news with your comments. It is strange to me, and even sad, that you are one of the very few commentators who can actually tell the whole truth no matter who gets hurt by it. I do not understand why so many of the radio commentators find it necessary to resort to downright lying in order to put over their distorted viewpoints.

The letter went on to tell of the hardships this man had suffered, moving from city to city selling pencils and playing an accordion on street corners until "Roosevelt and Hopkins" instituted Relief.

If you had been through the mill like me [the letter went on] you would see a parallel between the New Deal and the mystic statement about the "word made flesh." The Roosevelts have done and are still doing their best to translate words into deeds. . . .

These are dirty, dirty days. Honest men are convicted on the testimonies of admitted communists. It must be very hard for self-respecting people to choose between doing their duty by serving their government and obeying the first law of nature. . . .

P.S. Please drop me a line if you can, I'll get me one to read it.

Davis's reply has been lost but we may be sure there was one. He was conscientious about answering letters—even the attacks, if they were at all rational. Once he was called "inconsistent" because he defended a meeting which some so-called patriots broke up with violence.

How many meetings [the letter said] have the Reds and their Fellow Travelers tried to break up?

Davis answered:

The fact that Communists behave like Communists and try to break up other people's meetings is no reason why the rest of us should behave like Communists. This country was founded and has run pretty well for a hundred and sixty years on the principle of the rule of law, and on the doctrines set forth in the Constitution. I see no sign of such peril to the republic today that we need to throw away the Constitution in order to save it.

Letters from Thomas Velotta of ABC consistently defended Davis against those who wrote to the broadcasting company complaining of his views and threatening to write his sponsors. Velotta wrote that the sponsors approved the broadcasts and the hundreds of applauding letters from listeners fortified the company's support. It was evident that the hopes of Ed Murrow, expressed to Davis in 1939, "that broadcasting is to become an adult means of communication at last," had come true.

In 1951, Davis received the George Foster Peabody Radio Award and the citation recorded the tensions of 1950:

In a year of great anxiety and bitter partisanship it has been reassuring and edifying to hear the sanity, the horse sense, and the dry Hoosier wit with which Mr. Davis contemplates a troubled world. To his broadcasts he brings intelligence, integrity and a writing skill unmatched in radio today.

311

2

These qualities were more than ever necessary in the times that followed the Peabody Award. The outbreak of war in Korea had stirred up a hornet's nest on Capitol Hill. As the attention of the red-hunters turned to the Far East it became profitable Republican politics to follow up whatever charges the McCarthy-Jenner axis had made against the Americans who had tried to bring about a postwar equilibrium in China. McCarthy had followed his discovery of the "treason" of General Marshall because of his efforts toward Chinese coalition with lurid words about Professor Owen Lattimore of Johns Hopkins whom he called "the chief architect of our Far Eastern policy," and the "top Russian espionage agent."

In April, 1950, Lattimore answered McCarthy's charge that he was a spy by calling McCarthy a "base and contemptible liar" and a "madman" and saying that he was "accomplishing results for Russia which exceed their wildest hopes" and that the Soviet Union should decorate him. These were dangerous words: the Senator would not forget them.

Others who came under a cloud in the spring of 1950 were John Carter Vincent, Philip Jessup, John Stewart Service, Brigadier General Evans F. Carlson and Joseph Barnes, Davis's one time employee in OWI—the last two on the testimony of Louis Budenz, former editor of the *Daily Worker*. It was a time of triumph for the breast-beating ex-Communists.

How long [wrote Elmer Davis] will these ex-Communists and ex-sympathizers abuse the patience of the vast majority which had sense enough never to be Communists or sympathizers at all? They have a constitutional right, of course, to tell us what we must do to be saved—as they have always done. Twenty years ago they were telling us the direct opposite of what they tell us now; but they were just as sure

312

then as now that they had the sole and sufficient key to salvation and that those who did not accept it were forever damned. . . .

Congressional committees always seem willing to take the word of an ex-Communist—provided he has become a reactionary—against that of a man who never was a Communist. The preference may seem in contradiction to the McCarran Internal Security Act against the admission into this country of ex-Communists from abroad; but those provisions are only a phase of the protective tariff. The lucrative home market for exposures and revelations must be protected for domestic industry against the pauper labor of Europe. With this Congressional benediction there is some excuse for the ex-Communists to think they are a superior species.

In June, 1950, with the invasion of South Korea and the prompt action of the UN against the real Communists, Congressional committees became more than ever concerned with the phantom Communists of the past who had aided the President and the State Department in pursuing the disastrous Far Eastern foreign policy which somehow had brought all this to pass and on whose heads was the blood of "our boys" being killed in Korea. But there was one small subcommittee in the Senate that said it knew better.

This was the subcommittee of the Foreign Relations committee which had been assigned the job of investigating Senator Joseph R. McCarthy's charges of Communist infiltration in the State Department. On it were Senators Millard Tydings of Maryland (chairman), Theodore F. Green of Rhode Island, Brien Mac-Mahon of Connecticut, Bourke Hickenlooper of Iowa and Henry Cabot Lodge, Jr., of Massachusetts. On July 17, the subcommittee presented its majority report which Hickenlooper and Lodge refused to sign. The report was the result of four months' work with the eighty-one State Department loyalty files: files

313

which McCarthy had said would prove his charges should they be made available to him.

The report called McCarthy's one-man campaign

> a fraud and a hoax perpetrated on the Senate of the United States and the American people . . . perhaps the most nefarious campaign of half-truths and untruth in the history of this republic. For the first time in our history, we have seen the totalitarian technique of the "big lie" employed on a sustained basis.

The report cleared Owen Lattimore, Ambassador-at-Large Philip Jessup, State Department career officer John Stewart Service, State Department employee Mrs. Esther Brunauer, Judge Dorothy Kenyon and Minister to Switzerland John Carter Vincent of the charges against them. It recommended (1) Establishment by the President of a twelve-man commission to study the Federal loyalty program; (2) joint Congressional study of the immunity from civil suit enjoyed by Congress to stop "character assassination of American citizens."

The report, McCarthy said, was "a green light to the Red 5th column in the United States . . . a signal to the traitors, Communists and fellow travellers in our government that they need have no fear of exposure from this administration." Nevertheless, the report was accepted by a vote of 54-37 and though various Republicans denounced it as "political" and "insulting," yet no one in the Senate rose to defend McCarthy, even when Tydings accused him of perjury and offered to prove it with a phonograph record. Yet Tydings had used dangerous words and McCarthy never forgot them. In the fall, by means of a faked photograph, he engineered the end of Tydings's long and greatly distinguished career in the Senate. By the beginning of 1951, in spite of the bitter feelings against him, he had consolidated his power. He had scared a majority of the members of Congress.

In October, 1950, General MacArthur's forces crossed the 38th

Parallel and moved on toward the Yalu River. Before the end of November the United States 7th Division had reached the Manchurian border. In the spring of 1951, General MacArthur encountered the new look war had taken on in these changed years when military decisions had become subordinate to political ones. There were those in the United States who thought MacArthur was right in wanting to send bombers across the Manchurian border to destroy industrial installations there. (There are those who still think so.) But whether those who thought it right then would have wanted a full-scale war with Communist China in which hundreds of thousands of "our boys" might be killed—even if Russia did not come in—is, as Davis would say, not clear.

For the North Koreans had, after the UN forces had passed the 38th parallel, been reinforced by thousands of Communist Chinese "volunteer" soldiers, and President Truman and the State Department and the Joint Chiefs of Staff believed that further moves by MacArthur could bring on the third world war. So when MacArthur refused to concede, he was relieved of all his Far Eastern commands in April, 1951. He came home then, made his famous speech about old soldiers "fading away," resigned from the Army and went on an unsuccessful speaking tour to rally support for his position. Many wept at his dramatic words but there were few who wanted a third world war. It was a tragic business and even Joe McCarthy's remark that he was "the greatest American that was ever born" could not detract from the fact that Douglas MacArthur was one of our great generals.

3

All of these events and episodes accumulated a large amount of material for the presidential campaign of 1952. It was not the sort of material that would be likely to promote a clean campaign. The Democrats, being the incumbents, were obliged to adopt a defensive attitude and were thus the recipients of most of the smears, though they had their innings when the question arose of the vice-presidential candidate's supposedly illegitimate "fund." The Republicans concentrated on the tolerance of the Communist fifth column by the Truman administration. But the Republican smears were, as things turned out, superfluous; for their nominee, Eisenhower, was so popular an idol that nothing could have defeated him.

When the Democrats nominated Adlai Stevenson, McCarthy, on television, rose to the peak of his talents. Stevenson, he said, endorsed and "would continue the suicidal Kremlin-shaped policies of the nation."

> When I listened to that broadcast [said Elmer Davis] the past rose before me like a dream—a past I thought had been buried seven years before. I was reminded of another rabble-rousing broadcaster in another republic, who was taken up by rich men and conservative politicians because they thought they could use his talent for publicity against a middle-of-the-road government and then throw him over when he had served their purpose. But when he once got to the eminence for which he had been climbing, he threw them over when they had served his purpose. When I heard the applause for McCarthy that night an echo of memory seemed to give it an undertone—*Sieg Heil! Sieg Heil! Sieg Heil!*

The prophets, remembering 1948, were still cautious four years later.

> Nobody [said Davis on the eve of the election] is predicting with much confidence who will win—except the politicians who have to be confident; and I certainly don't know. Eisenhower had a good start with his world-wide reputation; but he labors under a handicap that no presidential candidate has overcome for many years—most of the newspapers are for him.

316

Eisenhower had made the usual promises and one unusual one; he would go in person to Korea to aid in the conclusion of peace. McCarthy, a Taft man before the Republican convention had, nevertheless, campaigned for Eisenhower. Though Eisenhower's intimates said he hated McCarthy, he had let himself be persuaded that it was good politics to campaign in Wisconsin and speak in Milwaukee "on McCarthy's issue," as Davis later said, "and very much in McCarthy's language."

There is a comment on this in Richard Rovere's biography, *Senator Joe McCarthy*.

He [Eisenhower] had from the start looked upon McCarthy as a cad, a guttersnipe, and he had planned a small gesture of defiance and disassociation. He would go into McCarthy's Wisconsin and speak a few warm and affectionate words about his old chief and patron, General Marshall, whom McCarthy had all but called a traitor. . . . Learning of Eisenhower's plans to dispute this view of Marshall—and trembling at what they were certain was the prospect of McCarthy's fury—the party leaders in Wisconsin and half a dozen other Republican politicians pleaded with him to omit that part of his speech, which he did. (In fairness, the President did, on other occasions stoutly defend General Marshall.) McCarthy's victory was made sweeter by the fact that he himself had played no part in gaining it. He had let it be known that Eisenhower could say what he pleased about Marshall and that he, McCarthy, couldn't care less. . . . But so great was the fear of him that Eisenhower gave in, even though McCarthy had magnanimously said that this would not be necessary.

On the day after election, Davis spoke without enthusiasm and it must have been evident to his listeners where his sympathies lay.

317

Our next President [he said] has been chosen; everybody on both the winning and the losing side has been saying the proper thing and making the proper gesture—and undoubtedly meaning them; so that there seems good hope that much of the bitterness of this exceptionally bitter campaign may wash out now that it is over; which is probably the thing which the nation most needs just now. . . .

The results clearly show that Eisenhower is much stronger than his party. It can be hoped that he will remember that, when many interested persons will be doing their best to make him forget it. He has received more than thirty-one million votes, and the highest figure on record. . . . But this enormous vote, and the fact that many Republican candidates for both Houses of Congress rode in on Eisenhower's coat-tails, gives him an opportunity to become the real head of the party, if he will take it. There was once another general in the same position, who declined to take that opportunity; but we can all hope that that won't happen again.

Davis went on to speak of the Republicans and Democrats in Congress. Senator Wayne Morse had resigned from the Republican party and there were some Democratic Senators who should resign from their party, "but preferred to stay in it and knife it in the back." McCarran, Daniel and Byrd were really "Republicans by political principle and would arouse more admiration in some quarters if they frankly said so."

This was scarcely "objective" reporting. He did not even follow the newsman's practice of putting the opinions he stated in the mouths of "important" persons. But Davis had long since ceased to be an orthodox reporter and "objectivity," he believed, "often leans over backward so far that it makes the news business merely a transmission belt for pretentious phonies." It was traditional, for example, for a newspaper to regard statements by a Senator

318

as news; they must be printed whether they are true or not—even if the person who writes the story knows that they are false—and it would be strictly against the code to print "This is not so" in parentheses at the bottom of the column. That would have to be said over on the editorial page. But over the air if you frankly acknowledged that you were a "commentator" or "interpreter," news and editorial could be combined in the same broadcast providing you were sincerely searching for the whole "three-dimensional truth."

On November 11, which, in 1952, was still called Armistice Day, he spoke of the prayers for peace.

Peace, though less important than freedom, seems more desirable than ever now that several letters have been published from eyewitnesses of the recent atomic explosion on a South Pacific island, presumably Eniwetok; they all say it was really something. Their impression seems to have been summed up by a sailor from Salt Lake City who wrote to his mother, "I think people are getting too smart."

Two days later, a tragedy brought him back to the Congressional spy-hunt. It was the suicide of Abraham Howard Feller, general counsel of the UN, after questioning by a lawyer of the McCarran Committee.

Any doubts [said Davis] of his loyalty would seem to me utterly fantastic. And even Senator McCarran didn't exactly *say* that there were any; when he heard of Feller's death McCarran said that if his conscience was clear he had no reason to suffer from what he expected from our committee. I don't mean to imply, Senator McCarran went on, that he has done anything wrong but anything may be expected in this investigation. Which is about as neat as possible a way for a Senator, when he is in a position where he is not

319

protected by his constitutional immunity, to leave a smear without taking the responsibility.

In this month, the case of Owen Lattimore was revived in the House Un-American Activities Committee's inquiry into tax-exempt foundations which had given grants to persons under a cloud.

Chairman Cox said today [reported Davis on the twenty-fifth] that they had made a great number of grants to persons disloyal to the United States; but he offered no evidence except that they had given money to the Institute of Pacific Relations for the researches of Owen Lattimore which, said Mr. Cox, was used for subversive purposes. The evidence of this is very far from convincing to most people; but Mr. Cox is not to blame, no doubt, if he confuses difference of opinion with subversion. . . .

Mr. Cox has to do what he can to save the country while the McCarran committee and McCarthy's government operations committee are getting no headlines; competition in the exposure business is going to be very hot this winter.

Soon after this Davis's attention turned to real Communists in a Russian satellite, and as we read the script of his broadcast we seem to see a kind of warning in this story of alleged treason in a police state.

The fourteen defendants in the Czechoslovak treason trials were of course convicted—you don't try a man in a Communist country unless you have decided, and arranged, to convict him—and eleven of them were sentenced to death.

A week later came another story from the same unhappy land.

Mrs. Kasenkina, the Russian schoolteacher who four years ago jumped to freedom from a window of the Russian

320

consulate in New York, has written to Vishinsky suggesting that it's not too late for him to break away. . . . The question has point. Vishinsky must remember that a couple of years ago the Czechoslovak Foreign Minister Clementis was a familiar figure around the United Nations Assembly; some of his friends advised him, when he was last in New York, that if he knew what was good for him he wouldn't go back to Prague. But he knew better, he went back, and yesterday he was hanged.

In this month of December, the character assassins in Congress were the target of some of Davis's most cutting irony.

These are great days [he said on the sixteenth] for Louis Budenz, the man so gifted at remembering what he forgot to mention last year or year before. Yesterday the Loyalty Review Board found a reasonable doubt of the loyalty of John Carter Vincent and today Owen Lattimore, whom Budenz had called a Communist, after previously denying it, was indicted by a Washington grand jury for himself denying before the McCarran Committee that he is a sympathizer and promoter of communism. This was only one of seven counts in the perjury indictment against Lattimore; the others all dealing with his statements about things that happened from seven to fifteen years ago when he talked to somebody, when or whether he knew that certain men were Communists and so on. . . .

Lattimore at once declared his innocence, and spoke of the vengeful harassment to which he has been subjected for almost three years since McCarthy first attacked him. Senator Mundt, however, assumes the guilt of both Lattimore and Vincent and joyously now says that some Congressional committee must now find out the names of the patron saints of both men, who protected them so long and so effectively

321

in their jobs in the face of what he calls all the evidence. Lattimore has had no government job for almost seven years. . . . But you can see Senator Mundt licking his chops in anticipation.

Actually, in the course of time the Lattimore indictment was withdrawn so there was never any trial, but recovery of his reputation from the damage inflicted on it in these years was difficult. Vincent was not indicted but the Review Board had "reasonable doubt" of his loyalty because, in 1945, of

what they call his studied praise of Chinese Communists and studied criticism of Chiang Kai-shek's government when it was the policy of the United States to support it.

From all this it looks as if Vincent's real offense is that he was the author of the program for General Marshall's mission to China in the winter of nineteen forty-five to end the Chinese civil war and arrange a coalition government. . . . The Marshall mission failed, so the plan might be regarded as a mistake. But there seems to be no such thing as a mistake in modern jurisprudence; if anything goes wrong it is the result of subversive activities if not of treason.

This was at a time when there was much discussion of American policy toward China, when the Chinese Communists had not yet shown themselves to be such a bad lot as they have since. . . . To have been mistaken then hardly seems to have been a crime, even if it does look like a mistake seven years later. But young men in the State Department, and the government service generally, will draw the obvious lesson from what happened to Vincent.

This is that no man who values his future can afford to do anything, or think anything, that may look like a mistake seven years later; if he does it may ruin his career and his reputation. And since few men can predict what ideas will be popular seven years ahead, the only safe course will be

322

to do nothing except under orders, and not to think at all. This already seems to be the practice in the Russian government service, and we are on the way to imitating it. And since people who are able to think like to do so, the tendency will be more and more to fill up the government service with people who can't think and don't want to anyway, for fear they might think wrong. Whether this would be a very competent government, able to direct the destinies of this republic, is a matter on which I suppose opinions will differ.

To Davis, it was evident that the long judicial tradition under which the courts had operated in the modern civilized world had gone by the board since Congress had taken over the inquisitorial function. The theory on which statutes of limitation, for example, had been based, no longer applied in the climate of fear that had proved so profitable to the congressional inquisitors. Once a Communist sympathizer always a Communist sympathizer *unless* one had beaten his breast in public and was ready to produce other criminals for the hungry spy-hunters. The fact that there was nothing to beat one's breast about was thought irrelevant. If a person was accused of fellow-traveling, that was enough.

Such a practice was peculiarly abhorrent to Davis. If all the Americans who, in the war, had accepted the Russian alliance and admired the Russian army were to be branded for all futurity as Communists and spies, there would hardly be room in the files of loyalty boards and the FBI for their dossiers.

At the end of December, Davis spoke about the new threat to academic freedom.

It promises [he said on the twenty-ninth] to be a merry winter for our colleges and universities, for at least two and probably three Congressional committees are going after them. . . .

323

The principal investigators were to be McCarthy, chairman of the committee on government operations, and Velde, who would head the Un-American Activities Committee in the House.

They are both looking for Communists in the colleges and the competition will be lively. The winner, of course, will be the one who can put the finger on the largest number, not of Communists, but of people who he says are Communists or something like it. Also Senator Ferguson, who hopes to succeed McCarran as chairman of the Internal Security Committee, intends to make sure among other things that educational institutions implant only sound ideas in the minds of students.

McCarthy has broadened the field; he said he would rather say he is looking for Communist thinkers than for Communists. This of course is a conventionally vague phrase; you don't have to have any proof that a man is a Communist, only that you think he thinks like a Communist. McCarthy admits that this will be an awfully unpleasant task; there will be a lot of screaming about interference with academic freedom. . . .

If, Davis went on, the committees should hit real Communists, they would not be interfering; for a true Communist has no freedom of thought. But if they choose to brand a person as a Communist thinker because he favors public housing or is unenthusiastic about Chiang Kai-shek there would be protests.

Well [he continued], what is academic freedom? The McCarran committee today publishes a definition by J. B. Matthews, a specialist on communism for the Hearst newspapers, who has been around as a denouncer for some years past. Academic freedom, he says, is something under which a very large number of our colleges and universities permit the employment of men who are subversive in their activities.

324

Who says their activities are subversive? Matthews. He has told the trustees of their universities about them and apparently the trustees didn't believe him. Which raises a dreadful suspicion; could trustees be subversive too?

So ended the turbulent year of 1952. There was hope in the hearts of many millions of Americans who had voted for a change of party. With the promised journey of the President-elect to the Far East, there would be a prospect of permanent peace—not merely a cease-fire—in Korea, and our war-weary boys could come home.

In the few years that were left to Elmer Davis, he would reach the peak of his life's achievement.

# 22 ]]]]]]

1

T HAS BEEN SAID that his intense and physically rugged
activity in the cause of freedom of the mind in 1953 and
1954 was responsible for Davis's final illness. Yet even later
in the difficult time of his long disability he must have known
some satisfaction—as the rest of us still know—in what he accomplished. For when the people finally woke from their postwar nightmare, it can probably be said that Elmer Davis and
Edward R. Murrow were the most effective alarm clocks. There
were many Americans at that time whose minds were too confused to read and to reflect on what they read; but these people
still had ears and eyes and the direct media of radio and television could do what, in this crisis, reams of printed words could
not.

Davis's life in these years, however, was by no means all grim.
He spent many a warm, happy evening in New York with old
friends at the Century Club or the Algonquin. At the New York
studios and offices of the American Broadcasting Company he
was always sure of a welcome. Thomas Velotta, his special friend
and admirer in ABC, used to go with him on some of his New
York stories—especially to the United Nations.

One day Davis and Velotta were riding together in a taxi to
Lake Success. At the stop lights, the colored driver would turn
his head to look at them with puzzled eyes. Finally, he said:

"I guess it's none of my business but the voice of one of you gentlemen is driving me crazy."

"Why?" said Velotta.

"Because it's just like a voice I hear every night but I can't place it. When I hear it now it's like some friend was talking to me."

The lights changed and they went on. But at the next stop the driver turned again.

"It's none of my business," he said "but just tell me you gentlemen's names."

"Why," said Velotta, "my name is Thomas Velotta. And my friend here is Elmer Davis."

The driver struck the steering wheel with the flat of his hand. "That's it," he said. "That's it! You just wait till tonight!"

"What," said Velotta, "is going to happen tonight?"

"Why," said the driver, "this evening when they turns on the radio I'm going to tell my wife and nine kids that I drove Elmer Davis himself to Lake Success!"

It was good to get away from Washington. The air there was alive with whispered rumors and venomous gossip. The daily round of interviews with Senators or ambassadors or the scared people of the State Department; the press conferences with the new President or the active, talkative Vice President—all this familiar routine palled except when there was real news or something that could be believed. It was bad enough for the newspaper reporters.

But even for us [Davis explained in his article "News and the Whole Truth"], with much more latitude than the ordinary reporter, it is becoming harder and harder to get at the three-dimensional truth in Washington—partly because the news becomes more and more complex, partly because so much of it is coming to consist of never-ending serial melodramas, like soap operas on the radio, or those newspaper cartoon strips that used to be comic.

327

In their large, rather gloomy apartment, the Davises did little entertaining. Although Fliss was a constant help to her husband in his work—watching the teletype in the apartment all day and selecting the ribbons that would give the most interesting news for the evening broadcast—she was not an orthodox Washington hostess. Unlike most cabinet officers' and ambassadors' wives who are able to turn on the charm even toward their husband's enemies, Fliss was reserved, sometimes stern, with sardonic humor and indifference toward those who bored them both. But when Elmer came home at tired day's end, she had his highball ready for him and some pertinent things to tell him.

In the spring of 1953, he was "going around the country, preaching sermons on the need of defending the freedom of the mind." He spoke at Vassar College, at Yale, at the University of Minnesota School of Journalism, the Twin Cities Press Club; and he gave the 1953 Phi Beta Kappa Oration at Harvard. Afterward he wrote that:

> An unforeseen dividend of my missionary journeys was that I made the acquaintance of so many of the best [of the good people in the world]—agreeable persons who were also good citizens, as unhappily is not always the case. I am afraid, however, that I was preaching mostly to just men and women who need no repentance.

In his modesty, Davis ignored the significant fact that words like his usually filter down to the people who need them most.

2

At Vassar in an address which forecast the title of his forthcoming book by paraphrasing the words of St. Paul, he said:

> More than eighteen hundred years ago a great historian wrote that "rare is the felicity of the times when you can think

328

what you like and say what you think." That felicity has indeed been rare throughout human history. Tacitus himself had lived through times when it was suicidal to say what you thought, and hazardous to let it be suspected that you were thinking at all; he survived into a more tolerant age, but that lasted for only a few generations till the lid came down again. Since then the lid has been on and off—mostly on. In the false dawn of the eighteenth century it was lifted once more; and the men who made our government thought they could guarantee that the lid would stay off by almost immediately writing into the Constitution as its very first amendment the guarantee of freedom of religion, of speech, of the press—all corollaries of the basic right to think what you like. That seemed to have settled that; with a great price our ancestors obtained this freedom, but we were born free.

As in so many of his speeches and writings, he was aided in this last sentence by his explicit familiarity with Scripture.

Then the chief captain came [it is written in Acts 22:27] and said unto him, Tell me art thou a Roman? He said, Yea.
     And the chief captain answered, With a great sum obtained I this freedom. And Paul said, But I was born free.

But times, explained Davis, have changed: is the lid going on again? The price, he said, of retaining the freedom into which we were born is "the eternal vigilance which has always been its price." The Vassar speech went on to repeat the story of the late inquisitions that he had told in many broadcasts.
     At Yale, he said:

In these times perhaps more than ever, except in the crisis of civil war, we need a government that can do what it has to do. It may be that, as optimists hope, the leaders of world

329

communism may some day abate their zeal and give up their hopes of world conquest. . . . But till that happy day comes we shall need a government that can do what has to be done.

It would seem that such a situation calls for as high a degree of national unity as is possible in a democracy, short of a shooting war. Instead of which . . . we have a good many citizens who seem to think that the enemy is their fellow citizens who disagree with them, rather than somebody abroad; and many others—some of them eminent, more of them rich—think that the enemy is not the government of the Soviet Union or the Chinese People's Republic, but the government of the United States. During the Roosevelt and Truman administrations it could be supposed that their enemy was only a liberal government; but since January of 1953 it has been evident that their enemy is no particular administration but government itself, and they are continually trying to weaken its power. . . .

At Harvard, he concluded his Phi Beta Kappa oration with these words:

I should perhaps have begun this sermon with a text, a text taken from the fourth chapter of the first book of Samuel, the eighth and ninth verses—the mutual exhortations of the Philistines before the battle of Ebenezer. "Woe unto us!" they said when they realized that the Israelites had brought the Ark of God with them to battle. "Woe unto us! Who shall deliver us out of the hands of these mighty gods?" But then, realizing that nobody else was going to deliver them, they said to one another, "Be strong, and quit yourselves like men; and fight." And they did fight, and delivered themselves. So may we; but only if we quit ourselves like men. This republic was not established by cowards; and cowards will not preserve it.

330

3

Interspersed among these addresses were some notable broadcasts. In January, 1953, citing a letter he had received, Davis said:

> One of my correspondents reminds me that the Salem witchcraft delusion spread out, with more and more important people getting hanged, till finally the governor's wife was accused; and then the authorities stepped in and stopped it. He wonders who in these days will be in the position of the governor's wife; he had thought that the attack by Jenner and McCarthy on General Marshall would bring an expression of disapproval from somebody whose disapproval would count. But now he concludes that the governor's wife will have to be nearer home.

In mid-June, following some remarks by President Eisenhower, he said:

> The President's warning on Sunday against joining the book burners seems to be subject to about as much interpretation as if it were a passage from Scripture. The most candid comment was that of Senator McCarran; he said the President's statement was a pitiful thing; he showed no knowledge of his subject. Well, the President took the same attitude toward freedom of thought and freedom of speech as did the men who wrote the Declaration of Independence and the Constitution; either Senator McCarran shows no knowledge of the subject or else—as his record makes more probable—he just happens to believe in book burning. . . .
>
> Senator McCarthy said, He couldn't have meant me; I have burned no books. And it is true that he is not known ever to have touched a match to any; he merely scared State Department employees into burning them. People who

heard McCarthy's attack on Dr. Conant yesterday on the matter of book burning got the impression that he did think the President meant him. Besides, State Department libraries have *burned* only a few books; they have removed many from the shelves, and McCarthy says obviously the President agrees with what his cabinet officers are doing or he would countermand their orders.

Senator Hennings, who does *not* like book burning, makes the same point; book burning is a totalitarian device, he says, but it's the President's own administration that has ordered it; all the State Department has to do is stop burning books. This however raises again the question whether the State Department is working for the President or for McCarthy.

The question must have impinged at times upon the Chief Executive himself. But Eisenhower was busy learning how to fill an elective office and, at the same time, be a leader. In the Army, there had been no problem: leadership had been easier there, for a general was exempt from criticism. It is true that he had been carefully briefed by his political advisers, but neither he nor they had been fully aware that snakes in the grass who had bitten his predecessor might turn and bite him. This knowledge must have been bitter indeed when it came to him but then, perhaps, it was too late; the snakes could be scotched only by the people.

The fact that the President had said in a speech at Dartmouth, "Don't join the book burners. Don't think that you are going to conceal thoughts by concealing evidence that they ever existed"— was, Davis conceded, one of the signs of the President's awareness of "something scandalous that he had not known was going on."

4

In the fall of 1953, the speeches Davis had made were gathered together, and with additions and editing were published in a book early in 1954. The title *But We Were Born Free* was not only a happy quotation from the Vassar speech: there was something about it that was essentially Davis—something stubborn, something that refused to be downed.

Before the book was published, E. B. White of *The New Yorker* wrote a review of it. James Thurber, a close friend of Davis's, got hold of an advance proof which, against all protocol, he sent Davis. Thurber remembers that *"The New Yorker* in its stuffy way, got a little stuffy" about this.

> Goodness gracious, just imagine! [Thurber recalls] Mr. Davis might have shown it to somebody! It might have been left in a taxi! *The New Yorker* has always had the jumpy nerves of a couple of elderly spinsters running a finishing school for all the Rebeccas of all the Sunnybrook Farms, and it has had all the daring of a Gibson girl at a lawn fete.

Davis wrote back to Thurber:

> Well, God bless you for that unauthorized enclosure. I have a terrible feeling that no book can be as good as most people are saying this one is, but it is nice to have them think so. This is the second time I am under obligation to Andy White —not counting reading his stuff which puts me under obligation every week. He was more responsible than anybody else for getting me into the government in war time, which qualifies me for inclusion in McCarthy's band of traitors.

E. B. White's review* in *The New Yorker* of February 20, 1954, says the final word about *But We Were Born Free* and far and away the most apposite words that were ever said about Elmer Davis.

> The human voice, even when its accents are familiar, does not always carry over onto the printed page with authority or

* *Copr. © 1954 The New Yorker Magazine, Inc.*

with grace. Usually the voice fades out in type, leaving only
the meaning, if by good fortune any meaning happens to be
there. Churchill's deliberate, brandied tones can be heard on
the page; Adlai Stevenson's meticulous voice carries, to
some extent, in his published speeches; once in a while
F.D.R.'s voice used to come through. But Elmer Davis—
reading him is almost the same as hearing him. When he
tosses a question into the air, you know that the next sentence begins with "Well comma" and you hear distinctly the
dry inflection of his contempt, the honest vibration of his
high principles, and the steady background music of responsible reporting. The experience of reading his new book,
*But We Were Born Free* (Bobbs-Merrill), is memorable; it
is the high fidelity of the publishing world. And the same
voice that in 1940 used to steady us at five minutes to nine,
quieting our goose pimples, now has the opposite effect—it is
the voice that stirs us with warnings of internal defeats perhaps more ruinous than war itself. As clear as the sound of
his voice is the sound, in this book, of his singleness of purpose. Mr. Davis is a devout man. His religion is the secular
religion that unifies America—faith in freedom, in self-
government, in democracy.

In the winter of 1953, Mr. Davis got so uneasy about the
state of the nation that he went on a speaking tour, to plug
the Constitution, introduce the Founding Fathers to some
people who hadn't had the pleasure, and slay a couple of
McDragons. He did all right, and you will find, here and
there around the country, the pug marks of some very strange
beasts and near them a drop or two of blood testifying to the
accuracy of Mr. Davis's aim. The sermons he preached on
that tour form the first chapter, and the principal part of his
book. His work is not done; the enemies of freedom are not
dead, and nobody knows it better than the author. He is over
sixty and his doctor wants him to taper off. Even a tapered-
off Davis is worth ten of most men. He has spent his life

334

tending the twin fires of liberty and justice in the drafty
rooms of politics; this book is his testament—a short, re-
sounding book, dogging the steps of the fearmongers, praising
that rare felicity, the right to think what one pleases and to
say what one thinks.

The review concludes:

> To the man from Aurora, Indiana (a name that means
> "light of morning"), the Founding Fathers are alive today.
> And he in turn, with his salt and his truth, makes them live
> for others. All through this noble sermon on the enemies of
> freedom there runs the cry "Don't let them scare you! Be-
> lieve what you believe! Say what you think! Love what you
> love! Despise what seems wrong to you! And don't let them
> scare you!"

The response of the public to *But We Were Born Free*—which
sold nearly a hundred thousand copies—was not a proof that the
tide had turned, but it was a sign. In the course of the year, Joe
McCarthy overreached himself and was washed up. He brought
about his final collapse by his behavior opposite Joseph N. Welch
in the Army-McCarthy hearings and Ed Murrow's television
cameras put the cap on it.

But Elmer Davis did not live to see the complete collapse of
McCarthyism. Perhaps none of us will live to see it: We only
know that in the years of McCarthy's rise and fall, the Republic
matured.

5

In February, 1954, before McCarthy's exit from power, the
Senator celebrated the birth of Abraham Lincoln by a speech entitled "Twenty Years of Treason." The title referred, of course,

335

to the administrations of the Democrats from 1932 to 1952. In response, Davis delivered one of the most eloquent broadcasts of his radio career.

But why [he said] do we worry about whether twenty-two hundred people are subversive or not when there are twenty-seven million traitors in the nation—if you believe McCarthy, and the Republican National Committee which is paying for his Lincoln Day speeches around the country. . . .

Twenty years of treason. You would think that would wreck even a country as big as this. But what happened in those twenty years? The Roosevelt administration came in when the national economy was at its absolute rock bottom; with farm prices lower than they had been for decades, with fifteen million unemployed; with a far larger and more dangerous Communist movement than there has ever been since; when people used to ask helplessly, Do you think there's going to be a revolution? . . . That year people were scared.

Was it treason to get out of that? There was recovery—slow and intermittent; but there was recovery, and a return of hope. Then the Japanese attacked us, the Germans declared war on us; and we licked them both, won the greatest war in our history. McCarthy calls that treason. . . . Does the Republican National Committee, which finances this method of celebrating Lincoln's birthday, think it was treason to lick Hitler and the Japs? Do they think we ought to have been on the other side in that war? No use expecting any answer from National Chairman Leonard Hall. But there must be many Republicans who are uneasy at this sort of thing; yet if a single one of them has protested, it hasn't got into print in the papers I see. After all, maybe the only way they can win this fall's election is to claim that all Democrats are traitors.

336

Davis was under doctor's orders at this time, to broadcast only once a week. The doctor was concerned about his hypertension. One night when he came to meet some friends in New York, they noticed that he walked with a limp and asked how he had hurt himself. Did he fall downstairs? they asked in a jovial mood as they sipped their cocktails. "No," said Davis, "it was what Winston Churchill called 'a cerebral incident.'" Quiet came over the group then but Davis would not let it stay so; he told a story that made them laugh and said to the waiter over his shoulder: "The usual—I. W. Harper on the rocks." So, he was gay enough that night and except for the limp he seemed in robust health, cheeks glowing and eyes clear, his mind sharper than ever.

But listeners to his broadcasts found that he would skip a word now and then and go back to pick it up. One night he coughed in such a paroxysm, in the midst of his talk, that a replacement was called in who finished the broadcast. For a time he was kept off the air entirely by a mysterious ailment that the doctors finally agreed was paratyphoid fever.

But his difficulties with the microphone did not keep him from thinking and writing. As he wrote in his essay "Grandeurs and Miseries of Old Age" included in *But We Were Born Free*:

> The steady physical deterioration that afflicts most of us is deplorable, but so long as it remains merely physical it is not disastrous. Far worse is the danger that in advanced years, a man's mind might go back on him at some unpredictable moment and drive him to make mistakes that would have been unthinkable a year or two earlier. . . .
>
> The older a man grows, the greater the danger that this will happen to him.

It did not happen to Elmer Davis. However much he might fail, physically, his mind remained sharply clear. He followed *But*

*We Were Born Free* with a book about the threatened thermo-nuclear conflict. Borrowing his title from the clock-face illustration on the cover of the *Bulletin of the Atomic Scientists,* he called it *Two Minutes Till Midnight.* Like his other book, it was a collection of amplified and re-edited pieces he had written for *Harper's,* the *Saturday Review* and the *New Leader* about the wholly new era that the bombs had brought into being.

> I have been told [he wrote in the introduction] that nobody wants to read about the hydrogen bomb, or even to think about it. But it will still be there, whether we think about it or not—perhaps especially if we don't; and a great many people are writing about it, in the evident hope that they will find some readers.

The book opens with the chapter "Year One, Thormonuclear Era."

> In August 1953 [the chapter begins] possibly the most important event in the history of the United States—certainly the most important since the Civil War—occurred outside the United States: the Russians made a thermo-nuclear bomb, and made it go off. This was far more important than our own production of the bomb a couple of years earlier, for most Americans think we would never use it first. . . . It was immeasurably more important than the earlier production of the atomic bomb, first by us and then by the Russians; for what is loosely and not quite accurately called the hydrogen bomb is so much more powerful, so much more dangerous, that the eight years of the Atomic Age in which we lived before the Russians produced it begin to look, in retrospect, like a Golden Age compared to what we are living in now.

338

The statement about the importance of the event in 1953 is debatable by those who think that the curtain went up on a new world with the explosions at Alamogordo and Hiroshima in 1945, but Davis makes a good case for his thesis. So much has happened, however, since this book was published that some of its value is that of a historic document. But in this chapter, there is a perpetually important passage and one which defeats for every thinking reader any suspicion of the author's Communist leanings.

There are optimists who hold that even if the Communists conquered the world they would eventually soften up, like the barbarians who overran the Roman Empire, and a new civilization would evolve. But it could evolve only out of what is in Communist culture now. The barbarians who overran Rome were backwoodsmen who knew they had much to learn from the Romans; the men who rule in Moscow have made it a matter of dogma that they have nothing to learn from anybody.

The essence of their system is not an economic or a political doctrine, or practice; it is a technique—the technique of seizing and retaining power. And despite what used to be heard about the state withering away, experience has proved —as George Orwell discerned—that the objective is not any purpose for which power might be exercised but power itself. The present association of the technique with Marxism is a historical accident—the accident that the political genius who invented it happened to call himself a Marxist, however he interpreted Marxism doctrine to suit his own convenience. . . . Lenin invented the whole thing; Stalin merely added a few embellishments. And his method could be used in the service of any totalitarian system—or, as the case of the Nazis proved, of no coherent system at all. An evil knowledge has been let loose on the world; and it could cause as much trouble, and for as long, as the atomic bomb.

This leads into chapter two—"No World if Necessary," Davis's answer to the symposium published in the first postwar year, "One World or None." Such a "one world" would, Davis was convinced, be inevitably a Communist world and worse than the total destruction the bombs would cause.

The erudition and pure essay style of *Two Minutes Till Midnight* set it far apart from *But We Were Born Free* with its eloquent exposition and exhortation. This, as well as the possibility that "nobody wants to read about the hydrogen bomb"—as Davis suspected in his introduction—undoubtedly accounted for its small circulation. But as the earlier book is a monument to Davis's courage and his interpretive skill, *Two Minutes Till Midnight* is the ultimate testimony of his gifts as philosopher and writer.

### 6

The book was his last great effort. The following year, he was obliged to give up broadcasting. His friends saw less and less of him. He continued to read books by his friends that they sent him and he wrote short notes to thank them. In 1956 he wrote to James Thurber to thank him for his book *Further Fables for Our Time* which he dedicated to Davis.

> My heartiest thanks. I am now reading it to discover which of the animals I am most like. At least theirs is a happier world than ours at present.

But his letters carried little hope.

> Sorry [he wrote again to Thurber], but I am not getting any better; every day seems to be worse. But why should I recite my troubles to a man who has plenty of troubles of his own?

340

He wrote again to Thurber in the same vein the following year.

I am sorry to say that no miracle of justice has come along so that I am as badly off as ever. But I am grateful to my friends who say such kind things to me.

After that, it was evident that he could no longer use his beloved typewriter. The notes were dictated to Fliss as the abbreviation ED/fd at the bottom attested.

The rest was slow tragedy. He lived until May 18, 1958. In the last month he was unable to speak or swallow; kept alive only by intravenous feeding. It was a late mercy that finally took him; for friends and admirers it singaled a loss that could not be replaced.

It is perhaps yet too soon to assess the full value of Elmer Davis's contribution to American life and the old American way. We live, still, in troubled times—more troubled in some ways even than his—but we see them more clearly than we did in those foggy years. He saw through the fog then and helped clear it away for us. And he helped us too to grow up. There used to be an old saying that every crisis produces a leader. We have lost some of our faith in that belief but Elmer Davis did much to restore it.

# INDEX

343

# Index

344

# Index

346

# Index

# Index

# Index